THE BEST LAID PLANS

Contemporary Approaches to Film and Media Series

A complete listing of the books in this series
can be found online at wsupress.wayne.edu.

THE BEST LAID PLANS
Interrogating the Heist Film

EDITED BY
Jeannette Sloniowski and Jim Leach

WAYNE STATE UNIVERSITY PRESS
Detroit

Library of Cataloging Control Number: 2017950916
ISBN 978-0-8143-4224-4 (paperback) | ISBN 978-0-8143-4225-1 (ebook)

Wayne State University Press
Leonard N. Simons Building
4809 Woodward Avenue
Detroit, Michigan 48201-1309

Visit us online at wsupress.wayne.edu

For
Zoya, Ethan, and Christian
James and Abigail

Contents

3. The Aesthetics and Ideology of the Heist Film

Acknowledgments

We would like to thank Rob MacMorine, film and video technician in the Department of Communication, Popular Culture, and Film at Brock University, for his help with the preparation of our manuscript.

William Denton, associate librarian at the York University Library, gave assistance with his amazing knowledge of hard-boiled slang.

Many thanks to Annie Martin, senior acquisitions editor at Wayne State University Press, for her patience and encouragement throughout the completion of our manuscript. And, of course, to our colleague at Brock University, Barry Grant, for his kindness and editorial advice. Thanks also to Sandra Judd for her thoughtful and thorough copyediting of the text before publication.

Jonathan Rayner's "Masculinity, Morality and Action: Michael Mann and the Heist Movie" was first published in *Criminal Visions: Media Representations of Crime and Justice,* ed. Paul Mason (Cullompton, Devon: Willan Publishing, 2003). Reprinted by permission of the author.

Hamilton Carroll's "September 11 as Heist" was first published in the *Journal of American Studies* 45 (2011). Reprinted by permission of the author and Cambridge University Press.

Introduction

. . . of Heists and Men

◇◇◇◇◇◇◇◇◇◇◇◇◇◇◇◇◇◇◇◇◇◇◇◇

Jeannette Sloniowski and Jim Leach

The heist—a carefully organized robbery of a bank, jewelry store, casino, or other commercial institution—has been a persistent and popular mainstay of popular cinema. The central question addressed by our contributors in this collection is why films about heists have proved so appealing to audiences over many years and in diverse cultural contexts.

In terms of genre theory, there is much uncertainty as to how to designate the heist film. Some critics have treated it as a genre, others as a subgenre of the gangster film or as a subgenre of the crime film more generally. Rick Altman, rather surprisingly, calls it a failed genre because it never developed "a stable syntax" (225) that could organize the semantic "building blocks" (219) into a coherent structure. This is odd because, in Altman's terms, the heist film has a very well defined syntax derived from the planning, execution, and aftermath of a major robbery, as well as a distinctive number of narrative variations such as the revenge, the comedy/parody, or the social issue narrative. Since this is the case, and because it shares many of its semantic features and much of its iconography with the gangster film and other crime films, such as the police procedural and the semidocumentary film noir, to say nothing of Westerns and war films concerned with crime, we think it most productive to see the heist film as a subgenre of the crime film, although, given the heist film's highly recognizable syntactic elements, it is not surprising that others, including some of our contributors, will continue to regard it as a fully fledged genre. This issue of generic definition is complicated in no small part due to what John Scaggs calls "the bewildering variety of different 'versions' of the crime thriller" (108). As we shall see, the heist subgenre is filled with hybrids of differing narrative structures and cross-generic conventions.

We have no wish to offer a prescriptive theory of the heist film, but it is useful to outline the normal features of the subgenre, acknowledging that individual films will deviate from these norms. All genre films are combinations of convention and invention but if the deviations become too great, the film may slip into a different generic territory: a film depicting a professional gang carrying out multiple robberies is best seen as a gangster or a bandit-gangster film. The most clearly definable heist films usually focus on one carefully planned major robbery; the gang usually consists of men who have been recruited for this one job and who may not have a criminal record; and the narrative is usually divided into three more or less distinct stages: recruiting and planning, execution, and aftermath. The amount of attention given to each of these stages can vary considerably, as in those films that concentrate mainly, after the heist is carried out, on the difficulties in getting away with the crime, the double-cross, or the revenge of the target of the heist (often the Mob).

As examples of the possibilities offered by these structural variations, we might compare *Dead Presidents* (The Hughes Brothers, 1995), in which the elaborate and bloody heist occurs only after long sections dealing with the coming-of-age of the protagonist and his experiences in the Vietnam War, with *Reservoir Dogs* (Quentin Tarantino, 1992), which omits the planning and the heist completely and deals only with the bloody aftermath. We might also distinguish between those heist films whose narratives are entirely from the criminals' point of view and those, like *Robbery* (Peter Yates, 1967) and *Heat* (Michael Mann, 1995), in which their actions are intercut with the police investigation. Martin Rubin calls *Heat* "a hybrid of heist film and police thriller" (34).

Tone is also a key factor, ranging from films that explore the social issues surrounding the thieves, including issues of race, capitalist exploitation, and consumer culture, to comedies where the ineptness of the gang clearly parodies the emphasis in the heist proper on competence, precision, and perfect timing. As Rubin suggests, what links the serious and comic films is the presence of irony, "with the protagonists defeated more often by twists of fate than by the forces of justice" (122). Taking his cue from the ending of *The Killing* (Stanley Kubrick, 1956), in which a small dog thwarts the getaway, Mark Bould refers to the quirk that brings the best laid plans to disaster as the "yappy little dog" (89). Most, but not all, heist films feature a yappy dog, and the variations in tone that this device makes possible contribute to the uncertainty about how to name the subgenre.

So far we have referred to the films in question as heist films, but many critics (including Altman) have followed Stuart Kaminsky and defined them as "big caper" films (79). According to the Online Etymology Dictionary, "caper" originally meant "playful leap or jump," then came to mean "prank," and was first associated with crime in 1926. The word "heist," used as a noun since 1930, originated in American slang and is "probably a dialectal alter-ation of hoist," meaning "to lift" in its slang sense of "shoplift." While the playful connotations of "caper" do capture the spirit of certain heist films, especially from the 1960s on, the term does not suit the many dark crime films to which it has often been applied. In these films, criminals often speak of the job as a "caper," as Doc does in *The Asphalt Jungle* (John Huston, 1950), but this is before the catastrophic series of events that ensue when the heist goes wrong. In *High Sierra* (Raoul Walsh, 1941), the gang similarly refer to the job as a "caper," but, during the robbery, Roy (Humphrey Bogart) tells a security guard to raise his arms, "Heist 'em, buddy," and then calls the job a "heist" as he flees from the police.

Neither "caper" nor "heist" necessarily refers to a crime committed by a gang, but both terms are usually used to describe films depicting such crimes, and they are often used interchangeably. However, "caper" also has been applied to quite different crimes, such as those involving confidence tricks (*The Sting* [George Roy Hill, 1973] is often so described), and refers less to the crime than to the spirit in which it is committed. "Heist" refers precisely to the crime and can even encompass those "caper" films that in-clude heists. For these reasons, we prefer to speak of "the heist film" as a single subgenre and, adapting the distinction suggested by Steve Chibnall in his discussion of recent British gangster films between Gangster Heavy, films that "strive for unvarnished authenticity," and Gangster Light, "films that cheerfully peddle myth" ("Travels in Ladland" 376–77), we prefer to think in terms of "Heist Light" and "Heist Heavy."

What is clear in many heist films is a ludic aspect where beating "the Man" is seen as a game created by the heist planner. Often this planner takes great pleasure in the creation of a seemingly brilliant plan that dupes au-thorities of all kinds. This pleasurable aspect, we argue, is passed on to the audience, which presumably enjoys the game, the planning, and what seems likely to be the absolute perfection of a brilliantly executed attack on main-stream institutions. The brilliance of the plan, and the demonstration of masculine competence and bravery, are perhaps a reflection of the war film. War films demonstrated the ability of the male group to impose their will on "the enemy." While this works only in part for the heist, since the brilliant plan fails on most occasions, part of the pleasure of heist films is watching the creation of the great plan. In *5 Against the House* (Phil Karlson, 1955), for example, the rich boy heist planner Ronnie (Kerwin Matthews) plans a heist using three of his Korean War buddies. Ronnie is obsessed with time and precision, but is interested in the heist only "because I wanted to see it work, to know if I was able to do it." The attraction of the heist is largely the pleasure of the challenge and an adventure to fight off boredom. He has no interest at all in the score. The heist fails primarily because one of the gang suffered a serious head injury during the war and cannot keep himself together emotionally while executing the heist.

The parallel with the war film was noted by Kaminsky in the first extensive critical discussion of the heist film, in which he argued that "the big caper film is a sub-genre of the adventure-process film . . . in which any small group of individuals of diverse ability . . . comes together to confront a massive establishment, be it prison, army, or secret installation" (74–75). Following Kaminsky's lead, several others, including Frank Krutnik and Kirsten Moana Thompson, have attempted to define the subgenre from various perspectives. Daryl Lee, however, is the author of the only book-length study of the heist film. Taking note of both the heist's "utility and pleasure," he argues that heists must be given "a flexible conceptual definition" (3) because of their hybrid nature, and that they must be studied historically to understand how their conventions have evolved over time. For example, the plight of returned veterans in the fifties can be compared to the plight of men today who cannot earn enough money to fund health care for their children or the down payment on a small business—and thus they steal. Different contexts, some changes in style, but at the core failed men still chasing their cultural dreams.

As with other kinds of crime fiction and film, Lee argues that there is pleasure in heist films because they "afford a powerful screen identification with criminals breaking the law," which satisfies a "desire to elude the oppressive aspects or limitations of contemporary mass society" (5). This pleasure in the ability to transgress is as clear in 2016's *Hell or High Water* (David Mackenzie) as it was in *The Asphalt Jungle*. Mackenzie's film is actually a hybrid of heist film and Western, and, as Fran Mason argues in *Hollywood's Detectives*, it has always been a purposeful strategy in the Hollywood genre film to mix various genres together to attract larger audiences, but also to prevent the audience from tiring of fairly rigid conventions that grow stale over time—hence the many variations in the heists that our authors have studied. These mixtures of generic conventions in many heist films not only demonstrate the flexibility of genre filmmaking but make extraordinary films and make them extraordinarily difficult to define.

Our authors offer a variety of approaches to the heist film, and the films have been chosen from a variety of national cinemas, from American and British to Italian, French, Japanese, and Canadian. We had originally envisioned this anthology to cover heist films in a broader international context. However, as with much popular cinema study, this work has yet to be done. It is our hope that this volume, along with Daryl Lee's book on the heist, will spur other researchers into looking at the heist film more internationally—Bollywood, for example, has a considerable number of heist films, and we believe that there is much to be learned about many cultures through the study not only of popular cinema but particularly of the heist film and how ordinary men, as opposed to important gangster characters, cope with lack of economic opportunity and the failure of their differing cultural aspirations.

The essays are organized in three parts, dealing with the heist film's international presence, the subgenre's social and cultural implications, and some theoretical ways of approaching it. Part One, "The International Heist Film," explores the subgenre in the context of four different national cinemas. Inevitably, given the worldwide popularity of the heist film, the choice of national cinemas is somewhat arbitrary, and it is to be hoped, as suggested above, that our authors' essays will inspire work on films from other countries.

Jeannette Sloniowski discusses the fifties heist film in America. Her essay concerns Hollywood films made during the Cold War and the McCarthy-era witch hunts. These American heist films, often made by directors and actors under scrutiny by the House Un-American Activities Committee, are gloomy and violent with little of the caper about them. The thieves bring to the heist complex plans and skills perhaps developed from their experiences in World War II or their previous participation in criminal activities. But no matter how well planned, fate or internal discord and betrayal cause the robberies to fail, and often fail badly, in films like *The Asphalt Jungle* (perhaps the first fully developed American heist) and *Plunder Road* (Hubert Cornfield, 1957), among others.

Jim Leach analyzes British heist films from the 1950s, arguing that the period of disillusionment following the elation of victory in the so-called People's War led to violent and gloomy heist films that end very badly in most cases. The complexity of fifties culture, particularly with respect to economic discontent and the aftermath of the war, followed by the emergence of consumer culture in the 1960s, produced some remarkably dark films in Britain, as in America and France.

Tim Palmer explores this darkness in postwar popular French cinema with his wide-ranging examination of the heist film in the context of French popular cinema. Palmer challenges traditional notions of French film history that emphasize critically acclaimed art films by pointing to the rich achievements of critically maligned and neglected, but extremely popular, crime films.

Scott Henderson takes on the Canadian heist film, produced in a culture that is not well known for genre films. He examines the few heist films produced in the English-Canadian and Quebec film industries, tracing the development from films of the 1970s and 1980s that depict the failed heroes also found in other Canadian films of these eras, to a more populist approach early in the first decade of the twenty-first century, to a more recent example that illustrates the impact of "a more globalized film industry in which national boundaries have perhaps become more porous."

Part Two, "Gender, Race, and Class in the Heist Film," examines the ways in which filmmakers have used the subgenre to address major issues in modern society.

Gaylyn Studlar surveys heist films in light of feminist theories that illuminate stereotypical characterizations of both men and women in the heist, calling the films "male obsessed" and about recovering "ideal masculinity." Acknowledging that male gangs are central to the iconography of the heist film, she argues that women play more important roles than previous critics have suggested, finally concluding that in "the neo-retro heist film" of our time, "tough" masculinity, although it has a lengthy history in the heist, is somewhat less important than it was in earlier films.

Jonathan Rayner's essay also focuses on masculinity, in this case in the heist films of Michael Mann, adopting an auteurist approach to the subgenre and relating these films to the vision developed in Mann's other crime films. He argues that Mann depicts a morally ambivalent world in which the activities of criminals and police distance them from the values that they are intended to sustain.

Jonathan Munby contributes an innovative survey of race in heist films, beginning with *Odds Against Tomorrow* (Robert Wise, 1959) and analyzing several films that have not been seriously examined before. Delving into issues of racism, racial profiling, and colonialism, Munby demonstrates the importance of heist films in raising and demystifying issues of race since

1959 in American films. As in several essays in our book, the heist is used to clarify a remarkable and important range of social issues.

Fran Mason writes about social class in a variety of heists featuring "underclass" crooks who come to represent "the struggle experienced by the dispossessed in capitalism." He argues that "disempowerment" is a feature of the heist film across cultures for men who see the heist as a way of escaping from their marginalized condition. Ascribing a "lack of professionalism" to the small-time heister, Mason identifies two kinds of criminal in heist films: the professional heister in the classic heist film and the amateur in the small-time heist movie, often with a comedic sensibility.

Part Three, "The Aesthetics and Ideology of the Heist Film," presents a series of more theoretical essays that make use of heist films to address aspects of the cultural, social, and political contexts in which they were made.

Homer Pettey's essay offers a comparative study of two films from different cultural and cinematic traditions, Stanley Kubrick's *The Killing* and Takumi Furukawa's *Cruel Gun Story* (1964). Using economic and gambling theory, he argues that these films are "allegories of modern capitalism" in which the criminals' plans mirror modern economic theory in an attempt to achieve financial security. Like many of the authors in our anthology, Pettey sees the heist, which fails despite elaborate planning and often competent execution, as a hopeless gamble to defeat the odds.

Andrew Clay's essay draws on phenomenological theory to examine possible audience responses to heist films, using five British films from the period 1970 to 2000 as test cases. He examines the heist film as an "aesthetic experience" in which the camera eye situates the viewer in relation to the depicted crimes. His essay seeks to establish how the films make us feel about them, particularly in terms of their address to a masculine subjectivity.

Daryl Lee extends his treatment of the aesthetic dimensions of the heist in his book to develop an argument about the heist film's relations to modernist traditions in the arts. Concentrating on Soderbergh's *Ocean's* trilogy (2001–2007), Lee explores "the relationship between art and criminality" through a detailed examination of the allusions to modern art in these films.

In the concluding essay Hamilton Carroll compares James Marsh's documentary *Man on a Wire* (2008), which draws on heist conventions to depict Philippe Petit's unauthorized tightrope walk in 1974 between the two towers of the World Trade Center, to Spike Lee's New York–set heist film *Inside Man* (2006). He argues that both films are responses to the 9/11 terrorist attacks on the World Trade Center, and both try to "work through" the pain and suffering of that horrific event using the conventions of the heist genre.

Here again an author examines the use of the generic conventions of the heist to open a conversation about a significant cultural moment.

What is clear from all of our authors is that "the heist" has been used for a remarkable number of purposes. These purposes include entertainment, of course, but also depicting the struggles of poor men in a world increasingly dominated by "big business," and the failure of the American Dream, or indeed any dream, in many different cultures. We need only to look at a few heists of 2014 to 2016 to see that social issues are still at the heart of the heist film. *American Heist* (Sarik Andreasyan, 2014) concerns the attempts of two down-and-out brothers to get on their feet. One brother tries to go straight and starts his own business, but his efforts are undercut by a banking system that has no interest in small businesses, only in high finance. In *Heist* (Scott Mann, 2015), a man plans (and gets away with) a heist in order to pay for medical treatment for his seriously ill child. *To Steal from a Thief* (Daniel Calparsoro, 2016) deals with a worldwide issue: heisting secret government documents to reveal government corruption, and it evokes this not uncommon activity for audiences who have seen this form of robbery even during the recent US presidential elections. The heist is uniquely positioned to draw attention to the trials endured by ordinary men and sometimes women.

PART ONE

◇◇◇◇◇◇◇◇◇◇◇◇◇◇◇◇◇◇◇◇◇◇◇◇◇

The International Heist Film

All for Naught

The American Heist Film in the Fifties

∞∞∞∞∞∞∞∞∞∞∞∞∞∞∞∞∞∞∞∞∞

Jeannette Sloniowski

The heist film is a hybrid form born in America in the 1940s. Along with the contemporaneous bandit gangster subgenre, it exhibits conventions drawn from older genres to create a formidable, desperate, and sometimes left-wing depiction of postwar American culture. Both subgenres show the influence not only of film noir and semidocumentary noir on the larger gangster and crime genres generally but also of the strongly held left-wing political views of some of their notable, sometimes persecuted, creators, among others: Abraham Polonsky, Bob Roberts, John Garfield, John Huston, Robert Ryan, Harry Belafonte, Burt Lancaster, Sterling Hayden, and even lesser-known character actor Marc Lawrence from *The Asphalt Jungle* (John Huston, 1950), who tried to get out from under by telling the House Un-American Activities Committee (HUAC) that he joined the Communist Party only "because I heard it was a good place to meet broads" (Server 47). It is virtually impossible to look at the cast lists, directors, and writers of these downbeat and often angry films without becoming aware that several of them were blacklisted, were hauled in front of HUAC, and had serious questions about American culture of their time. It is believed that John Garfield's untimely death at thirty-nine can in part be attributed to the emotional trauma of being investigated and consequently unable to find inspiring work as an actor. My essay will be a brief survey of some important fifties heists and will address a few others at greater length. This will be done from the point of view of their left-wing politics and social critique, but will also take note of the varying narrative positions and uses of the heist itself in a number of fifties films. I will also argue that the films depict the unreality of the American Dream and that the effects of the postwar consumer culture give many of the fifties heist films their particular power.

The Origins and Conventions of the Fifties Heist

Much of the history of the American crime film in this era is documented in the detailed and important work of Paul Buhle and Dave Wagner in books such as *Radical Hollywood* and *A Very Dangerous Citizen: Abraham Lincoln Polonsky and the Hollywood Left*. Jonathan Munby and Fran Mason have also authored important reassessments of the gangster film with historical, ideological, and close cultural readings of the more consequential films of various periods in the genre, including the fifties. These analyses provide breadth and detail to other recent analyses of the influence of left-wingers in Hollywood, despite the blacklist, to create a more factual, industry-driven critique of the crime genre and film noir historically, including the many politically motivated censorship battles that surround the crime film in its various forms. Because crime fiction and films are concerned with crime and "justice," however defined, they have expressed controversial ideas in many time periods. The anthology *"Un-American" Hollywood: Politics and Film in the Blacklist Era*, edited by Frank Krutnik, Steve Neale, Brian Neve, and Peter Stanfield, also adds detailed analyses of the Cold War era and of the semidocumentary noir in particular, so central to heists of the fifties. Will Straw's and Thom Andersen's essays in that anthology are remarkably detailed analyses of the aesthetic and ideological issues surrounding the reappraisal of the politics of noir, film gris, and the semidocumentary.

In "Red Hollywood" and "Afterword" Thom Andersen defines a small group of films as films gris. He refers to film gris as a genre but it might also be seen as a small subgenre of film noir. The essence of his definition is that film gris is a noir film that concentrates very concretely in a leftist way on important social issues. In "Red Hollywood" he names only thirteen films as films gris, but in "Afterword" he expands the list considerably and argues that we probably do not yet know all of the films that might be included in the "genre." He defines them as films that have "a greater psychological and social realism" ("Red Hollywood" 257) than noir, that are related to the thirties "social problem film" (259), that "implicate the entire system of capitalism in their criticism" (259), and finally, in which "the unreality of the American Dream is a constant theme" (260).

Film noir and particularly the noir-influenced gangster film are also an important and potentially radical departure from other kinds of films of their time and are a crucial part of the heist hybrid. This is a complicated inheritance, since both film noir and film gris have complex origins ranging from German expressionism to French existentialism to hard-boiled fiction and social issue films of the thirties. The semidocumentaries, in something of a turn away from noir, are often made as dark law-and-order police procedurals, such as *He Walked by Night* (Alfred L. Werker, 1948), a film that in large part paid tribute to modern, seemingly corruption-free, scientific policing. Gone are the "hunches" of the private eye film and earlier procedurals and even the genius of the Sherlock Holmes–style investigator, replaced by ballistics, fingerprints, modern surveillance technology, and computers, all signifying scientific policing, supposedly error and bias free, unlike the more corrupt cops of film noir.

Nonetheless, film noir itself contributes to the heist generally, in that fifties heists never succeed. Painful experience from the Depression, the war, and the Holocaust (to say nothing of the blacklist) taught Americans that humans' best laid plans can easily fall victim to cruel fate, to hatred, and to incompetence. The last great film gris heist of the fifties was Robert Wise's *Odds Against Tomorrow* (1959). It is a heist that goes horrifically wrong because of the racism of the white "muscle" of the heist, played chillingly by Robert Ryan. Harry Belafonte, who was central to getting this film made, plays the first African American heister—a brilliant blues musician but what is known in gangster circles as a "degenerate gambler" who steals to support his habit but also his estranged wife and daughter. The heist fails as the Ryan character, snarling all the time about Belafonte's false, racially attributed incompetence, refuses to allow him to carry the car keys. Unfortunately, the man who is carrying the keys is killed and this deprives the remaining two of their means of escape. The film ends, rather didactically, with Ryan and Belafonte shooting at each other in a chase through the grubby suburban streets of small-town New York State and dying in a huge gas tank explosion, an apparent reference to *White Heat* (Raoul Walsh, 1949) where it was a last defiant gesture by a larger than life, mad bandit gangster. Ironically and in a heavy handed manner, in the Wise film the police claim that they cannot identify the bodies because they are burned beyond recognition. Now the robbers are merely two dead men, their race indecipherable, the stupidity of racism debunked.

Fran Mason, in *American Gangster Cinema*, argues that the gangster genre, having exhausted the classical form, fragmented into a number of subgenres, including "the death of the big shot" (51) in *High Sierra* (Raoul Walsh, 1941) and *Dillinger* (Max Nosseck, 1945), among others. Another offshoot is the bandit film that Garner Simmons refers to as "the Bandit-Gangster Film" (67), including the male-female bandit couple, as in *Gun Crazy* (Joseph H. Lewis, 1950) or *They Live by Night* (Nicholas Ray, 1948), that also shares a strong connection to the Western, as do some heist films. The fifties heist is filled with failure, brutality, and death. Not a single one of the approximately twenty-five films features a successful heist, in that even if the robbers get off with the money or the jewels, most of them die nasty deaths during or after the robbery, commit suicide, or end up in jail for life. In fact, a successful heist produces little other than dealings with dishonest fences, violent double crosses, and more death. Dave Purvis in *Armored Car Robbery* (Richard Fleischer, 1950) runs into the propeller of his escape plane, no doubt ending up in various pieces on the tarmac. The ending of *The Killing* (Stanley Kubrick, 1956) in an airport is particularly black and ironic, as the cash, for which many people have died, blows away in the wind as a small dog knocks the suitcase filled with money onto the runway.

Gone in these films are the high-flying gangsters of the classical period—violent, aggressive, ambitious, and dressed like dandies. Gangsters were covetous of territory, marshaling armies of thugs to patrol their borders. The heister is a small-time guy with no territory—in fact, part of the failure of his life is his homelessness as he drifts from place to place, spending much of his time in seedy lodgings. He has no fancy wardrobes or palatial residences, and for company only a few ex-cons who perform the technical work of the job. He has little charm and less bravado than the gangster, often an evil temper, and he would not seem to be the hero that audiences pull for as he rises up in the world of crime, although the audiences may well like to see the precisely planned and executed robbery succeed, having no great love of big banks, jewelry stores, or casinos, all institutions that serve the rich. Rather than dying in a blaze of glory in the street like most gangsters of the period, he generally meets an inglorious and miserable end, like the heister in *Plunder Road* (Hubert Cornfield, 1957), who tries to escape by jumping off an overpass onto the top of a fast-moving transport truck. He fails. Badly. Why audiences like these films is only slightly puzzling, since they can, perhaps, identify with these struggling, working-class everymen, living in dumpy cabins or shabby motels, eating greasy take-out food, and only in the money between heists. They move from crummy place to crummy place, in rural or suburban areas, always short of cash but dreaming of the big score that will take them to glamorous places or allow them to reclaim the family farm. Perhaps they are not that different than many in the audience, dreaming of better times and the ready cash that greater consumer power could provide.

One of the key heavily loaded phrases used in *High Sierra* (and elsewhere in the period) is "crashing out." Originally the phrase meant staging a jail break, but in *High Sierra* Ida Lupino, playing Marie, Earl's working-class girlfriend, co-opts the term to mean something that poor, desperate Americans like her, and Bonnie Parker after her, long to do—to escape poverty, abuse, and failure for a better life. Many of the heisters of the fifties and after do exactly this: they try to "crash out" though pulling off a big score, often to fund an escape from America to foreign places. Importantly, the heist subgenre also has a number of characters crash out by committing suicide when the grand dream fails—Emmerich, the corrupt lawyer in *Asphalt Jungle*, shoots himself, and Swede, in *The Killers* (Robert Siodmak, 1946), allows hired thugs to kill him with hardly a word of protest. Even Roy Earle (Humphrey Bogart) can be considered here. He must know that his life is finished when he entraps himself in the mountains in *High Sierra*. And there is Gino (David Clarke) in *The Great St. Louis Bank Robbery* (Charles Guggenheim, 1959), who suicides in a wild fit of terror and rage in the bank's expressionistically rendered rat trap of a vault. Many of the fifties heist films look like documentaries, and these suicides are shocking, brutal, and moving.

Daryl Lee calls the heist a "process film" (51–52) owing debts to both the war film and the musical—stories about a group of characters trying to pull off a significant job of work requiring great technical skill. The war film is perhaps the more important, along with film noir, since almost all of the heist personnel are male and of an age to have served in the military. However, the only fifties heist to have an all-veteran crew is *5 Against the House* (Phil Karlson, 1955), a story about five attractive thirtysomething veterans in college on the GI bill who are starved for excitement. This film, as well as *Six Bridges to Cross* (Joseph Pevney, 1955), is perhaps a foreshadowing of the heist films of the sixties, whose lead characters are more personably portrayed and whose plots are more caper-like than those of the miserable fifties. The heist fails in *5 Against the House* because one of the veterans breaks down, suffering from what is now called post-traumatic stress disorder (PTSD).

As in the war film, but unlike the bandit-gangster film, the "workers" in the heist movie seldom know one another well, if at all, before the robbery. In *Kansas City Confidential* (Phil Karlson, 1952) a masked Tom Foster (Preston Foster) summons various crooks to a secret meeting in a hotel. The crooks never see his face at all in the film. All have technological skills related to their role in the well-planned robbery, just as military personnel were trained for specific, specialized duties. A crucial scene in many heists is the planning sequence where architectural drawings and blueprints are shown to the robbers and their specific roles rehearsed many times, after which the joint is cased over and over until everyone knows his job. The bandit-gangster robberies are far more ad hoc, with Bonnie and Clyde even trying to rob a failed bank that has absolutely no money at all. Bandit gangsters roam the countryside knocking off banks seemingly chosen at random. Heisters have a plan, often a complex one, with a large score at the end.

Protoheists and the Fifties Cluster

Generally speaking, the fifties heist "cluster" (Mittell 122) or "cycle" (Elsaesser 127) consists of a downbeat, action-oriented, and always violent series of films building on a few notable predecessors of the forties, such as *High Sierra*, a combination of the early heist and early bandit-gangster subgenres, and Robert Siodmak's *The Killers* and *Criss Cross* (1949), significant noir melodramas featuring heists. Daryl Lee traces the heist farther back to American Westerns and jewel thief films (1–6), and it is even possible to go much farther back in history to recruit Robin Hood and his gang of Merry Men into the generic mix. But it is my intention in this section to spend some time looking at a few important fifties heists: *The Asphalt Jungle*, *Armored Car Robbery*, *He Ran All the Way* (John Berry, 1951), and *Plunder Road*, all examples of variations within the heist formula. These variations generally concern style, where the heist occurs in the films, and whether the heist is the center of the narrative or is a strategically placed semantic unit, important to the film's overall meaning but not its center. These films also differ in the amount of empathy asked from audiences, some humanizing the criminals, others more critical of the masculinity depicted and relating it to the gender struggles of those times.

 The Asphalt Jungle, for example, uses the heist at the center of the narrative with all of its various and what would become conventional elements: putting the gang together, discussing and perfecting the plan, the heist itself, and its aftermath—fencing the score and escaping (or not). *Armored Car Robbery* is similar in this way but rather than a film noir is a noir-inflected semidocumentary police procedural lacking the intense character psychology of *The Asphalt Jungle*. The amount of empathy asked for in this film is far less than in *The Asphalt Jungle*. *He Ran All the Way* is yet again different. It is a film gris, family melodrama/social issue film that spends a very short time on the heist, although it is key to understanding the main characters, and concentrates on defining issues of social class, working-class life, and gender in the aftermath of the crime. It has a more obvious political message than the other three films, as film gris often does. *Plunder Road* is another semidocumentary that differs from many semidocumentary police procedurals in that it concentrates on the gang alone and their inability to master the newly constructed and widely admired American highway system, deconstructing the idea of the open road and all that it seemed to mean to the culture of the fifties.

Other fifties heists, like *Violent Saturday* (Richard Fleischer, 1955), reduce the time spent on the heist but use it semantically to underscore other important issues. For example, the hero of *Violent Saturday*, Shelley Martin (Victor Mature), is forced to stay out of the army during the war by government officials because of the importance of his job at home to the war effort. Some in the small town where he lives consider him a coward and torment his son about his father's suspected cowardice. After a particularly nasty group of heisters, including the vicious Dill (Lee Marvin), come to rob the town, Martin is redeemed by fighting off the very violent gang almost single-handedly, and thus takes his proper and honorable place in the town, his heroic masculinity established. The significance, duration, and placement of the heist thus varies with its importance in the films.[1] *Violent Saturday*, a more conservative film than many others, places us firmly on the misunderstood Shelley Martin's side, and we are likely to be appalled by the viciousness of the heisters, career criminals whose motivating reason is avarice alone.

Most of the heist films made in the United States in the fifties show these variations, as do several notable international films such as *Rififi* (*Du Rififi chez les hommes*, Jules Dassin, 1955), *Piccadilly Third Stop* (Wolf Rilla, 1960), and *La Città si Difendi* (*Four Ways Out*, Pietro Germi, 1951), the latter written by Federico Fellini. The fifties heist cluster, like its European counterparts, is characterized by downbeat films that end badly. The heists fail because of incompetence, greed, internal discord and double crosses, or pure bad luck. Most of the heisters end up dead, the loot gone and all the planning and precision come to naught. This is characteristic of the American heists of the fifties and is relieved only by the more caper-like films that appeared in the sixties, like *Ocean's 11* (Lewis Milestone, 1960),[2] where only one heister dies (of a heart attack) and the money burns in his coffin (the others all go free), and *Seven Thieves* (Henry Hathaway, 1960), where all go free save for the heist planner (Edward G. Robinson), whose plan works brilliantly but whose heart gives out in the end as he celebrates the brilliant success of his plan. Both of these films mark the advent of glamour and "stars" into the heist, unlike the spartan, for the most part cheaply made, documentary-like noir atmosphere of the fifties films. These films are almost free of humor, the comic heist coming later in a more parodic cluster.[3]

In the postwar context, downbeat crime films might well come as no surprise, with the plight of returning veterans suffering both physical and mental disability, joblessness, and the discontent of liberation-seeking women, who were often negatively, but erotically, depicted as femmes fatales, like Ava Gardner in *The Killers*, Yvonne De Carlo in *Criss Cross*, and the ironically named stripper Yvonne Le Doux (Adele Jergens) in *Armored Car Robbery*. This cultural context contributed an atmosphere of despair and failure to the heists and noirs of the time, as the country adjusted to the enormous changes taking place in the late forties and fifties. The profound shock created by both the Holocaust and nuclear fears, as well as the Cold War and the Kefauver[4] revelations, created further angst in a culture that was still recovering from the Depression, and the birth of consumer culture added both anxiety about the acquisition of money and "things" and an intense pressure for male success in fifties heists.[5] This context had a strong effect on the documentary-like aspects of many fifties heists like *Plunder Road* and *The Big Caper* (Robert Stevens, 1957), so that, when combined with the many relatively unknown actors in these films, they almost seemed like docudramas or documentaries about troubling issues of the time in a culture recently so taken with documentary depiction of the war.

One of the little known and absolutely gloomy heists made toward the end of the decade, *The Great St. Louis Bank Robbery* is gay-themed in an era when gay characters, including those in this film, were mostly ugly stereotypes. The heist in this film is led by a middle-aged and brutal ex-convict, John Egan (Crahan Denton), who is both a bad-luck, serial jailbird and a very disciplined heist planner. His brutality is primarily directed toward Willie, a pudgy young criminal who was his protégé in prison and probably his lover both in and out of jail. When the very young George Fowler (Steve McQueen) joins the crew, Egan is clearly attracted to him, even planning a potential double-cross escape for the two of them to Mexico after the heist. Egan, abused by his mother in his childhood, has an intense dislike for women and brutally murders Fowler's ex-girlfriend by throwing her off a fire escape, very graphically depicted, just to be rid of her before the heist. It is implied that he murdered his mother as well by throwing her down a flight of thirty-three stairs (like many heist leaders, Egan is very precise in his calculations). When the heist goes horribly wrong, Gino, another serial ex-con, blows his brains out rather than face a return to jail. Egan is killed by the police, and a wounded Fowler has become unhinged. Willie, Egan's lover, in a jealousy-inspired fit, drives away in the escape car, abandoning the others to their fate. The serious mental and emotional problems of all of the men are central to the fifties cluster and a noir depiction of unstable and troubled masculinity. The film, directed by a liberal documentarist, looks like a combination of semidocumentary noir and neorealism and is set in actual locations and mostly shot outdoors. It is also based on a true story and includes many actual citizens and police officers from Kansas City in the cast. It is typical of the grim fifties cluster notwithstanding the gay subtext, very openly depicted for the time.

High Sierra and The Asphalt Jungle

The forties and fifties American heist films, several of them notable, tackle many important social issues of the postwar period, from the first significant film of that period, *High Sierra*, screenplay by John Huston and starring lefties Humphrey Bogart and Ida Lupino. The representation and critique of one of America's most important mythologies—that of the return to the mythical agrarian heartland—is played out in moving and emotional terms. Roy Earle, the big shot of *High Sierra*, a famous bandit and colleague of John Dillinger, unlike the mostly anonymous small-time heisters of fifties films, is released from prison through the influence of an old and dying gangster to commit one last large jewel heist, the last big heist becoming a staple in the heist film thereafter. Earle has spent most of his miserable life behind bars and is now older but no wiser, living on nostalgia and fantasies of his failed life in the rural, pre-Depression past. Embittered by the loss of the family farm in Illinois, Earle has dreams of returning to the country and settling down with a beautiful young wife. When he is first released from jail, rather than immediately pursuing the new heist, he seeks out a local park to see "if the grass is still green." This nostalgic longing for the natural world, and his desire for the young, but deceptive, daughter of an elderly farmer who has also lost his land, leads him to greater failure and death as he falls, shot by a brigade of police, from a rocky peak in the Sierras. Bogart's remarkable performance in this film made him a star but also demonstrated a truly heartfelt, nostalgic love of the American landscape and its "pure" life outside of the urban jungle of the gangster film and the oppressive darkness of film noir. *High Sierra* was remade twice, as *Colorado*

Dix (Sterling Hayden) lies dying amid his fantasies of a rural past at the end of
The Asphalt Jungle.

Territory (Raoul Walsh, 1949) and *I Died a Thousand Times* (Stuart Heisler,
1955) but never managed to summon up the grandeur of Bogart's "rush
toward death" in the original.

    This longing for the mythical heartland is duplicated in *The Asphalt
Jungle*, remade three times as *The Badlanders* (Delmer Daves, 1958),
Cairo (Wolf Rilla, 1963), and *Cool Breeze* (Barry Pollack, 1972) and considered by many to be the first true American heist. This time directed by
Huston, it exhibits the same longing for a mythical America by Dix Handley (played by Sterling Hayden), the "muscle" in a jewelry heist that, of
course, goes wrong. There are strong similarities to Huston's *High Sierra*
script, as each of the main characters, Dix and Roy Earle, have lost their
family farms during the Depression and have resorted to crime to help
buy back the past and their version of the American Dream. The main female characters in both films are also similar: down on their luck dime-
a-dance girls, they have been forced to live by their wits, but long for a
respectable life with, alas, two unsuccessful criminals. Both Ida Lupino
(*High Sierra*) and Jean Hagen (*Asphalt Jungle*) play decent, but terribly
sad, working-class women who always seem to find the wrong man.

Settling down with a man, apparently any man, is a preferable option to the dime-a-dance world.

In writing of *Public Enemy* (William Wellman, 1931), David Thomson argues that this film was key in inducing "the public's ambivalent feelings toward the criminal classes" (128). This ambivalence is a striking characteristic of both the gangster film and the heist. Theoretically the audience should be on the side of law and order; however, and perhaps for different reasons in the fifties, we seem to have at least one foot in the criminals' corner even when they are vicious. Elsaesser (127) and Thomson note the popularity of James Cagney and his lively performance as the gangster/thief whose stunning rise from poor working-class boy to wealth and success is a Horatio Alger–like story. Cagney's performance is key to audience sympathy. In the fifties heist, however, there are few performers like Cagney. Instead, *The Asphalt Jungle* subtly creates sympathy for Dix and Doll, both down-at-the-heels failures; Louis Ciavelli (Anthony Caruso), the safe cracker, who needs money to feed his family and buy medicine for his son; and Gus, the disabled driver, who scrimps out a living working in a diner. While not excusing their behavior in a film that is extraordinarily sensitive to their plight, the film delves into their lives in a way that creates sympathy. Little sympathy is created for the greedy, corrupt lawyer Emmerich, who bankrolls the heist in order to buy his way out of debt. This debt is the result of high living and having to support both a sickly, complaining wife and a beautiful, young, but expensive, girlfriend. Emmerich plans to double-cross the gang to take all the spoils but kills himself when he is found out by the police. It is not that the film has no feeling for this character, but it depicts him as a victim of both capitalism and his own greed: he wants more and more and will do anything to support his grand lifestyle and clear his debts. Caught between his own sense of dignity and importance and having to buy his girlfriend's affection, he is a man in a trap, but a trap not entirely of his own making. It is the trap of fifties consumer culture. The girlfriend, well played by a very young Marilyn Monroe, expertly works Emmerich for jewels and vacations but cannot bring herself to call him anything but "Uncle Lon," hardly a sexually charged response to an aging man trying to retain his sense of virile manhood. The last sequence in a film of moving characterizations shows Dix, slowly bleeding to death, driving back to his childhood home to see his beloved Kentucky and the beautiful horses of his youth. He dies of exsanguination in the grassy fields with the horses milling around him.

These two early and historically important heists, created in part by John Huston, represent the bitterness of a generation expelled during the

Depression from a pastoral life in the heartland, which is so important in American mythology. The dreams of the past are shown to be a comforting illusion but still a powerful, motivating mythology that is part of the foundation of American culture as well as emblematic in both the heist and bandit-gangster film generally. These same myths are movingly represented in later bandit-gangster films like *Bonnie and Clyde* (Arthur Penn, 1967), where the emotional and elegiac picnic in the dust bowl, the last time that Bonnie will see her elderly mother and family, demonstrates the expulsion of working-class Americans from their rural roots, and a leftist view of the illusory nature of the American Dream, at least for those who live desperate lives of poverty and frustrated aspiration in a failed America seen through left-wing eyes. Bonnie's love of Hollywood musical fantasies also resonates in this fantasy life of the dispossessed, and so do the more despairing moments of heist and other bandit-gangster films where these sustaining myths are demystified rather than propagandized.[6]

Armored Car Robbery

Armored Car Robbery is a very different kind of heist film than *The Asphalt Jungle*. It is a semidocumentary police procedural depicting the activities of a brutal heist gang, mostly unknown to each other, wearing masks when together and showing their faces only toward the end, and the equally brutal police officer who pursues them. Charles McGraw, a gravelly voiced character actor who played police officers as often as he was cast as thugs and heavies, is an angry, obsessed, and violent cop who shows little compassion even for his fellow officers. When called to the scene of the racetrack payroll heist, he abandons his mortally wounded, longtime partner to chase the thieves. His job is his life, and we see no family or friends around him ever. He treats his new, younger partner with disdain until he proves himself by almost being shot to death. Only at the end of the film does he express any affection for the young cop, and it seems too little too late. As in *The Asphalt Jungle*, the police are portrayed as brutal. *Armored Car Robbery* is a film where both the police and the crooks are cruel thugs and there is little compassion created for them or even much character development for either. The world of cops and robbers is a brutal one, but the thrill surrounding the heist and its aftermath is always intensely gripping, maintaining a high level of interest in the final outcome.

As a form, the semidocumentary was popular for a short time after the war. It was popular with audiences accustomed to documentaries, with studios who made them cheaply, and even with directors, who often found these "B" films somewhat less subject to censorship than more expensive "A" features with famous stars. Thus a bit more critical commentary on American society sneaks through in the semidocumentary heists, but even more in film gris. Will Straw, in his enlightening essay on this form, notes that semidocumentaries were unemotional, or, as he puts it, the form has "a more generally puritanical resistance to melodramatic intensities to reduce main characters to the institutional settings in which they worked" (140). This lack of emotion in the semidocumentary extended as well to the many police procedurals so popular on American television in the fifties, shows such as *Dragnet* (1951–59) and *The Lineup* (1954–60), as well as to many cinematic heists. Straw also notes that the semidocumentaries are somewhat "incoherent" in their politics because, as I argue for *Armored Car Robbery*, they depict an often ambivalent picture of both the police and the heisters. As Straw argues, the tension in these films "does not map easily onto that between left and right, as if the semi-documentary film enacted the struggle between an ascendant security state and a populist, neorealist opening onto social life" (141). Alternatively, semidocumentaries have also been seen as the right wing of often leftist film noir because of their depiction of thorough, scientific policing and law-and-order plots. Comparing semidocumentary to neorealism, Rebecca Prime believes that the two are very different because "in direct contrast to semi-documentary's emphasis on aesthetics over ethics, Italian Neo-Realism was an 'ethics of aesthetics'" (146). *Armored Car Robbery*, because it is critical of both the police and the crooks, cannot easily be seen as purely a conservative law-and-order film. Both groups are deficient in their feelings, both robotic in their lack of ethics and emotions. Modern men are measured only by their competence and jobs; feelings and ethics are left behind.

He Ran All the Way

Ethics becomes a major consideration in *He Ran All the Way*, and the film has by far the most left-wing narrative of all of the fifties heists, with the possible exception of *Odds Against Tomorrow*. Like Abraham Polonsky's *Force of Evil* (1948), it is an earnest film about the conflict between love, family, and money. A film gris/family melodrama/heist, it stars John Garfield in his last film. Produced by Bob Roberts, written by Dalton Trumbo (as Guy Endore), and directed by John Berry, *He Ran all the Way* involved the cream of the Hollywood blacklist. It is a tense and intense film that begins with a sweaty and seemingly hungover Nick Robey (John Garfield) awaking after a nightmare in a rumpled bed in a disaster of a cheap apartment to the grating sound of his slovenly, alcoholic mother's voice berating him for being jobless and sleeping in, with "If you were a man you'd have a job." Robey replies, "If I were a man I'd kick your teeth out." This is our introduction to a small-time hood who is poor and riddled with anxiety. He immediately goes into a small heist with a friend. Needless to say, it goes very badly. The friend is killed, and Robey kills a police officer in retaliation and to save himself from arrest.

Shot with many noir lighting effects and several extreme close-ups of anxiety-ridden, sweaty faces, this is an unsettling film, perhaps intended to be, as identification with the characters is difficult. Hiding after the robbery in a public swimming pool, Robey meets Peggy Dobbs (Shelley Winters), a lonely working-class woman who works in a bakery and lives with her mother, father, and younger brother in a walk-up apartment, not wealthy but certainly better than Robey's catastrophe of a home. Robey ends up holding the family hostage for a few days, alternately terrifying them and trying to fit into a family life he has never experienced. The father labors as a print setter at a newspaper, the mother is a homemaker, the ten-year-old son is inquisitive, and Peggy is a pretty but unhappy girl with no suitors and an uninspiring job on the assembly line in a bakery. She is both attracted to Robey and afraid of him, having little experience of men. In many ways she is the most interesting of the characters, as she is clearly attracted to the brash Robey but at the same time is trying to be a "good" girl and is very protective of her family. In the end she seems to love him, or, as her father thinks, pretends to love him to get him to run away with her and save her family. She does take some of his money and buys him an escape car. Robey is completely unaccustomed to love or family life and trusts no one. At the end of the film, overwhelmed by anxiety and fear of capture, he does not believe that she has bought the car, and screams, "Nobody loves anybody," as he drags her down the stairs into the street. In a gun battle, Peggy shoots him and he dies in the gutter, having just noticed that she did, in fact, buy him a car. Would she have run away with him? The film is ambiguous in this regard. Clearly she is attracted to him, clearly she is afraid of him. She labors at a miserable job, has no social life, and longs to be happy in a traditional relationship, something that is impossible for Robey.

One of the key ideas in the film is that Robey begins to learn about family life with the Dobbs family. He has conversations with the mother, father, and young boy. He tries to be social with them but is unable to connect. After the mother is injured using her sewing machine, the boy

At the end of *He Ran All the Way*, Robey (John Garfield) lies dying in the street, where money can't buy love.

becomes hysterical, thinking he must defend her. Robey, trying to patch things up, sends the child to the local store to buy food for a grand dinner. When the family sits at the table they will not eat the turkey and fixings because they refuse a family dinner furnished by a killer. Robey forces them to eat, threatening violence. The message here is clear: brought up in the slums by an alcoholic, abusive mother, he has been deprived of the most basic of human feelings: love of family. He is interested only in money, thinking that money might buy love, and is planning to escape to Florida and after that to skiing vacations in the winter. The politics here are hammered home, as in *Force of Evil*: pursuit of money despoils love and family. The heist at the beginning of the film colors everything else that happens, and in the end Robey lies dying in the street, while Peggy is filled with despair.

Plunder Road

The last film I will address is *Plunder Road*, a remarkable heist described by Edward Dimendberg in *Film Noir and the Spaces of Modernity* as a film that demystifies the fifties "great narratives of centrifugal space" (203). This film is a demonstration of the power of the B film to open significant issues of its time. Only seventy-two minutes long, it makes the heist and particularly the escape its central concern. The film opens with a lengthy heist sequence where there is almost no dialogue (in a nod to *Rififi*), and dialogue is sparse throughout the film. The heist sequence itself depicts a highly competent, meticulously timed train robbery. The loot is a very large number of gold bricks belonging to the American mint. The heist is tense and very engaging, taking place in the dark of night during a terrible rainstorm. The mechanics of the heist are complicated, as the robbers must force the train to stop and then gas members of the crew before they use nitroglycerine to blow open the doors. A crane is used to remove the bars quickly, but also to demonstrate how heavy they are. The heist leader, Eddie Harris (Gene Raymond), makes a daring jump onto the top of the moving train. The heist comes off without a hitch. They drive off to a prepared barn, divide the loot between three different trucks, and then begin the nine-hundred-mile trek to Los Angeles.

Two of the trucks do not make it. One falls foul of a police roadblock because an illegal radio is found in the truck. Another ironically ends because the truck, which they claim is hauling a load of coffee, is required to stop at a weigh station and the police are amazed that a load of coffee weighs forty-five hundred pounds more than it should. The heist leader makes it to his hideout in Los Angeles and decides that the only way to save the remaining gold bricks is to melt them down and make them into parts for his car. The emphasis in this film is on how competent and thorough Harris, a college graduate, is. On the drive to the port where the two remaining heisters and a girlfriend plan to escape with the gold, Harris giddily celebrates his own brilliance. Almost immediately, the extraordinary (but not unusual) traffic on the freeway produces a traffic accident, and a middle-aged woman rubbernecking the wreck rear-ends the car with the solid gold bumpers. The two heisters make a run for it after the police notice the gold shining through the rear bumper. The driver is shot, and in an odd kind of irony, Harris, the precise timing man, mistimes the speed of a transport truck when he tries to jump from the freeway onto the top of it on the highway below.

Dimendberg argues that the fifties saw an enormous expansion of the interstate highway system. Mythically these roads were intended to promote commerce and enable Americans to travel freely and easily across the country; they were also essential to the development of suburbs and the huge growth in the auto industry. As a demystification of what Dimendberg sees as a utopian mythology, *Plunder Road* debunks much of the mythology around highway development. The road system itself seems to frustrate and

Harris (Gene Raymond), the precise timing man, mistimes the speed of a transport truck at the end of *Plunder Road*.

end the heist. Extraordinary in its ability to enhance police surveillance, the highway system makes it possible for the police to block all of the trucks in their escape. Rather than promoting the freewheeling ability to travel, the highway frustrates it with a traffic jam, even preventing Harris from escaping down the road. Dimendberg argues that this modest heist film "is a rare work of social criticism that punctures the generally affirmative character of 1950s American culture" (206). In this I would argue *Plunder Road* is another of the fifties heists that demystify American culture.

This is a very competently made and attractive film, where the heisters steal for money and think about foreign travel and the high life. One of them is violent and kills a clerk in a gas station, but they are generally quite civil, although they still have the burning desire to get the gold bars at any cost, despite their enormous weight and how difficult they are to transport. Only one of the heisters that we know of is a serial ex-con; the others seem to have had respectable, but clearly not lucrative enough, jobs. The burning need for money and the good life portrayed in this film is characteristic of a society driven by consumer culture. Even the waitress in a roadside diner tells the assembled customers, including two of the robbers, that she hopes that they "get away with it" as she talks about glamorous vacations in Europe. For the heisters and women like her, such a life is well beyond their means but never beyond their desires.

Conclusion

Each of these four early fifties heists takes a strong, left-wing position regarding how working-class Americans live by or die of the American Dream and are corrupted by the rabid pursuit of money. The desire for money at any cost drives most of the characters to their deaths. Some characters seek money only in order to reclaim the family homesteads; others, like Emmerich, Purvis, and Robey, are afflicted by greed for consumer goods and the good life, widely advertised in the America of the fifties. Joseph Losey argued during this period that America had been afflicted with "false values. About the means justifying the end and the end justifying the means. '100,000 bucks, a Cadillac, and a blonde' were the sine qua non of American life at that time and it didn't matter how you got them—whether you stole the girl from somebody else, stole the money and got the Cadillac from corruption" (quoted in Thomson 2011).

These often uncomfortable heist films, derived from the noir period of the gangster film (which, itself, is also about the ambitions of lower-class men and their need for the success that only money seems to bring, but with no way of getting that success outside of crime), were created by directors, writers, and actors accused of being communists. Made by small studios and often cheaply made, but still often visually arresting, they seemingly managed to escape the watchdogs that plagued more expensive, prestigious films. While heist films are not large in number, they are still being regularly made in our own time. Many are humorous and caper-like, others, like *American Heist* (Sarik Andreasyan, 2014) and *Heist* (Scott Mann, 2015), still take on pressing, working-class social problems. Although the heist subgenre might be relatively small, the fifties cluster certainly initiates the depiction of a strong discontent among working-class men (and women) around the newly minted consumer culture of that time. It is a tradition that continues into our own time.

Notes

1. Another more recent and powerful heist, *Dead Presidents* (The Hughes Brothers, 1995), leaves the heist until the very end of a long film, after the despair of the African American characters is movingly demonstrated. The heist, which fails, seems the only way out.

2. It may be that the director of *Ocean's Eleven* had thought to let the crew get away with the loot, but Frank Sinatra, the film's star, says on a clip from the *Tonight Show* (1962–1992) included on the DVD that letting the crooks get away with the money was not acceptable at that time.

3. Perhaps the first American comic heist was *Larceny, Inc.* (Lloyd Bacon, 1942), where Edward G. Robinson, head of a gang of ex-cons, tries to dig his way through the brick wall of his sham luggage business to get into the bank next door. Things go

badly in a comic way. This film is, perhaps, also referred to in Woody Allen's comedy heist *Small Time Crooks* (2000). The heist film seems a perfect target to parody because of its strict insistence on competence and precision.

4. The Kefauver Committee, which existed from 1950–51, was a Senate committee charged with investigating the existence of organized crime in the United States. The committee did conclude that there was such an organization, adding to the paranoia of the Cold War years. The fact that the committee meetings were televised on early American television spread word of the covert crime syndicate widely throughout the United States.

5. One of the key novels and films of this era is *The Man in the Gray Flannel Suit* (Nunnally Johnson, 1956). It is about a returned veteran who struggles to find his way through a changing world. Pressured by his wife for a better house and the finer things, he has to choose between success in business and family life.

6. Perhaps the most ideologically driven evocation of this mythology is shown in Ronald Reagan's "It's Morning in America Again" (1984) presidential advertisement where the Reagan campaign broadcasts a glowing and highly partisan vision of a white, well-to-do middle America to which white Americans would presumably return during a second Reagan presidency—a retreat from the urban corruption and the dangerous "other" of the inner city and a return to the "real values" a of pre-Depression America. It is extraordinary and has a very different meaning than the views expressed in many fifties heists.

"What Price Glory?"

Postwar British Heist Films

◇◇◇◇◇◇◇◇◇◇◇◇◇◇◇◇◇◇◇◇◇◇

Jim Leach

In July 1945 the British public went to the polls in the first postwar general election. The result was a resounding victory, not for the Conservative Party under Winston Churchill, who had led the nation through the so-called People's War, but for the Labour Party, which promised social changes that would ensure there would be no return to prewar conditions of poverty and class privilege. However, despite the implementation of the "welfare state" and major initiatives in the fields of health, education, and housing, a feeling of disillusionment soon began to creep in, with complaints that the social structure had not changed as much as people had hoped and that the reforms had brought with them more state control and an ever-expanding bureaucracy. According to David Kynaston, "within a year of VE Day there had set in not only a widespread sense of disenchantment—with peace, perhaps even with the Labour government—but also a certain sense of malaise, a feeling that society, which broadly speaking had held together during the war, was even starting to come apart" (109).

The euphoria of victory and the promise of new beginnings made the reality of the difficult postwar years seem all the more dispiriting. Crime films, of many different kinds, began to appear in numbers, reinforcing this feeling that British society had emerged from the war in a state of disarray and moral collapse. As early as 1947, Roger Manvell lamented the tendency toward "films of violence" and suggested that, "deprived of our war films, in an increasingly civilian world, we must find our violence, they say, in studies of crime and sadism" (13). War films, which had disappeared in the immediate postwar years, made a comeback in the 1950s, and their popularity attested to widespread nostalgia for the sense of urgency and community associated with the People's War. However, these were not usually regarded as "films of violence," and critics continued to deplore the prevalence of crime films.

My interest here is in a group of British heist films released between the early 1950s and mid-1960s in which memories of wartime come into conflict with the forces that led to the consumer society, which emerged in full force in the late 1960s. These tensions reinforce the two main appeals of the heist film that always, at least potentially, contradict each other. On the one hand, there is the teamwork, men working together according to an elaborate and ingenious plan, that makes the heist possible in the first place. Then there is the acquisitiveness, the desire for wealth, that motivates at least some of the robbers and often leads to the breakdown of the gang once the heist has taken place. In postwar British heist films, the former is likely to be associated with the war, when the nation supposedly worked together to overcome the threat of Nazism. The individualist drive for monetary gain that motivates most of the thieves gradually moves to the fore and is associated with the modernization that succeeded the austerity of the immediate postwar years.[1]

About thirty heist films were made in Britain between 1951 and 1964, as well as a number of films depicting heists that are not central to the narrative structure. As Christine Geraghty has pointed out, there were also several "crime comedies" that drew on the conventions of the heist film (68–75) and exaggerated the element of the absurd often present, as an undercurrent, in more serious films. Most of the heist films were B features, shown in the double bills that were the most common form of exhibition at the time. These low-budget productions vary considerably in quality, but they effectively represent the tensions at work in the society in which they were made. In what follows I will refer to many of these films to bring out the key concerns of the British heist film, but I will focus mainly on how these concerns are worked through in five major contributions to the subgenre: *The Good Die Young* (Lewis Gilbert, 1954), *The League of Gentlemen* (Basil Dearden, 1960), *Piccadilly Third Stop* (Wolf Rilla, 1960), *Payroll* (Sidney Hayers, 1961), and *A Prize of Arms* (Cliff Owen, 1961).

Does Crime Pay?

During the pre-war years, the British Board of Film Censors kept crime films in check, insisting that "they must be about the detection and punishment of crime, with no criticism of the authorities and no sympathy for the criminal" (Richards 113). Although similar censorship rules developed in the United States as a result of the moral panic over the gangster films of the 1930s, the British censors treated Hollywood crime films more leniently than their British counterparts because crime and violence were seen as the products of a society supposedly quite different from Britain, where the police did not even carry guns. However, "the post-1945 social scene rendered that policy virtually untenable," and "the knowledge of profiteering and racketeering, a legacy from the war, was too extensive for their existence to be convincingly ignored" (Robertson 17). Although there was little criticism of the police in postwar crime films, many did focus on criminals and their activities, as heist films did virtually by definition. The extent to which these films promoted "sympathy for the criminal" is a difficult issue that I will discuss at the end of this chapter

Although critics at the time tended to treat British heist films, as they did most genre films, as slavish imitations of the Hollywood model, there have been attempts to differentiate them in terms of their structure (or syntax).[2] Kirsten Moana Thompson, for example, claims that, "unlike the American heist film, most British heist films emphasise the events before or after the robbery, and focus on the gang's interpersonal conflicts" (47). However, she provides no examples, and the emphasis on each component of the heist film's three-part structure, planning—execution—aftermath, varies from film to film as much as it does in Hollywood films. In *Naked Fury* (Charles Saunders, 1959), for example, the robbery has already taken place, and the opening sequence shows the men speeding away with a woman they have taken hostage, while, in *Calculated Risk* (Norman Harrison, 1963), the planning and execution of the heist are depicted at length, only to come to a very abrupt end when a bomb obliterates the men just as they have cracked the safe.

A more fruitful way of approaching the specific qualities of British heist films is to examine the ways in which the semantic features of the subgenre interact with the social and cultural contexts within which the films were made. Thus the basic rhythm of the heist film, in which the euphoria of the successful robbery is usually followed in short order by the disintegration of the gang, must have resonated strongly with audiences who had lived through the end of the war and the postwar disappointments. Similarly, the insistence on split-second timing that is vital to the planning and execution of the heist would have reminded British audiences not only of the regimentation of military service but also of the ways in which postwar society depended on schedules and time management, associated with both the new welfare state and "time and motion studies" imported from the United

States. Although a key element of all heist films, the importance of good timing, in the British context, could be seen as looking back to the need to work together during the war or looking forward to the more efficient (and more Americanized) ways of organizing the economy and everyday life. As we shall see, other typical features of the heist film take on distinctive overtones in the British context.

War and Peace

The shadow of World War II hangs over British heist films even more than it does their Hollywood counterparts. It frequently determines the actions and motivations of the gang members, who apply methods they learned in the army, and it is also very often visually present in the damaged cities in which the heists take place. In *The Secret Place* (Clive Donner, 1956), for example, the jewels from the heist end up in a young boy's "secret place" in a derelict building on a bomb site near his home, a stark contrast to the construction going on in the more well-to-do parts of the city. The thieves in *Calculated Risk* tunnel into a bank from a bomb site, where they find an unexploded bomb that has been there since the war.

The involvement of men returned from the war is, however, the most common way in which criminal activities are represented as a perverse acting out of wartime behavior. Thus, in the earliest British heist film, *Dangerous Cargo* (John Harlow, 1951), Harry (Terence Alexander) blackmails Tim (Jack Watling) into becoming the inside man on a heist at the airport where he works, reminding him of their time in a German prisoner-of-war camp and then manipulating him into accumulating gambling debts. Pliny (Karel Stepanek), the gang leader, insists on using men from the services, who will have "a sense of discipline," and calls the job "a commando raid," referring to the day of the heist as "D-Day" and saying that he feels "like a general going into battle."

In *The Good Die Young*, all four thieves have served in the war, but the omniscient narrator tells us that none have criminal records. Their leader, Miles Ravenscroft (Laurence Harvey), known as Rave, convinces the others that their misfortunes are due to the ingratitude of a society in which only the people who stayed home from the war have prospered and that they can solve their problems by holding up a post office van. The ex-soldiers who come together to rob a bank in *The League of Gentlemen* are equally discontented with the way society has treated them, and the film depicts the heist as a perverse version of the kind of operation seen in many war films.

In this film, Jack Hawkins, the star of many British war films, plays Hyde, a former army officer, who gathers together a gang of men, all of whom were cashiered from the army for a variety of offenses, but only after acquiring the skills necessary for his planned bank robbery. The link to the war film is underlined by Philip Green's musical score that evokes the scores of numerous war films, notably *The Dam Busters* (Michael Anderson, 1955). Hyde contacts the men by sending them each a letter, along with a copy of a crime novel and bank notes cut in two, inviting them to a meeting at a London hotel. As the men receive this message, the film shows the uncomfortable lives they are leading in postwar society. At the meeting, Hyde carefully mentions their former ranks and points out that they are "all crooks" and were "trained at public expense" to do jobs that are "frowned on in peacetime."

Although the film has been described as nostalgic for the excitement of the war, it forcefully reminds us that, as Raymond Durgnat puts it, "these officers and gentlemen . . . are a pressgang of moneygrubbing or dishonest scoundrels, largely caddish, seedy and mean" (35). Hyde insists that he is different from the others, asserting, "I served my country well," but his bitterness about being made "redundant" has led him to plan the perfect crime. When he shows the men a film of the bank he plans to rob, he says this will be "our finest hour" and insists that the heist should be planned like "a textbook military campaign." "What price glory?" he asks, and then answers the question himself: £100,000 each, which will be "tax free," and "you won't even have to sign a form for it." The heist is carried out using gas masks to protect the thieves from the smokescreen they use to cover their escape, which, along with the explosions used to take out the alarm system, creates imagery that evokes the Blitz.

A Prize of Arms also looks back to the wartime experience of two of the gang members but places the heist in the context of Britain's humiliation in 1956, when troops were deployed in a futile attempt to prevent Egypt from taking control of the Suez Canal. The film depicts a modern Britain in which the army is a relic of the past, struggling to maintain the illusions of empire. In *The League of Gentlemen*, the gang members impersonate army officers to steal weapons from "our late employer," but the army becomes the main target in *A Prize of Arms*. Turpin (Stanley Baker), who plans the heist of the payroll on an army base, reveals that he fought in World War II but received a "dishonorable discharge" when he was stationed in Hamburg after the war, where, he explains, it was "one gigantic fiddle." The army base is already in crisis mode, with soldiers mobilizing for a military

The robbers enter the bank wearing gas masks in *The League of Gentlemen*.

intervention in the Middle East: not the Suez debacle but a similar situation supposedly taking place in the near future (the very near future if we take literally Turpin's reminiscences about being in Hamburg fifteen or sixteen years earlier). As Turpin explains, there is an unusually large payroll to take care of the "expeditionary forces," while the crisis provides "a flap to hide behind." A radio newscaster reports that the government's aim is to preserve "the rule of law," and the base commander responds to the heist by muttering, "As if imminent war and international tension weren't enough." The heist becomes a tragicomic parallel to the political situation.

Foreign Accents

The patriotic associations of the leader's speech in *Dangerous Cargo* are rather undercut in that Pliny speaks with an accent that would have been taken to be German (although the actor was Czech). European actors who had fled from the Nazi regime appeared regularly, usually as villains, in postwar British crime films, but the changing status of the nation was more apparent in the casting of American actors to increase the chance of success in the ever more important US market. The heist films most obviously aimed at this market were *A Prize of Gold* (Mark Robson, 1955), for which the British producers imported an American director, and *The Day They Robbed the Bank of England* (John Guillermin, 1959), produced by MGM's British studios. In the former, an American soldier (Richard Widmark) in occupied Berlin persuades his British colleague (George Cole) to take part in the heist of gold bars left behind by the Nazis, and, in the latter, a rare period heist set in the early twentieth century, an American mercenary (Aldo Ray) is brought in to assist an Irish gang with a heist financed by the Irish Republican Army. American actors routinely appeared in other heist films, playing characters who were only sometimes identified as American (or Canadian).

The accents of the British characters often draw attention to the class system that remained a strong presence in the national cinema, as in the society at large, despite the promise of an end to class distinctions. In *The Bank Raiders* (Maxwell Munden, 1958), the bank clerk who fears for his life because he has seen one of the gang during the heist, his middle-class family, and his fiancée are contrasted with the underworld characters by their clipped accents, and, in *Ambush in Leopard Street* (J. Henry Piperno, 1962), when Johnny (James Kenney) wants to provoke a quarrel with Gina (Jean Harvey), the jeweler's assistant he has been dating to get information for the heist, he objects to her "posh voice."

At the beginning of *The Good Die Young*, the narrator describes Rave as a "gentleman of leisure," and his aristocratic background sets him apart from the other gang members, two of whom are American: Joe (Richard Basehart), a "clerk," and Eddie (John Ireland), an "airman." Their nationality and accents place them outside the class system, but the fourth gang member is Mike (Stanley Baker), a former "prizefighter" whose left hand has been amputated, and Rave's assumption of leadership makes it clear that the opportunities for working-class men like Mike are no more promising than before the war. While all the men in *The League of Gentlemen* are English, from various social backgrounds, Hyde describes the book that has inspired his plan as "an American thriller," and his second-in-command, ex-Major Race (Nigel Patrick), at first objects, "You can't pull a stunt like that in this country." There are also no Americans in *A Prize of Arms*, although the original audience would certainly have remembered that the United States virtually ended the Suez invasion (and Britain's imperial illusions) by refusing to support the illegal military operation. The main problem with accents in this film involves Swavek (known as Con), Turpin's Polish friend whom he met in Hamburg after the war, played by German actor Helmut Schmid, whose accent becomes a liability once they enter the base in a stolen army truck and wearing British uniforms.

The film in which clashing accents make the most impact is *Piccadilly Third Stop*, which was made in the same year as *The League of Gentlemen* and released five months later. It makes only marginal references to the war, and the score, also by Philip Green, emphasizes jazz and dance music, in keeping with the cosmopolitan milieu of leisure in which the heist plan is hatched. The opening sequence takes place at a society wedding reception, where Dominic (Terence Morgan), a small-time crook, wanders around, overhearing snatches of inane conversation in upper-class voices, and then palms jewelry from the gift table. As Steve Chibnall suggests, Dominic is "a well-bred wastrel," much like Rave in *The Good Die Young*, who represents "the terminal decline of a social class" ("Ordinary People" 106), and the international cast only adds to the suggestion that social change has not produced a renewed sense of national identity.

Preedy (John Crawford) is an American, a smuggler who looks down on the effete Englishmen at the gambling club to which Dominic has introduced him. His wife, Christine (Mai Zetterling), has a Swedish accent that is never accounted for, and Fina (Yôko Tani), the woman Dominic seduces into helping the thieves enter the foreign embassy in which her father is ambassador, has a Japanese accent (although the character comes from "one of the spice republics"). Dominic is something of an "angry young man" and says he is "sick of being lectured to by people who have had it all handed to them on a plate." However, Preedy, who is equally angry, regards him as a "society type" and an "amateur," despite Dominic's pride in the "skill and ingenuity" that enabled him to come up with the plan to use the London Underground tunnels to break into the embassy. It soon becomes clear that Preedy's claim to the virility often associated with Americans in British cinema is only a pose, undermined by the fact that Christine is also Dominic's mistress, and he finances the heist only because of his losses as a gambler.

Films of Violence

Since the crime genre was generally regarded as American, the casting of US actors would seem quite logical, but the association of American culture with gunplay also raised questions about the alleged social effects of the violence in Hollywood films—and British genre films. In *Gelignite Gang* (Francis Searle, 1956), Jimmy (Wayne Morris) is an American who, working for a company called "Anglo-American Investigators," tries to find the leader of a gang of jewel thieves that, as newspaper headlines make clear, has no qualms about using guns. He suspects Popoulos (Eric Pohlmann), the Greek owner of a nightclub, but the leader, he eventually discovers, is no foreigner but Rutherford (Patrick Holt), Jimmy's English boss. More commonly, gang leaders insist that their men not take guns on the job, although this stipulation is not always taken seriously. Thus, in *Three Crooked Men* (Ernest Morris, 1958), Vince (Michael Mellinger) insists he won't "work on any job with guns," but Masters (Eric Pohlmann again), the gang leader, assures him they are only to scare people and won't be loaded. He then loads the guns outside the shop from which they plan to break into the bank next door.

Similarly, in *The Good Die Young*, the decision to carry guns on the heist becomes a key issue. When Rave hands out guns before the job, the others, who have agreed to take part only because of their financial needs, are reluctant to take them. Rave assures them that they will not have to use them, but he starts shooting immediately when a policeman asks him to move their car when they park outside the post office. An apparent allusion to this sequence in *The League of Gentlemen* brings out the superiority of Hyde's planning and organization. When the men are casing the bank, a policeman comes up to a parked car in which ex-Captain Porthill (Bryan Forbes), who was cashiered for killing political prisoners in Cyprus, sits waiting. He starts to pull a gun, and smiles at the officer just as Rave did, but he restrains himself, and the policeman moves on with a polite warning. Although the gang's first action is an elaborately orchestrated theft of guns from "our late employer," the discipline that Hyde has instilled means that they do not have to use them in the actual heist.

The question of guns also comes up in *Piccadilly Third Stop*, in which Colonel Whitfield (William Hartnell), an older man who presumably served in the war, agrees to join the gang as the safecracker on condition that they not carry arms. However, Preedy secretly decides to take a gun and plans to escape with the entire proceeds. When Christine tips him off, Dominic also takes a gun and, when the two men struggle over the loot, he shoots Preedy as the American tries to push him onto the electrified rails. In *A Prize of Arms*, the guns belong to the army (although the troops are apparently short of ammunition), and the only weapon used by the thieves is a flamethrower, with which they set fire to the payroll office to distract attention from the theft.

Men and Women

As will be clear by now, heists are usually committed by men, and the women in the films are often simply window dressing—literally in *Date*

With Disaster (Charles Saunders, 1957) and *Calculated Risk*, in which thieves are distracted by women undressing in front of windows. However, in these male-dominated films, women can have an impact on the outcome quite disproportional to their numbers, especially since, as in many postwar crime films, the heists often seem to be undertaken to shore up the masculine credentials of the gang members now that the war is over. Thus, in *Naked Fury* the men's character is tested by their responses to the woman they have kidnapped during the heist, while in *The Day They Robbed the Bank of England* the success of the heist is threatened by the jealousy of two of the men over the woman who is organizing it. Women take more active roles in two films directed by John Gilling. In *The Frightened Man* (1951), Amanda (Barbara Murray) is a modern woman who wears trousers, but her attraction to the feckless Julius (Dermot Walsh) undermines her desire for independence. In *The Challenge* (1959), the gang boss is an American woman (Jayne Mansfield) whose leadership is called into question when the men turn against her.

At the beginning of *The Good Die Young*, as the men are about to start the heist, the narrator asks why they are there, and a long flashback depicts the situations that have brought each of the men to a state of desperation, all of which have to do with the women in their lives. Joe has been fired from his job in New York because he wants to go to London to bring back his English wife, Mary (Joan Collins), who is reluctant to leave her hypochondriac mother. Eddie is still in the US Air Force and is being transferred to Germany, but he deserts to deal with his wife, Denise (Gloria Grahame), a would-be film star who is having an affair with her leading man. Mike's wife, Angie (Rene Ray), has used their savings to provide bail for her brother, who promptly skips the country. Rave is married to Eve (Margaret Leighton), who decides she will no longer cover his gambling debts. They all feel emasculated: after he loses his hand, Mike's wife tells him the court has impounded the money he earned as a fighter, and he asks, "What sort of a man does that make me?" while Eddie's first quarrel with his wife takes place when she comes home late and ruins the dinner he has cooked for her. The film thus depicts a crisis in postwar masculinity in which the women are implicated, although only Denise can be called a femme fatale in the Hollywood sense.

Women are less prominent in *The League of Gentlemen*, figuring only in the opening sequences before the men sequester themselves to plan the job. These brief cameos establish that none of the men have satisfying personal lives, but this is attributed less to the women than to the overall drabness of the society in which they live. The book that gave Hyde the idea for the heist is called *The Golden Fleece* and has a drawing of a scantily clad woman on the cover, implying that the men can prove their masculinity by escaping from the reality of their lives into the glamour associated with American popular culture. The film has been accused of misogyny because of a scene in which Race asks if a portrait of a woman in Hyde's house depicts his wife; he then asks if she is dead, and Hyde replies, "No, unfortunately, the bitch is very much alive." Yet, there is no reason to assume the film endorses this aspect of his character. After the final briefing, Hyde walks through the cellar of his house past a rocking horse and a harp, and the film suggests that this outburst may be a defense mechanism against his memories of a past family life. At the end, when the telephone rings to announce the presence of the police, a photograph of his wife is seen beside it, suggesting that Hyde's bitterness is the result not just of being made "redundant" but also of the breakdown of his marriage. In a sense, the heist enables the men to "retrieve their 'manliness'" (Kirkham and Thumim 100), but only at the cost of spending several years in an all-male prison.

In *Piccadilly Third Stop*, Dominic is a womanizer, and his affair with Fina makes the heist possible, but his relationship with Christine ensures that the tensions that will tear the gang apart are apparent early on in the film. Women certainly cannot be blamed for the final disaster in *A Prize of Arms*, since, apart from a few workers on the army base, they are completely absent from this film, but, like the Suez crisis itself, the film makes clear that postwar Britain is no longer a major world power and that the traditionally male institution of the army, however efficient, has become increasingly irrelevant.

The film in which women play the most active role in the outcome is *Payroll*, which reverses the usual gender dynamics of the heist film. In the first half of the film the preparations for the heist are intercut with the suburban lives of two families. Harry Parker (William Peacock) has designed a new armored vehicle that he has demonstrated to a large company, and he returns home to find his wife, Jackie (Billie Whitelaw), in the bathroom with their children. He is delighted with the new contract, which will be lucrative because the payroll he will deliver is well over £100,000, but she is worried that he will be running a risk by driving the van himself. Dennis Pearson (William Lucas) is the "inside man" on the job, and, when he comes home to a similar suburban house, he offers his Austrian wife, Katie (Françoise Prévost), a holiday in Majorca. She doesn't believe him and complains, "Out of two occupying powers, I chose you." After she starts an affair with Johnny (Michael Craig), the leader of the heist gang, she explains that she married

Dennis only "to get out of Vienna, to escape from the ruins." When the thieves ram the new van, Harry is impaled on the steering wheel, and one of the gang also dies. A few days later, Johnny suggests that the newspapers are losing interest because "there's no sex angle," but it is the women who will prove to be his downfall, as we shall see.

Getting Rich Quick

The transition from heists that take place in the context of the memory of war to those that emphasize the lures of the affluent society cannot be seen as a linear movement. As early as *The Frightened Man*, Julius, who has been sent down from Oxford, declares, "I'm going to make money and make it fast." He is not interested when his father (Charles Victor) offers him a partnership in his antique store, apparently setting up a theme of youth rejecting the values of their elders. Only six years after the end of the war, the thieves represent the emerging consumer society as opposed to the values of the antique dealer, but it is later revealed that the father has raised the money to send Julius to university by acting as a fence for thieves and that he is now the leader of the gang ("crime is a habit," he says). Similarly, in *No Road Back* (Montgomery Tully, 1957), John (Skip Homeier) returns from the United States (with an American accent) and discovers that his deaf and blind mother (Patricia Dainton) is the leader of a gang and has used the proceeds to finance his studies to become a doctor.

In both of these films, the criminal activities are traced back to the parents, who want to see their sons rise in the social order. The transition from the austerity of the immediate postwar years to the affluence of the later 1950s only added to the frustrations of those who felt they were missing out. This is clearly brought out in the opening sequence of *Three Crooked Men*, in which the men planning a heist drive past a factory and houses under construction and speak of wanting their share of the "boom."

In *The League of Gentlemen*, Elizabeth (Nanette Newman), the wife of ex-Major Rutland-Smith (Terence Alexander), luxuriates in a bubble bath and tells him, "The war's been over a long time. There's no more rationing. There's plenty to go round." Her comments suggest that, for all the apparently nostalgic allusions to the war, the main motivation for the heist is the men's feelings of being left out of the economic revival. Alexander Walker even suggested, "*The League of Gentlemen*, with its target of quick capital gains, was the ideal comedy for a boom-time economy" (103–4). However, as we have seen, the comedy is very dark, and the only visible signs of an affluent society are the bustling London streets the men drive through on their way to the bank.

The signs of the times are much more evident in *Payroll*, in which Harry comes home after his first run in the van carrying presents for his wife and children and exclaims, "Easy come, easy go." When she tells him she is worried, he insists, "It's the only way to make real money," a comment that creates an uncomfortable link between his business success and the motivations behind the robbery. Similarly, in *A Prize of Arms*, the heist mirrors the government's actions, driven as it is by Turpin's bitter insistence that, "If you want anything in this world, you've just got to go out and take it." Cliff Owen had already made a heist film, *Offbeat* (1960), in which thieves organized themselves like businessmen and the lines between police and criminals became blurred, a vision that would reappear in his comic heist film, *The Wrong Arm of the Law* (1963). The more upbeat mood that was emerging in the 1960s was accompanied by new questions about the social order, which the earlier films had seen as stifling but clearly defined.

Conclusion: Endings

In all of the films discussed here, the heist is successful in that the robbers achieve their objective, but they end up either dead or facing a long jail term. While this outcome is partly due to censorship requirements, it leaves the viewers in an ambivalent state to the extent that they have identified with the criminals. Because heist films depict the action from the perspective of the thieves, they tend to set up a tension in the spectator between wanting them to succeed and a respect for the social order that almost always prevails. However, postwar British heist films depict characters with whom it is difficult to identify, and what Barry Forshaw says of *Piccadilly Third Stop* applies to many other films: "The audience scrutinises Dominic for one action which will redeem his strictly utilitarian view of other human beings, but Rilla is simply not interested in providing such banal excuses" (37).

If the audience identifies at all, it is less with the characters than with the job, as the films appeal to the spectator's own desire for material security in a society undergoing rapid and disorienting change. The moral dilemma that they set up is also related to the issue of tone: the noir world within which the heist plans are hatched is both undercut and reinforced by comic elements related to the absurdity of elaborate plans that always come to nothing. Although the final effect is, to some extent, determined by whether the gang is betrayed by internal divisions, by police intervention, or by sheer chance, the ending is always ironic and usually does not resolve the moral and social issues that the film has addressed. To suggest the possible impact of these endings, I will briefly discuss how they work in the five films on which I have mainly focused.

In *The Good Die Young*, the heist itself takes very little time (partly, it seems, as a result of censorship), and its disastrous consequences follow very quickly (Harper and Porter 171). As the police arrive, Mike tries to surrender but Rave shoots him in the back. When the three remaining robbers escape across electrified railway tracks, Rave pushes Eddie to his death, and he and Joe both die in a shootout at the airport, where they go to make their separate escapes. The loot remains hidden in a tomb in a churchyard, and, with all the men dead, the film ends with a shot of the tomb, as the narrator's voice intones that it contains "an illusion called money, which would never have done them any good, would it?" This is presumably a rhetorical question to which the implied answer is, "No," but the rest of the film suggests otherwise, and the spectators are free to decide for themselves.

By the time the members of *The League of Gentlemen* meet in Hyde's house to share the proceeds from the heist, the men, unlike those in *The Good Die Young* and most heist films, are united in their mutual respect for each other and their leader, who has whipped this disparate crew into shape like an officer in a war film. Despite the precision with which the gang has carried out Hyde's plan, the police, acting on information received from a small boy who had been collecting car license plate numbers outside the bank, pick them up as they leave their celebratory party in small groups. With its whimsical title sequence in which a man in evening dress climbs out of a manhole in a dark city street, the jaunty tone of this film is very different from the gloomy noir imagery of *The Good Die Young*, and viewers are more likely to identify with the characters, despite their failings. Andrew Clay cites the film as an example of a "caper" as distinct from a "heist" ("When the Gangs" 82), and another critic casually refers to it as "a caper comedy" (Dux 201), but if this is a caper film or a comedy it is a very dark one.

As the heist begins in *Piccadilly Third Stop*, Preedy grumbles that it is "the blind leading the blind." The outcome seems to support this assessment. The men enter the embassy through the Underground after it closes down at night, but the carefully timed operation is delayed, and the trains have started running when they leave in the morning. After the safe is opened, Fina appears, and, while Dominic is distracted, Preedy clubs the colonel and takes off with the bag of money. Dominic pushes Fina aside,

The men enter the London Underground tunnels in *Piccadilly Third Stop*.

ignores the wounded man, and pursues Preedy. As we have seen, they fight beside the rushing trains, and Dominic is finally able to shoot his opponent. He manages to reach the station, where Christine is waiting in the escape car. However, she drives too fast and crashes into a truck, killing them both in front of a sign that reads NO ENTRY. This outcome has been aptly called "one of the bleakest endings in British crime film" (Forshaw 37), although the endings of many other British heist films are close rivals.

At the end of *Payroll*, it is the women, whose lives have been ruined by the heist, who bring about Johnny's downfall. After Dennis, consumed with guilt for his role in supplying information, tries to burn his share of the money, setting the house on fire in the process, Katie persuades Johnny, who has killed the surviving gang members, to take her with him to the boatyard from which he plans to escape. She tries to double-cross him and drugs him so that she can leave with the case of money from the heist, but he is suspicious of her motives and has switched cases so that she finds only a bundle of old newspapers. Meanwhile, Jackie has been conducting her own investigation into her husband's death and has hastened Dennis's breakdown by sending him anonymous letters. She tells a policeman friend that she doesn't want justice, fearing that Johnny will receive just a few years in jail; she wants "vengeance," which she pursues with a zombie-like

At the end of *Payroll*, Jackie (Billie Whitelaw) holds a gun on the man who killed her husband.

obsession. She tracks him down to the dockyard, where he is still feeling the effects of Katie's drug. On the boat, Jackie holds him at gunpoint and, when he falls overboard, watches gleefully as the boat runs him down. In a final image, typical of the subgenre, the money floats away in its wake.

In *A Prize of Arms*, the thieves succeed in joining a convoy in their truck, with the money hidden in a tire, and they reach their hideaway thinking they are "home and dry." However, their departure from the convoy has attracted the attention of a motorcycle escort rider, who has disobeyed orders and stopped for a drink at a nearby pub. As troops surround the place, Turpin decides to crash through in the truck, but Fenner panics and starts using the flamethrower before they leave. When Turpin tries to stop him, the flames set fire to the truck, but they drive out in the burning vehicle, unaware that it is carrying explosives. All three men are killed in the explosion, and the money literally goes up in smoke. This obliteration of the gang is the culmination of a series of incidents inside the camp that upset Turpin's careful planning, leading one critic to suggest, "the film could have been subtitled, 'The Three Stooges Pull a Heist'" (Keaney 160). But the overall effect is far from comic, and although it is possible to see the depiction of the army as "not unaffectionate" (Forshaw 144), Turpin's "obsession/determination, combined with a sense of fatalism and dark visual style is what gives the film a noir sensibility" (Clay, "Men, Women" 59). The mixture of farce and tragedy parallels the vain attempt during the Suez crisis to sustain the illusion of British imperial power.

By the mid-1960s, these dark heist films gave way to films that offered the spectacle of crime as an amoral expression of the new consumer society. *Robbery* (Peter Yates, 1967) and *The Italian Job* (Peter Collinson, 1969), both produced by Stanley Baker's production company, are very different films: the former, based on the real-life heist in 1963 that became known as the Great Train Robbery, mixes the heist film with elements of the police procedural, docudrama, and action movie; the latter is a lighthearted caper in which British robbers steal a gold shipment in Milan during an England-Italy soccer match. Both prominently feature spectacular car chases and, unlike the earlier films that were all made in black-and-white, the bright color cinematography sweeps away the shadows and anxiety that permeated the postwar British heist film.

Notes

1. It should be noted that a similar tension was already present during and immediately after the war in the ambiguous figure of the spiv, a small-time crook who acted as a "an intermediary in the transfer of black market goods from army camps, docks, railway yards, lorry parks, industrial depots and so on, to a grateful mass of consumers" (Wollen 186).

2. I am referring here to Rick Altman's distinction between the semantic and syntactic dimensions of the genre film, as discussed in the introduction to this volume.

The Joy of Burglary

Wealth Relocation Strategies and Other Entertainments in the Postwar French Policier

◇◇◇◇◇◇◇◇◇◇◇◇◇◇◇◇◇◇◇◇◇◇◇

Tim Palmer

Midway through Jean-Pierre Melville's *Bob le flambeur/Bob the Gambler* (1956) is a ninety-second sequence that epitomizes the power, and pleasures, of the postwar French crime film *policier*. Bob (Roger Duchesne), an aging gentleman-kingpin, fallen upon hard times, has recruited a motley assortment of henchmen for a heist of the Deauville resort casino. After Bob drills his lackeys through lengthy rehearsals, culminating in a practice walk-through on a floor plan painted onto airport wasteland, Melville himself interjects a droll piece of voice-over: "Here's how, according to Bob, everything would happen." Fade in next to a series of strange yet beguiling tableaux: the gang's two black Cadillacs pulling into Deauville at dawn; a whip pan left and cut to the casino's entrance hallway, where the men draw their pistols and take up their stations; cut to a medium long shot of Bob himself, dressed in an immaculate tuxedo, leaning on the banister at the top of an opulent stairway, gesturing imperiously for his team to advance; then the leading four men congregating, then freezing like statues, in the main casino office, where, as the camera tracks in, Roger (André Garet) sets about cracking the safe. All the while, no words are spoken and there is no diegetic sound of any kind; instead we hear an ethereal minor-key musical quartet—strings and bassoon set against a reverberating xylophone and shrill lilting flute—echoing over the soundtrack. The casino itself is oddly deserted. The gang meets no resistance at all; nothing impedes their progress. A fast horizontal wipe right then concludes the segment, whisking us back to diegetic reality, with Melville's quip: "But Roger had already improved his system . . ."

Bob (Roger Duchesne) leads his team in a hypothetical heist of the Deauville casino in *Bob le flambeur*.

This *Bob le flambeur* sequence—Melville's tongue-in-cheek hypothetical flash-forward aside—distills the policier's materials, and how it engages its audience, in a suite of ways. Most brazen, the film signals its awareness of the central heist as its load-bearing set piece, what we're all waiting for, the literal and figurative jewel in its crown. Like a well-designed clockwork timepiece, the policier's main burglary goes off in predictable crescendo. But the swaggering Melville raises the stakes: he teases his expectant viewer by presenting his heist not once but twice, the former a perfect success, but only in Bob's subjective fantasy; the second time, for real, a generically prescribed debacle, with Bob too distracted by the roulette wheel to lead his gang, whose scheme has already been leaked to the police. In addition, *Bob le flambeur* highlights the textual attractions of the theft act as pure procedural choreography: Bob dictating proceedings like a director blocking his actors, leading the troupe through practiced maneuvers, each man perfectly syncopated, in control, in his element, united in pursuit of illegal wealth. Performed in total diegetic silence, yet set to an exaggerated non-diegetic score, Melville's sequence also takes the musicality of the heist performance to the verge of pastiche, self-parody. Entering the casino stage, each chorus thug strides over to his place, turns, and strikes a pose, firearm clutched and face set, as if performing a droll version of an underworld ballet. All the while, the staccato rhythms of the musical accompaniment make the foregrounded Bob a kind of virtuoso orchestra conductor, setting the pace, the man from whom everyone takes his or her cue. Lastly, there are Melville's arch omniscient remarks, with their self-reflexive panache: the filmmaker calling the shots over his own on-screen exploits, talking the sequence up then tossing it away peremptorily, underlining his stature as knowing policier impresario, a carnival barker bantering with the crowd, one step ahead of Bob's toiling mob, clearly the most expertly versed in the minutiae of the policier genre at hand.

With *Bob le flambeur*'s remarkable generic flourishes foremost in our minds, we can begin to think more broadly about the postwar French policier, setting out the case that this chapter will pursue. Our argument here is that, belying its reputation for intellectual zeal and cerebral self-consciousness, the textual pleasures of French cinema are actually legion, often as codified and ritualized, honed and alluring, as anything in classical or contemporary Hollywood. Exploring the idea of the French policier as entertainment text will be this essay's agenda. Right away there are ingrained essentialist assumptions to combat. The misguided belief that French film is inherently elitist, an art cinema to its core, with its many long-lived popular formats either dismissed as unworthy or else ignored entirely, is a perennial default to many. T. Jefferson Kline's overarching framing argument, for example, in *Unraveling French Cinema* is, befitting its loaded title, that French cinema is fundamentally an evasive discontinuous complex, rife with textual snares, always to be approached with caution, "forewarned with the sober knowledge that the medium *needs unraveling*" (192; his italics). Colin Crisp, similarly, in his ostensibly expansive *Critical Filmography* encyclopedias of classical French cinema, attempts nothing less than an anti-mass-culture coup d'état. Crisp openly shuns "some extremely popular film and series," deeming such fare "no longer watchable except by the committed historian," which leads him to expunge the likes of *Fanfan la tulipe* (Christian-Jaque, 1952) from the record entirely and to argue that among French crime "action parodies" barely a single entry, the Eddie Constantine star vehicle policier, *La Môme vert-de-gris* (Bernard Borderie, 1953) is "still tolerable" (*A Critical Filmography* 20–21). Stern and stark, lessons like these are clear: French cinema means high art cinema, and if what you're watching is enjoyable, it's not only bad for you but not truly French anyway.

In contrast, this chapter contends the opposite: that popular French film can be just as sophisticated as its rarefied arthouse counterpart; that its pleasures are fascinating, valuable, and salient to contemporary audiences; and that the process by which French film entertains is overlooked and worthy of our attention. With this particular template embodied for us by the policier—as reliable a popular mainstay as any yet produced by French cinema—there will be none of Kline's sober knowledge here, but rather our consideration of a carefully crafted entertainment system, a playful yet deliberate generic vernacular, and refined escapist idealism (with certain deflating, yet still gratifying, disclaimers). Most obviously, the policier's assets exist at the level of plot and iconography: its endlessly recycled patterns of jaundiced gendarmes pursuing inveterate thieves, the exchange of wealth and gunfire set amidst the teeming underworld of Paris, the city of lights recast on-screen as an alluring communal labyrinth of avarice and vice (T. Palmer). As long as there have been French filmmakers, indeed, there have been policiers: from the serial crime texts of Louis Feuillade (most famously *Fantômas* [1913–1914], *Les Vampires* [1915–1916], and *Judex* [1916]), the backbone of Gaumont's early studio output, to a profusion of twenty-first-century gangster narratives, distributed internationally, made by figures like Jacques Audiard, Fred Cavayé, and Olivier Marchal. France's new wave of twenty-first-century television exports is also led by hit policiers, such as *Engrenages* (2005–) and *Braquo* (2009–) (Guérif; Massonat).

For our purposes here, however, we will look at how the policier genre found particularly rich expression—arguably its decisive manifestation—in the immediate postwar period, a major reason for the revival of France's post-Liberation cinema. Central to our analysis will be the policier's main stock-in-trade: the heist sequence, the cycle's quintessential tour de force, its pivotal act of crime and—inevitably, subsequently—punishment. From the celebrated extended jewelry store robbery of Jules Dassin's *Rififi/Du Rififi chez les hommes* (1955), carried out in complete silence, to the outlandish casino antics in *Bob le flambeur*, the policier heist looms as large as any in the canon of French cinema's most iconic sequences—the mass genre equivalent of the climactic beach freeze-frame of Truffaut's *Les 400 coups/The 400 Blows* (1959)—beloved by cinephile connoisseurs and casual newcomers alike. In sum, our framing questions here are: What ingredients are fundamental, endemic to the French policier heist? Why do audiences, both historical and contemporary, revel in these particular segments of film? What textual qualities make the heist so critical to this most popular French screen format?

To start, we need salient contextual data, a brief counter-history of France's cinema of the Fourth Republic (1946–58), a period still in need of rehabilitation, from which our case studies originate. For despite its reputation as an era of stagnation—a bias drawn from François Truffaut's "tradition of quality" epithet, still widely used as if it were an objectively accurate term, as if all popular or critically successful pre–New Wave films warrant scorn sight unseen—the postwar period is actually one of the richest and most dynamic in French cinema history. From an industry in ruins by 1944, France's film trade rebuilt on an unprecedented, and still uncelebrated, scale. This growth, over the post-Liberation decade, was on the one hand institutional, with a network of state-supervised organizations established: the Centre national de la cinématographie (CNC) in 1946, which immediately diverted revenues to reconstructing French movie theaters; the Institut des hautes études cinématographiques (IDHEC), France's national film school, inaugurated the same year; France's central film export body, UniFrance, opened in 1949; and, crucially, the Cannes Film Festival, revived in 1946 after being on hiatus for seven years, where certain more prestigious policiers found positive reception: Dassin won the Best Director festival prize in 1955 for *Rififi*, while Jacques Becker's *Le Trou* premiered there in 1960 (Vezyroglou). Buoyed by this industrial investment, as well as a slew of state-sponsored projects, postwar French cinema bloomed and diversified, encompassing short filmmaking, nonfiction forms like essay films and documentaries, pedagogical films, animation, and commercial productions alike. Most importantly, however, across the span of this new French postwar cinema ecosystem, mass audiences returned with a renewed appetite for film—and they were often hungry for policiers. From 1944 to 1958, annual film-going attendance doubled, from two hundred million to four hundred million, or nine visits per person per year (Crisp, *Classic French Cinema* 68), while during the same time frame French crime film production rose to twelve to twenty genre pieces made each year, a new staple of the industry, making up about a fifth of the country's annual film output (Bessy, Chirat, and Bernard; T. Palmer 223–24). One iconic tent-pole policier production, Jacques Becker's *Touchez pas au grisbi* (1954), drew 4.7 million viewers in 1954 alone, the fourth biggest hit of the year, grossing 96 million francs at the box office and underlining the genre's vitality.

Based upon this dramatic upturn in the policier's fortunes, a strong current in the revitalized postwar French film industry, what factors of its design proved enticing to so many? How to quantify the genre's entertainment determinants, its organization of enjoyment? Richard Dyer's classic study, "Entertainment and Utopia," originally published in 1977, provides us with initial headway, a useful way in. Dyer's main pitch, that "because entertainment is a common-sense, 'obvious' idea, what is really meant and implied by it never gets discussed" (19), is actually sharply relevant here. Dyer's account uses evidence from Hollywood mass culture, a more obvious high-profile source, whereas the entertainment mechanisms of French mainstream cinema remain more willfully obscured, given that its popular genres are, as we have seen already, prevailingly written out of the equation, willed away, made to vanish, rather than being seen as of consequence.

Principally, Dyer argues that entertainment works by offering its audiences outlets of "escape" and "wish-fulfillment" (20) that manifest specifically via "categories of utopian sensibility" (24). Thus, social tensions and sources of real-world malaise are articulated in the entertainment text in neatly packaged form, compartmentalized on-screen, and then countered with a utopian solution. Ideologically "playing with fire," entertainment, to Dyer, is thereby a complicated balancing act that must "take off from the real experiences of the audience," yet resolve the problematic aspects of those experiences without overt contradiction in order "to 'manage' them, to make them seem to disappear" (27). Using tropes derived from the song-and-dance numbers of classical Hollywood musicals, which have widespread currency throughout American popular culture, Dyer discerns five configuring types of these utopian pressure valves:

> *Scarcity* (poverty, income inequality) vs. *Abundance* (equal wealth)
> *Exhaustion* (work as grind, urban pressures) vs. *Energy* (work as play)
> *Dreariness* (monotony, predictability) vs. *Intensity* (excitement, affectivity)
> *Manipulation* (social constraints, roles) vs. *Transparency* (open spontaneity)
> *Fragmentation* (isolation, disempowerment) vs. *Community* (collective action) (26)

While the generic rapport between American film noir and the French policier has received close attention—Ginette Vincendeau itemizes its "rich network of intertextual relations, ranging from imitations, reworkings and parodies, to mere allusions, and autonomously parallel forms" (69)—Dyer's entertainment paradigm puts this international dialogue in a compelling new light. How, then, does Dyer's model account for the pleasures of the French policier? The heist sequence, a perfect counterpart analogy to Dyer's

classical Hollywood musical numbers, allows us to explore the French policier entertainment system versus its American rival.

Take the famous heist and focal point of Jules Dassin's *Rififi*. This robbery sequence, which runs twenty-seven minutes, almost a quarter of the
entire film, is often held up as a veritable pièce de résistance of the entire
policier format. Alastair Phillips singles out *Rififi* as a genre master class, a
"blueprint for the heist film," built around its central burglary as "an extraordinary feat of filmmaking" (3, 44). Equally, Dassin's heist demonstrates how
a trope Colin McArthur ascribes to Melville as an auteur—his predilection
for a logistically protracted "cinema of process" (191)—is also a component
of the policier format itself. Within *Rififi*, the heist comes after Tony (Jean
Servais), a veteran thief, washed up after a five-year jail term, is recruited by
Jo (Carl Möhner), his young criminal protégé, and Mario (Robert Manuel),
their gangster comrade, to join with César (Dassin), a master Italian safecracker, and loot the elite Mappin and Webb Parisian jewelers. After days
of preparations, the quartet successfully break into the store in a nocturnal
raid, shown at length on-screen, before all four eventually die after Grutter
(Marcel Lupovici), a rival racketeer, tries to steal their plunder for himself.
Rififi ends, in a typically Pyrrhic policier denouement, with Tony slumped
dead over the wheel of his car, fatally wounded after avenging his fallen
team by murdering Grutter, the robbery takings untouched in a suitcase
behind him on the backseat.

Rififi's heist is a veritable mother lode of policier entertainment gam-
bits, a trail of textual bread crumbs for its audience. We start with a pref-
acing setup: just like *Bob le flambeur*, *Rififi*'s direct offspring, the robbery
follows an extended rehearsal segment, in which the audience's appetite
for the obligatory forthcoming crime act is whetted, as the gang learns to
overcome the challenges ahead, at first hypothetically, then on the actual
job. Vital to the heist sequence, the current in its narrative circuitry, is the
fragmentation-versus-community trope of Dyer's formula. The burglary is
the most rigorously enacted course of mutual cause and effect: Tony's gang,
coming together in perfect collective alignment, must check off sequential
tasks, all completed, by necessity, without error. Individually, each character
is limited in his specialization (Jo is the muscle, Mario has money and inside knowledge of the neighborhood, César is a safecracker, and Tony is the
brains) and/or generically circumscribed as a dysfunctional-incomplete (Jo
is callow and needs the traditional policier senior mentor, Tony, whom we
first encounter by himself, not among comrades, drunkenly losing at cards
to rival thugs). In isolation these men are marginalia, flawed ne'er-do-wells,

but together they are consummate unstoppable practitioners of the burglary dark arts. Mid-heist, moreover, all roles and designations, vestigial
job titles, disappear. Hence, the heist is an ideological as well as a logistical
obstacle course, in which the team cooperates by playing to their combined
strengths. Laid out for us step-by-step, then, united in body and mind, the
quartet must: subdue the target building's concierge couple; access the jewelry store through its only weak point, the ceiling; bypass the shop's sensor
detectors by descending from on high (led by Tony, our messiah of crime)
via knotted ropes from the apartment above; disable the shop's alarm system with meticulously applied foam from a fire extinguisher; then drill into
the safe and overcome its locking tumblers, all the while completing their
tasks before dawn and avoiding detection from outside as they go. Alternat-
ing between long shots and closer-view inserts at moments of heist micro-
crescendo—the first penetration of the jewelry store roof; the group man-
aging to lower the safe from its wall housing onto Jo's broad back—Dassin's
editing amplifies the impression that these actions are so behaviorally communal that the men seem like fingers on the same hand, limbs on the same
body, driven by but one shared thought, one shared goal.

Similarly foundational to Rififi's heist is its notorious and insistent lack
of speech—deeds not diction. Reinforcing the men's collated skills here is
a trio of Dyer's tenets: energy, intensity, and transparency displacing, respectively, exhaustion, dreariness, and manipulation. The men's silence is
self-willed, a voluntary choice of stringent self-discipline, a statement of
empowered harmony and taut concentration, but also the premise for the
burglars creating their own nonvocal language, a seamlessly unified rep-
ertoire of gesture, movement, and action. (The affinity between ritualistic
Parisian master criminals and Japanese samurai is an idea Melville would
pursue in Le Samouraï [1967]). Like high-wire walkers inching forward
above an abyss, despite the beads of sweat that multiply on their faces the
men never flag, deviate, or lose their focus; they maintain perfect protracted poise even in the face of the constant, and rising, risk (highlighted
by cutaways to patrolling gendarmes on the streets outside); they improvise
fluently, in tandem, in unison, all social and linguistic differences dissolved
(César, the Italian safecracker, cannot even speak French) in combined
behavioral spontaneity. There is no hierarchy here, never a need for one.
During one stage of the proceedings, indeed, as the men gather around
the burrowed opening in the apartment floor, they act like a team of sur-
geons carrying out together a high-stakes medical operation: handing each
other specialist implements (a multipart extended chisel, industrial-grade

sheet metal cutters) without needing to be asked; assembling and exchanging tools from their suitcase just before those objects are needed; and encouraging each other with brief glances, curt nods, and small upturns of the corners of their mouths, buoying each other along with sheer force of will. If words are so obviously superfluous to these experts, the audience's invested pleasure comes from our striving to keep up with them, to grasp the significance of each tool, the consequence of each dexterous action, arcane heist rituals that are occasionally opaque (or even miraculous) to us, but always logical to them. We are neophyte initiates, vicarious apprentices; they are masters.

Lest the group's stoic prowess seem overly, or tediously, hypermasculinist, *Rififi*, like *Bob le flambeur*, *Touchez pas au grisbi*, and many of the most enduringly popular policiers, takes pains to highlight the men's capacity, even (or especially) when under the most pressure, for tiny moments of delicacy and grace, offsetting accents of subtle finesse. As Dyer would conceive it, this is entertainment at its most eloquent: work as play. Like the sock that Jo uses to cover the hammer handed to him by César, muffling his chisel blows, or the trickle of oil deftly caressed into the safe by Mario to cushion César's drill, the heist's central motif is the velvet fist, the diamond in the rough, measured patience prevailing over brute force. Surveying our team in action, these are coarse, aggressive, self-destructive thugs elsewhere, but within the confines of the unfolding heist, their criminal activities are elegant and cultivated, beautiful to behold. An exercise in constrained form and controlled performance, the policier heist is at moments of peak scrutiny a haiku, a sonnet, something instinctively impressive to apprehend, but even more delectable for the connoisseur.

If spoken language is too brutish for the heist, then *Rififi* and its peers celebrate instead other, more refined or precise (and difficult to render cinematically) senses: sight, touch, and sound, in particular. In *Touchez pas au grisbi*, most outrageously, which depicts no heist, only its immediate aftermath, Becker substitutes the burglary with a scene of commensurable length and design, just as beloved as *Rififi*'s robbery, in which two gangster comrades sit down together, eat, and revel in, at length, Jean Gabin's stash of gourmet pâté. Literally and figuratively, we thereby exult in, mouthful by mouthful, their superior (French) criminal taste. In *Rififi*, similarly, when Jo finally tunnels through the jewelry store's roof, Tony, unprompted as always, plucks from his jacket pocket a gossamer-thin handkerchief, more translucent tissue than practical cloth, and places it over the hole, as if he's setting the table. All four men huddle above the opening in overhead medium

Tony (Jean Servais) descends via rope into the jewelry store in *Rififi*.

close-up, conjoined in purpose again, and when the delicate square ripples gently, stroked by a tactile upsurging current from below, the men wordlessly exult with more shared glances. The spiraling wisp of air on fabric signals triumph—they're in.

The heist's latent lyricism insistently teases out its musicality, underscoring again the policier's links with Dyer's utopian song-and-dance routines. *Rififi* and *Bob le flambeur* are highly symptomatic in the links they make between violence and music, acts of criminality and the performance of dance numbers, all permeated by a steady, understated wit. (The fraught "transforming energy" of entertainment, as Dyer depicts it, recalibrating real-world pain as on-screen pleasure, is carefully mediated in the French policier with a bone-dry, occasionally caustic sense of humor [31].) In this context, in *Rififi*, after the gang initiates their heist by using direct aggression (chloroform rags pressed to faces) to subdue the husband-and-wife concierges, their next two actions immediately counter such boorish, loutish behavior. First, Tony makes sartorial adjustments: swapping his formal suit's dress shoes for lightweight white athletic pumps, readying himself for his cue to swing down the rope onto the jeweler's open shop floor, bathed in a subtle spotlight from the hole in the apartment floor above, taking the stage, as it were, like a revue acrobat in costume. Second, upstairs in the opulent apartment, the gang's instigating physical task is, of all things, to prepare their space by manipulating an enormous gleaming grand piano. Tony concomitantly carries off a giant bouquet of flowers from a vase, a performer receiving floral tribute from an offscreen appreciative audience. *Rififi* now uses this piano as a punctuating refrain. Jo strikes notes on it, inadvertently, twice: the first time, job barely begun, it makes the gang reflexively flinch, but second time, well on their way, Jo and Mario share small smiles, acknowledging, it seems, this tonal accompaniment to their own group recital. Throughout the heist, moreover, its participants co-opt banal everyday objects like skilled dancers incorporating props within routines: Tony's handkerchief, for instance, becomes a fluttering barometer of success; and then, most famously of all, César opens an inverted umbrella underneath Jo's carved-out hole, catching its debris to circumvent the motion sensors underneath. Almost every action performed in the heist, it seems, is laced with what Dyer calls the "sensuous materialism" of "non-representational" textual forms: the agreeable "oomph of music and movement" (29, 30).

So fundamental is creative musicality to the heist that *Rififi* extends it outward, embedding it within the surrounding film, beyond the nondialogue robbery itself. Virtuosity is what matters, the representation of sheer inventiveness, the policier heist as song. *Rififi*'s crucial prompt, nearly ten minutes before the actual heist begins, is the last spoken line, Mario's rasped exclamation, "We're all set, guys," his delighted response to Tony's breakthrough final idea, immediately seized upon by the whole gang, of using fire extinguisher spray to deaden the store's alarm. Problem solved, thanks to Tony's flash of inspiration, and from here on out, to sustain that crescendo, that level of genius, music accompanies the defining situating events. Next, we hear the rising ululations of nightclub chanteuse Viviane (Magali Noël), who, nondiegetically at first, reprises the film's title number "Rififi," an ambivalent siren's song that is essentially an ode to living hedonistically, in the moment, embracing joie de vivre. ("It's not an ordinary word / You won't find it in the dictionary.") Her humming accompanies images of the gang assembling—Jo leaving his apartment while his children sleep; Mario kissing his girlfriend goodbye—and then we see Viviane playfully rehearsing the song, clad in a full black body stocking, a wry visual reference to Musidora's notorious costume in Feuillade's *Les Vampires*, a criminal screen maestro if ever there was one. Reworked by a single accordion, then supplanted by a full orchestral score, musical themes then embellish shots of Tony stealing a getaway car (beforehand), then the gang speeding off through

Paris at dawn, ditching their tools and the vehicle, and repairing delightedly to Mario's apartment (afterward). Running over thirty-one minutes without a single line of dialogue, then, *Rififi*'s full heist segment, complete with musical preface and postface, ends with another sardonic joke: the long wordless span is finally broken only when Tony, at last, opens the small humdrum bag of stolen jewels and, in pure awe at what has transpired—taking us in policier terms from the sacred to the profane—declares simply, "*Merde!*" Mario and César, unable to contain themselves, now immediately burst into song themselves, performing a gleeful impromptu waltz around the living room. Their partners look on, elated. Like the drumroll sting, an aural punch line payoff, which concludes Melville's *Le Samouraï* with pitch dark percussive humor, it is only through the communal constituents of music—instruments, rhythm, melody, singing, dance—that the full flair of the policier heist can be fully conveyed.

Tony's gang's victory dance also reminds us of another primary driving force behind the policier heist—pure economics: the opportunity to, if not exactly get rich quick, then certainly get rich quick*er*. Returning to *Bob le flambeur* and *Rififi*'s burglaries, alongside most of their genre peers, their core trajectory—a physical space that must be traversed, down and up, side to side, generating an instant payday—highlights a key aspect of the policier-as-entertainment: Dyer's scarcity-versus-abundance formula, the lure of quick transformative rewards. The heist itself, moreover, as a spatial analogy, an environment to be quickly and profitably crossed, accelerates and compresses on-screen the most abiding capitalist principles, making the hard (or impossible), drawn-out, lifelong process of upward social mobility perceptible, attainable, literally just within reach. This notion of the postwar French policier heist being the liveliest of economic parables has compelling social evidence. These are films produced and exhibited, of course, at the height of the so-called *Les Trentes Glorieuses*, or thirty glorious years, a maxim coined by French economist Jean Fourasté to describe the historic prosperity enjoyed by France between 1946 and 1975. As catalogued by historian Jean-Pierre Rioux, during the modernizing 1950s alone, France roused itself from economic doldrums for a period during which "gross national product and national income grew by 41 per cent . . . the volume of consumption increased by 47 per cent, exports grew by 44 per cent, and gross fixed capital formation was up by 57 per cent" (Rioux 318).

Cold economic data, even when labeled glorious, seldom entertains, however, so the postwar policier's task is to make such figurative gains palpable and exciting, vividly demonstrable to anyone, with additional illegal frisson. (The transformative process from *abstract* to *tangible*, representing either fiscal or romantic screen activities in dramatic physical terms, makes a useful sixth category, in fact, to Dyer's overall entertainment complex.) Exactly like the Depression-era utopian musical numbers at the heart of Dyer's model, the heist's goals as aspirational micronarratives are abundantly clear: we're in the money. Whether it is bank couriers loaded down by, and soon relieved of, stuffed satchels of banknotes, in *Le Rouge est mis* (Gilles Grangier, 1957); the glittering stacks of absurdly heavy gold bullion hoarded and fought over in *Touchez pas au grisbi*; the enormous rectangular casino chips Bob stockpiles during the climax of *Bob le flambeur*; or the dazzling diamond miniatures gloated over by Tony and colleagues in *Rififi*, the stakes of the policier heist make the sped-up process of wealth accumulation overt, concrete, visible to the naked eye. Step-by-step, bypassing the usual tedious social proprieties, the heist makes a lifetime's struggles toward prosperity condensed, explosive, immediate.

Speaking more broadly, furthermore, beyond postwar French cinema's policier genre in isolation, this process of instantiating opulence on-screen—canceling out austerity with affluence, erasing the specter of Occupation-era privations—is a much more fundamental textual system than Truffaut's facile pejorative tradition of quality. Lavish material abundance is the coin of postwar French cinema's realm: celebrated transtextually amidst the rippling sheen of expensive costumes and finery, the culmination of fortunes made on-screen before our very eyes, the life force of *tableaux vivants* of hedonistic Parisian nightlife. Bottom line, in the policier and elsewhere, France's postwar cinema is obsessed, varyingly ironically, with a dynamic of sumptuous prosperity, an expansive, lustrous fecundity taking hold of diegetic France. In its postwar regenerating phase, in other words, France's is a cinema of largesse. (These antidotes to economic adversity might also account for the postwar policier's revived fortunes in the early twenty-first century, for depressingly obvious reasons.)

These policiers being products of postwar French culture, there is a striking philosophical dimension to the heist, and its execution, as well. Mesmerizing when active in the field, Tony, Bob, and other heist initiators project a popularized version of France's ubiquitous post-Liberation philosophical model: the existentialism of Jean-Paul Sartre, debated in conjunction with Simone de Beauvoir, Albert Camus, and other like-minded Parisian intellectuals. On this front, our heist leaders embody a mainstream equivalence of Sartre's good-versus-bad-faith idiom, famously discussed in his 1943 bestseller, *Being and Nothingness*. The key to Sartre's existentialist dilemma, put simply, is that authentic freedom, good faith, can be attained only with constant self-vigilance, staunch integrity in the face of a slippery slope toward capitulation, a refusal to acquiesce to the social baggage foisted upon us. On the one hand, Sartre's iconic test case of bad faith, the path to be avoided, is the figure of the professional café waiter, unctuous, oily, obsequious, overly solicitous, a consummate fraud whose very identity has been surrendered in favor of social ingratiation to paying customers: "We need not watch long before we can explain it: he is playing at being a waiter in a café" (82). (Cynics might speculate whether Parisian waiters have taken heed of Sartre's warning, reversing their behavior, ever since.) Moment by moment, deed by deed, the true good-faith course, by contrast, entails striving to avoid such compromised self-deception, testing ourselves when in social situations, to be true to our existence, through the informed instincts of our revitalized behavior to define our contingent essence. There is no God, Sartre declares, no overarching binding social contracts save those that we internalize, so the individual is very much on his or her own—an emancipating yet intimidating idea. As Sarah Bakewell outlines the consequences of the existentialist position, "we should remain passionately, even furiously engaged with what happens to us and with what we can achieve. . . . We should not expect freedom to be anything less than fiendishly difficult" (157–58).

Clearly there are shades of Sartre's good-faith course in the conduct of heist practitioners, immersed in the throes of what Dyer would call their utopian set pieces. At their finest and most engaged, when on the job, these figures are incandescent with attuned authentic being, lawless and alert to but one immanent task at hand, consumed with its completion alone. Tony in *Rififi* and Bob in *Bob le flambeur* are notable candidates already, but even among less-exalted policier outings there are similar appeals to the sheer in-the-moment integrity of the crime act itself. Take the opening heist in veteran (and usually grimly dedicated) policier director Gilles Grangier's *Le Rouge est mis*. Distilled once more into a ninety-second flash point, the four-man robbery here takes place outside the Banque National Industrielle. Again there are no words spoken; again the taut editing highlights the tight pacing and geometry of the heist; again we proceed via microgestures (a tipped hat, terse nods, brief glances) only the participants discern; again the plan is perfectly carried out with minimal, deemphasized violence (two bank guards overcome with quick blows obscured by Pepito [Lino Ventura], on guard in the shot's foreground). Two fast cutaways—one to a shot of a startled passing family recoiling, the other to a nearby bartender informing the police by telephone ("There's a holdup happening on the Rue de la

Grange aux Belles!")—emphasize by contrast the banality of the binding social contract unfolding elsewhere, a surrounding mass of stooges unthink-
ingly perpetuating legal norms, going about their tedious daily business,
succumbing without resistance to the humdrum conformist expectations of
the everyday. As gang leader, Louis (Gabin), manning the shining getaway
car, pulls off and accelerates, weaving through traffic (cuing jazz music and
a title sequence that propels us around Paris), he models in definitive policier guise, not without pungent amoral irony, the dynamic Sartre good-faith
human. Eyes on the prize, Louis, alongside his policier comrades within the
heist, is bound by no bourgeois compromises, groveling to no one, a perfect
confluence of authentic action and self-willed self-determination.

Inevitably, though, beyond the actual heist, such idealized self-being
cannot last forever: things fall apart. The final part of our case for the policier as quintessential French film entertainment text must then be to consider not the successful heist but rather its unsuccessful aftermath. Clearly,
this is a genre that parades before us conclusions of inexorable disaster, dis-
unity and death, gangs undone by fatal flaws and jealousy, the wiles of de-
ceitful women or foolish male pride writ large. In *Rififi* we end with a blood-
drenched Tony, the last crook standing, expiring at the wheel of his car. In
Le Rouge est mis former gang-mates Louis and Pepito shoot each other and
perish in a tenement stairwell. *Razzia sur la chnouf* (Henri Decoin, 1955), in
a rather desperate reversal, stages its customary climactic murderous cross-
fire, only to reveal that its lead gangster villain, Henri (Gabin), is actually
an undercover cop. *Échec au porteur* (Gilles Grangier, 1958) has its nominal
hero, Bastien (Serge Reggiani), a drug peddler trying to go straight, alert
the authorities to a bomb hidden in a soccer ball but be mortally injured
while so doing. Best-case-scenario policier denouements offer redemption
through dark irony and gallows humor. *Touchez pas au grisbi*, most well
known in this category, leaves us with Max (Gabin) losing his entire gold
bullion loot to a burning car after a shootout with a rival gang, and then
simply returning to his usual routines, expensive dinners, and dates, habits
designed to project his apparently enduring social stature. *Bob le flambeur*,
similarly, concludes with Melville at his most customarily arch: Bob, finally
a big winner at the roulette table, is arrested after his heist collapses and
his young protégé dies in his arms, but he then suggests wryly to his old
crony, the presiding Inspector Ledru (Guy Decomble), that with a "really
top lawyer," instead of jail time he might actually "sue for damages." Inevitably, though, in the policier's summary accounts, heists pay but crime does
not; gangs stockpile profits but never get to spend them; splendid burglaries

Max (Jean Gabin) watches the loot go up in flames at the end of *Touchez pas au grisbi*.

lead to dismal incarceration or death in the gutter. How, then, to reconcile the policier's spectacular heists with its typically bleak final reckonings?

Obviously, among these doom-laden finales, the French policier diverges most sharply from its Hollywood genre counterpart, the studio-era musical whence Dyer's entertainment tenets derive. Classical musicals uplift us with the prospect of utopian continuity; policiers confirm, staunch and deadpan to the bitter end, that entropy is utopia's bigger, nastier older brother. Hollywood entertainments lie, their dazzling sleights of hand distracting us from the truth, while France's screen diversions sooner or later always return us to the sadder facts of life. But schadenfreude aside, even within these policier calamities there is still authenticity and inarguably jubilation—a refusal to conform or compromise, an urge to live fast and go down blazing in your vestigial prime, to leave behind you that perfect heist as your culminating creation, a communal masterpiece that can never be replicated or bettered. This, then, is the true joy of burglary, the reason it entertains us so. Like the drab little purse of gorgeous jewels Tony opens in *Rififi*, the cue for his gang to dance and sing together one last time, the point of the policier heist is that it crafts a glittering, fleeting work of performance art in an enduringly sordid context. These heists never instigate a viable long-term outcome but rather an immaculate set piece on its own terms, a self-contained stand-alone interlude with rapturous residue, an afterimage of an extraordinarily realized act of concerted civil disobedience, a middle-finger salute to the world. Death, on these policier terms, is the domain of the victor.

A final perspective on the policier's disintegrating heist comes from Sudhir Hazareesingh, whose masterful history of French cultural sensibility sets out what is, for him, the bedrock upon which France's many national expressions build. Hazareesingh's book, *How the French Think*, discerns repeatedly the French proclivity for "conceptual juggling acts . . . delicious oxymorons [that nourish] yet another cherished feature of Gallic thinking: the love of paradox" (16). Although Hazareesingh attends chiefly to politics and France's loftier discursive ideologies, this deep-seated principle of French internal contradictions—a nation that has, after all, given us "violent moderates, secular missionaries, spiritual materialists, *spectateurs engagés*, patriotic internationalists" (16)—actually finds profound rendition in the postwar French policier, especially among its poetically dystopian resolutions: brilliant heists leading to terrible dissolutions. This fundamental French affiliation with paradox, as Hazareesingh expresses it, champions, "by virtue of the sometimes unfortunate fate of French armies on the battlefield, from Vercingétorix to the battle of Waterloo, perhaps the most exquisite [paradox] of them all: the glorious defeat" (16). Tony, Bob, and their like-minded policier comrades-in-arms, then, are antiheroic icons redolent not just of French genre cinema but also of France herself. These are figures summoned forth by genius but compelled to destroy themselves, freethinking titans undone by their own vainglorious natures, monuments to superb misadventure, spectacular failure. Like the Arc de Triomphe edifice that looms over the western Paris skyline, a testament to fantasies of battlefield victories as much as actual lasting triumphs, the policier's heist protagonists are self-defeating emissaries of a fierce nation, shaking their fists at the sky, defiant to the last. With their panoply of glorious defeats snatched from the jaws of victory, moreover, the policier's heists ultimately speak most resoundingly to our image of French cinema itself. Overhauling the standard account of authentic French film being born of high art alone, in the form of its postwar policier we discover a source of entertainment cinema that is deliberate, gripping, thoughtful, and insightful, yet above all has the enduring capacity to delight us all.

From Nickel Mines
to Plastic Vaginas

The Heist Genre in Canadian Cinema

∞∞∞∞∞◊◊◊∪∪∪◊◦◦ϙ◠∕∖∩◇◇

Scott Henderson

While assembling his heist crew in *The Art of the Steal* (Jonathon Sobol, 2013), art thief and motorcycle daredevil Crunch Calhoun (Kurt Russell) contacts a Paris-based forger, Guy de Cornet (Chris Diamantopoulos). The excited Guy indicates that he is happy to come to America to work with Crunch. "Not exactly America," responds Crunch. "Canada." "Meh, America light," is Guy's reply. In many ways, *The Art of the Steal* and the other Canadian heist films addressed in this chapter provide a version of "America light." Each responds in its own ways to the influences of American culture and capital on Canada, as well as the influence of American genre cinema on Canadian national cinema. Very often, there is a self-conscious awareness of national borders and of the notion that Canada, sharing many similarities with its southern neighbor, does often appear as "America light" in film and other visual media. The films analyzed here all engage in distinct ways with this cross-border relationship. In fact, the heist film may be an apt genre for working through the nuances of this relationship. As Daryl Lee argues for the heist film, it "may be read as a locus of mass-art in which the business of film tries to work out its relation to art," and the heist film's "social function" is a "common yet consistent reflection on the status of film art in a consumer society" (10). These concerns regarding the role of art, particularly in a national cultural context, and the influence of commercial imperatives have long been central to any understanding of the Canadian film industry. As Jim Leach has noted, "the tension between commercial and artistic or cultural goals in Canadian film policy remains a highly contentious topic" (4).

There have not been many heist films produced within Canadian cinema, but the ones examined here allow for a consideration of the role of genre within the national context. Additionally, these five films permit analysis of the changing nature of genre cinema within the English and French Canadian cinema industries, each of which has developed its own unique trajectories owing to distinct economic and cultural influences. Earlier films, such as *Between Friends* (Don Shebib, 1973) and *Pouvoir Intime/ Blind Trust* (Yves Simoneau, 1986), align with the arguments made about the emergence of more clearly defined Canadian cinemas—the nascent English Canadian cinema of the late 1960s and early 1970s, and the rapid maturation of Québécois cinema in the 1980s, respectively. The relationship between Canadian cinema and its American counterpart is continued in films such as *Foolproof* (William Phillips, 2003) and *Le Dernier Tunnel/ The Last Tunnel* (Erik Canuel, 2004). Both demonstrate ways in which Canadian cinema attempted a more populist, genre-focused approach in the latter part of the twentieth century and the early part of the twenty-first. *The Art of the Steal*, which opens with a heist in Warsaw, Poland, and which features an international cast, including Russell, Matt Dillon, and British actor Terence Stamp, demonstrates how Canadian cinema is now positioned within a broader global cinema industry, driven by international coproductions.

Despite the social and political changes that have occurred over time, culturally and economically, arguably all of the films examined here provide examples of a common Canadian cinematic trope, that of the failed hero. While failure is a staple of the heist film more broadly, this particular Canadian failure is connected to the protagonists' inability to live up to the admittedly problematic ideals of the American hero. In the case of the aforementioned "Crunch," his attempts at art theft have landed him in a Polish prison, and his daredevil reputation is based on his frequent failures and the accompanying broken bones that lend him his moniker. To return to Guy's "America light" response to being invited to take part in a Canadian heist, Canada, and the Canadian film industry, do not provide the illusion of glamour and excitement so often associated with Hollywood genre film. Instead, a different sensibility has emerged, one that involves examining the relationship between commerce and art, and one where the commercial imperatives of genre can be harnessed to probe concerns related to national cultural identity.

Lee's examination of the heist film, and his articulation that the heist film works as a genre in its own right, is tied to the "social functions" that he identifies. The place of art in a consumer society is the second of these listed by Lee. The first is "a critique of the socio-economic order through mostly likeable characters achieving something extraordinary from marginalised social position" (8). If the protagonists of heist films are usually marginalized, then those of Canadian heist films may be doubly marginalized. They are outsiders in a society that itself is often outside of mainstream genre representation. If, by Lee's definitions, the heist film itself has introspective tendencies, particularly in asserting marginalized voices against the cultural dominant, then Canadian heists may be even more prone to this tendency. Leach has identified precisely this sort of relationship in assessing the role of genre in Canadian cinema: "It was precisely because of the close association between popular genres and American culture that Canadian filmmakers could use these genres to explore the impact on Canada of the powerful cultural influences from south of the border" (83–84).

The heist is not an exclusively American film form, as Lee and others have noted. There is a long history of heist films in a multitude of national cinemas. Yet, the dominant concern in Canadian cinema has been with the influence of American popular cinema, as both an economic and a cultural force, and genre tropes, when borrowed, are inevitably filtered through that American lens. That said, the Canadian film examples here borrow their references from a range of sources, but each positions itself in relation to the dominant syntax of the genre. In fact, in all of these examples, the Canadian protagonists are cast, in some way, against more successful and affluent criminal counterparts, whose character is often defined by recognizable genre traits. In *Foolproof*, for example, a group of friends in their early twenties, Kevin (Ryan Reynolds), Sam (Kristin Booth), and Rob (Joris Jarsky), continue to play a game called Foolproof that they had developed as students. The game involves designing and executing elaborate mock heists of real-world locales. When their plans are inadvertently stolen by a real-life criminal mastermind and his associates who have used them to perpetrate a successful jewel heist, the friends are forced to work with this criminal to implement a large heist. The mastermind, Leo "The Touch" Gillette (David Suchet), is a highly stereotyped caricature. The class differences are made blatant via his refined British accent and his mannerisms, taste in fine wines, and expensive cars. Additionally, *Foolproof* employs a number of the semantic aspects of heist films in slavishly adhering to the genre. In fact, in reference to the execution of their stolen plans, Kevin refers to the different parts of the plan as "beats," echoing the screenwriting terminology most prevalently employed in mainstream genre films.

The film itself was part of a concerted effort by Telefilm Canada[1] to develop a more mainstream, popular cinema that could compete with

American blockbusters in Canadian theaters. It was a process that ultimately failed, and *Foolproof* was a box office failure that failed to resonate, not only with Canadian audiences but with any audiences. As Charles Acland has argued in examining Canadian exhibition and spectatorship practices, "there has been a too-rapid agreement that access to Canadian films through theatrical exhibition will build a currently underdeveloped Canadian popular film culture" (15). Acland's point is that the Canadian industry is intertwined with the American, and, as *Foolproof* demonstrates, a Canadian genre film easily gets lost in the broader popular culture realm rather than gaining any particular spectatorial sympathy (in the form of box office revenue) from Canadian audiences. Replete with action sequences, explosions, a pulsating soundtrack, high-stakes international criminality (the heist is of $20 million in German bearer bonds), and a known star in Ryan Reynolds, *Foolproof* is very much a mainstream genre film. In effect, it does seem a case of "commerce over art." Nonetheless, unlike the many products of "Hollywood North" (the name employed to describe the use of Canadian locations to film American film and television productions), *Foolproof* does not hide its Canadian origins. The Toronto setting is made evident through shots of the cityscape, including the iconic red, white, and black streetcars of the city's transit commission. Additionally, the dialogue includes intentional Canadian references, such as an allusion to a mock heist to steal the iconic hockey trophy the Stanley Cup. *Foolproof* is very much a Canadian genre film, and unlike with the other films addressed here, its relationship to genre is far less ambivalent. As noted, the key distinction may be in the contrast between the Canadian protagonists and the stereotyped criminal mastermind. The Canadians have appropriated the genre elements and have turned them into a game, unlike the "real-world" aspirations of the genre archetypes against whom they are pitted, who are in it for the money and the typical "big score." There is an overt acknowledgment of the genre machinations of the heist film, and the group's training exercises mimic the stereotypical actions of heist films. The film ends with the Canadian trio recovering the evidence that linked them, via their game, to the original jewel heist. The millions in bearer bonds become irrelevant to their success and are left behind with Leo "The Touch," whose arrest they have orchestrated.

It is possibly disingenuous to refer to the protagonists of all of these films as "losers" and their heists as failures. Instead, there seem to be varying degrees of "failure," and instances where the failure to achieve the "big score" is set against more modest personal goals. In *Foolproof*, the recovery of the stolen plans and the arrest of Leo are seen as a victory despite the absence of a monetary reward. The main characters themselves are depicted as "losers," or at the very best as marginalized figures. The only one of the three who appears to be employed is Reynolds's Kevin, who is a beleaguered insurance adjuster whose job and life clearly lack excitement outside of the Foolproof scenarios he and his friends concoct. The gangs assembled for the heists in the other films analyzed here comprise the sorts of marginalized, misfit characters that are typical of the heist genre. As noted, Crunch Calhoun of *The Art of the Steal* has not only been in prison in Poland, following a failed art theft, but is now reduced to accepting insignificant payoffs to purposely crash during his motorcycle stunts, as a means of "thrilling" the audiences, who have come to expect such failure from him. The rest of the heist gang he assembles is filled equally with misfits, often played for comic relief. In one scene, Francie Tobin (Jay Baruchel), wearing a poorly attached fake beard, bluffs his way through a United States border crossing by claiming the beard is part of his costume as an actor in *Witness! The Musical*. While *The Art of the Steal* plays these types more for comic effect, the film, like the others, adheres to the sorts of characters that Lee identifies as central to the heist film's semantics: "this group of social misfits and societal castoffs traditionally embraces serious craftsmen, such as safecrackers, mechanics, drivers, demolitions experts and other technicians" (5). Despite his comic characterization, Guy de Cornet proves to be a master forger, and despite his absurd story and false beard, Francie manages to smuggle Crunch and his brother Nicky (Matt Dillon) across the American border, while the other members of the gang also perform their assigned roles to perfection.

Of the other four films analyzed here, it is only in *Between Friends* that the heist might be described as a complete failure, as two of the gang are killed during the heist, while a third succumbs to heart problems before the heist takes place (the illness and eventual death of an aging crew member is another of the semantic elements of many heist films). Even then there is a degree of ambiguity, as the final surviving member of the heist crew, Toby (Michael Parks), is left with the loot, but in stasis, staring into the frozen Canadian landscape (more specifically, the barren nickel-mining landscape outside of Sudbury, Ontario) while reminiscing about surfing in his home state of California. The "failure" in *Art of the Steal* is revealed to be a purposeful one, where the complex plot is revealed to have been orchestrated by Crunch as a means of getting revenge on his brother, Nicky, whose own opportunistic actions years earlier had led to Crunch's Polish imprisonment. The finale of the film reveals that there has also been a heist within a heist. While the ambitious Nicky ends up the "loser" and is arrested, the

Nicky (Matt Dillon) confronts Crunch (Kurt Russell) in *The Art of the Steal*, the Tim Horton's sign behind his head providing a Canadian touch in the globalized urban landscape.

remainder of the gang actually profit by peddling fake versions of a Georges Seurat painting that Nicky had stolen earlier. While the gang make their money on the sale of fakes, the original Seurat is gifted by Crunch to Samuel Winter (Terrence Stamp), a retired art heister who has been forced to work with Interpol as they attempt to unravel Crunch's gang's convoluted plans. Social marginalization is again highlighted, as Samuel's passion had been formed in childhood, and he notes, while explaining his lifetime love of art, that he was aware that such fine objects were financially out of his reach from an early age. So while the gang has made their money selling fakes, Crunch honors his comrade by sending him the original Seurat. The film's comic tone and the nature of its characters suggest that they are marginalized, but with the exception of Nicky, they, in fact, come away as winners.

While not unique in English Canadian cinema, the more optimistic ending of *The Art of the Steal* does run counter to the traditional notions of what might be expected from Canadian protagonists, who often are contrasted with the notion of the Hollywood hero. Christine Ramsay has summed up this line of thinking as a "metaphoric/allegoric assertion that men's losing and victimization (vis à vis an American standard of romantic masculine heroism) is not only all that goes on for *all* men in Canada, but it is also all that goes on imaginatively in the text" (36). This comparison to the United States returns us to de Cornet's invocation of "America light," although in *The Art of the Steal* failure, an ineffectual masculinity is used as an advantage. This is perhaps made explicit via a piece of art that features prominently in the film. A presumed modern art cube sculpture of a plastic vagina becomes the hiding place, first, of a fake, allegedly valuable antique book (a supposed Guttenberg version of the "Gospel According to James") and then of the genuine Seurat painting. The appearance of this odd work of art recalls an earlier exchange in the film. Winter has been tasked with aiding a bumbling Interpol agent, Bick (Jason Jones). During an early exchange between the two, Winter undercuts Bick's authority, stating, "You wouldn't know a vagina if it was four feet tall and staring you in the face," aligning Bick's authority with his masculinity. Later, when the two first encounter a picture of the artwork, Bick inquires, "What the hell am I looking at?" to which Winter responds, "It's four foot high and staring you right in the face." The book heist is fake, while the vagina sculpture is employed to hide the Seurat, a fact overlooked by both Bick and Nicky, a bluff that offers rather Oedipal overtones to their respective failures. As brotherly authority and revenge are at the heart of the dispute between Crunch and Nicky, the role that masculinity plays here is reinforced. The ultimate success of Crunch's convoluted plan not only reverses some of the expectations around English Canadian cinema but also runs counter to the tendency in heist films more widely, where, despite the engaging cinematic actions of the heist itself, it is the rare film that ends well for the perpetrators.

The spectacular failure of a heist provides the culmination of *Between Friends*, which is frequently cited as a film that exemplifies the failed masculinity evident in earlier English Canadian cinema. Piers Handling refers to the main characters of the film as "born losers" (84), while Marshall Delaney calls them "young men blundering into a rather stupidly organized crime" (14). Not all of the main characters of *Between Friends* are Canadian. Toby is an American who has sought an escape to Canada from a life in California that seems to be going nowhere. The relationship between him and his Canadian counterpart, Chino (Chuck Shamata), is referenced by Robert Fothergill as part of a postscript to his influential take on masculinity in Canadian film, "Coward, Bully or Clown: The Dream-Life of a Younger Brother." In describing the film's plot, Fothergill notes that the film "shows a strong and candid girl abandoning the flabby, inconsiderate dope she has been living with, for the sake of a visiting American whom he has idolized as hero, mentor, special buddy—in short, as older brother" (249). While *Between Friends* does provide contrast between the United States and Canada, and between its American and Canadian leads, it does so in a manner that questions the very validity of such comparisons. The supposed "older brother" does not live up to expectations.

Among the expectations that are established are those related to genre. *Between Friends* opens with the concluding moments of a heist in California, for which Toby is seen working as the driver. The scale of the heist is evident in the film's opening shots, as a helicopter lands on a beach and pallets of money are quickly offloaded into a waiting van, which is then hijacked by the gang employing Toby. This opening suggests the genre excitement of the "big score," and, as Toby receives his payoff for his involvement, there is indication that he will be rehired by the same gang. The success of this opening heist is in sharp contrast to the later, ill-planned heist in Canada. Yet these comparisons are very quickly muted. Despite the genre thrills, what little is seen of Toby's life in California is far from glamorous. He delivers his cut of the heist to his ex-girlfriend, who lives, along with Toby's son, with her own new boyfriend. In the following scene, Toby stands along the beachfront, watching surfers. Again, there is no idealization of the California locale. The sky is overcast, the coast is rocky, and, judging by Toby's jeans and heavier jacket, the weather is far from ideal, making this the antithesis of the stereotyped world of sun, surf, and sand. A surfer acknowledges Toby as having once been "really good," and from this, combined with Toby's melancholy gaze, it is evident that the "dream-life" is not only one pursued by the Canadian Chino but also one that his American counterpart seeks to reclaim. Peter Harcourt identifies the personal aspects in Toby's nostalgia: "Toby, who throughout the film has seemed directed towards the past, is speaking to his son in California on the telephone. 'Do you want to hang up first? Or should I hang up first?' He is trying, as if for the last time, to recreate those playful games of domestic intimacy which he himself has lost" (215).

If the American dream is something that Toby has lost, for Chino it is something that still drives his imagination. When Toby first arrives in Toronto to visit Chino, the two men drunkenly attempt a skateboard slalom course on a darkened city street. In the dark, swerving around broken and breaking beer bottles, it is evident that the two are attempting to recreate their surfing past, primarily for Chino's benefit. As they skateboard, music emanates from the house of Chino and his girlfriend Ellie (Bonnie Bedelia). Ellie turns off the music at one point, owing to the late hour, but turns it back on again at Chino's urging. The songs themselves are revealing. The first is "Catch a Wave" by the Beach Boys, a clear invocation of the imagined California dream, while the second is the nostalgic doo-wop number "In The Still of the Night" by the Five Satins, again a genre evocative of American culture. Neither song elevates the scene above the mundane as the two pathetically skateboard. This is a microcosm for the characters' efforts throughout the film to call upon American cultural ideals as some sort of escape from a less exciting Canadian life. They fail to live up to the task.

As made evident by Toby's own situation in California, life in the United States is no better. All of this is enhanced by the film's realist aesthetic, again in contrast to the escapist polish of Hollywood genre cinema. This aesthetic is described by Christine Ramsay in relation to an earlier Don Shebib film, *Goin' Down the Road* (1970). Ramsay identifies the "typical aesthetic markers of a film's traditional 'Canadianness' (*i.e.*, stark, if not 'depressing' social realism; documentary flavour; eccentric and off-beat characterizations; contemplative treatment of the landscape)" (34). Ramsay's own analysis raises questions about Shebib's use of realism, pointing to *Goin' Down the Road*'s self-awareness about marginality and the construction of a sense of nation. As Leach has indicated, "the dominance of realism in Canadian cinema has been much exaggerated, but the persistence of this notion has played an important part in shaping how Canadian films have been interpreted and how questions about the national cinema have been posed" (17). In this sense, it is possible to see *Between Friends* as not so much a realist depiction of Canada as a stylistic choice with thematic implications. The film's use of Toronto is a case in point. Shebib purposely chooses locations that capture a gritty, more working-class Toronto, rather than the financial center that the city was already becoming by the early 1970s. Shebib's locations shun the city center, and instead the film lingers in the margins. Toronto-based scenes are set in working-class neighborhoods of early-twentieth-century row houses, in backstreet diners, and in rocky, disused industrial landscapes along Toronto's waterfront. In fact, when Toby first meets the plotters of the heist, Ellie's father Will (Henry Beckman) and his friend Coker (Hugh Webster), the waterfront locale is rocky and windswept, similar to that scene in the earlier images of Toby in California, emphasizing the lack of escape on either side of the border.

This waterfront meeting, and the apparent (though reluctant) formation of the "crew," is one of the rare moments in which *Between Friends* aligns with the semantic elements of the heist genre. As Lee notes, in borrowing from Rick Altman, "semantics . . . refer to recurring 'building blocks' of the same film genre, 'common topics, shared plots, key scenes, character types, familiar objects or recognizable shots and sounds'" (4). Most of these are missing when considering *Between Friends* as a heist film, yet that seems purposeful in terms of its relationship both to the genre and to the American culture the film's characters wish to emulate. Lee points to the alignment between the audience's reception and Altman's notion of "generic 'syntax'": "The syntactic dimension of Altman's model for analysing genre is crucial: vocabulary (semantics) varies with relative ease . . . but syntax often matters more in figuring out form and meaning, especially over time" (6). *Between Friends* promises its audiences a heist film. It does so with its opening shots of the successful California heist and via the plans led by Will and Coker, alongside the semantic moments that do appear in the film. Its "syntactic dimension" is the failure of these elements either to be fully realized or to coalesce. The attributes of the idealized American genre fail to function in the realities of the Canadian setting. They do not belong, nor, as Toby's home life indicates, are they any more fulfilling in an American setting, perhaps outside of the Hollywood mythos. A number of commentators identified that *Between Friends* was a commercial failure, and it might be possible to relate the audience's rejection of the film, or distributors' reluctance to better promote the film, to those syntactic elements and its ultimate lack of "generic affiliation," which is part of the film's "form and meaning." As Leach notes, "the film's commercial failure could be attributed to this refusal to meet expectations, although, as so often, it was also a victim of poor distribution."

There are numerous points in the film where the semantic expectations of a heist film are disrupted. This is evident from that first meeting, as described by Barry Keith Grant:

> The group never comes together as a team. . . . In place of the genre's typical professionalism, Chino and Toby, although not complete amateurs—Toby, we learn, has "done time"—certainly do not display the cool competency of American movie hoods. Will reassures Toby that he's not an amateur, that he's "done this kind of thing before," but when Toby asks him why then he isn't rich, Will's reply—"I figure you can't lose all the time"—hardly inspires confidence in his abilities. (10)

This amateur incompetence continues through the planning of the robbery, the heist of the payroll of a nickel mine in northern Ontario. The group drive to Sudbury in an effort to case the mine and plan for the robbery. Coker is said to have previously worked there, and knows the place. The group does go on a public tour of the mining facility, but the lessons learned about the nickel-mining process have no bearing on a robbery of the payroll office. Instead, the visit descends into a weekend of drinking, womanizing, and partying. Will and Coker take the group to a local bar, where they meet up with a pair of women and return to their home. The evening turns into a drunken party, Will at one point falling and breaking a chair as he attempts to execute a dance routine. Rather than showing the professionalism anticipated by the genre, this gang demonstrates their amateur hedonism, and the dream of a "big score" is one that is woefully misplaced and unlikely to be realized by a group more focused on partying than planning.

The same house party is also the starting point for a relationship between Toby and Ellie, which creates friction with Chino, promoting jealousy that creates a distraction during the actual heist. The clear distrust between Chino and Toby (combined with the poor planning) triggers the disastrous events of the heist, leading to Will and then Chino being shot dead. As Grant identifies, "the robbery itself, usually the showcase scene of caper films, is treated more like an anticlimactic afterthought" (11). The expectations of the heist, of the "big score," are ones fueled by genre expectations, both for audiences and also, clearly, for the protagonists of the film. Lee's description of the characteristics of the heist film is revealing. He identifies "the crime unfolding as process and often presented through special descriptive moments, elliptical montages and extended sequences, sometimes using thrilling parallel or rapid editing for captivating the audience and at other times long takes for dilating the temporality of activity" (7). These cinematically attractive and elliptical elements belie the work and the professionalism that might be anticipated in the actual execution of a heist, and the failure of these to translate to the Canadian landscape and to Canadian cinematic traditions becomes evident. Cinematic genre depictions are slick, engaging, and meaningful, and even where heists fail, the execution tends to be vibrantly presented. Grounded in an aesthetic of realism, the heist of *Between Friends* is reduced to a sad attempt, by an inept gang, to pull off a robbery in a bleak northern Ontario mining town.

The bleakness of the landscape and the misplacement of genre codes are reinforced during the scene detailing Coker's funeral. With the barren, cold landscape of mine tailings, a grey sky, and the smokestacks of the distant nickel refineries, the setting of Coker's burial is one that underlines the grim realities of the film. As the handful of mourners move away, Will begins to sing "Shall We Gather at the River," a song frequently employed in John Ford's Westerns. The song clearly evokes the ideals of community, usually set against the rugged, epic American wilderness of Monument Valley, that are iconic of Ford's films. In *Between Friends*, Will is left on his own, and the image is one of despair rather than hope.

The same landscape marks the end of the heist. Following the robbery of the payroll office, the three men flee into this remote, snow-covered milieu. Will has been shot during the heist, while Chino is shot as they drive off. Shebib intersperses shots of the getaway car with shots of the industrial backdrop of slag heaps and mining equipment. The final shot of the gang is a long shot, with the two cars (they have met up with Ellie, who was waiting with a different getaway car) and the two dead bodies of Will and Chino in the snow. The film ends with Toby dreaming of surfing in California. This conclusion takes him back to the life he had hoped to escape, and in its circularity suggests that the escapism of Hollywood genre film remains out of reach for these marginalized characters. The film thus becomes a critique of the heist film, and of genre more broadly. It suggests that the American dream is a falsehood on both sides of the border. The futility of chasing Hollywood dreams may resonate more strongly within the Canadian film industry, but it also aligns with Lee's observations about the heist genre more broadly, in that it is one that pits the marginalized against the constraints of the bigger system.

This sort of critique takes on more political significance in the two Quebec heist films to be considered. In both *Pouvoir Intime* and *Le Dernier Tunnel*, marginalization extends beyond aspects of class, with the failed heists serving to raise larger sociocultural issues that each film explores. More specifically, each film deals with aspects of marginalization in respect to French Canadian identity, particularly in terms of power relations. *Pouvoir Intime* opens with two shadowy figures, one of whom, H.B. (Yvan Ponton), identifies himself as "chief of security for the Ministry" while the other, Meurseault (Jean-Louis Millette), works as a fixer. Meurseault has been hired to retrieve a bag from an armored truck, although it is never made clear what the exact contents of the bag are. They appear to be incriminating documents that H.B. needs returned. Meurseault hires an ex-con, Théo, to steal the bag, arranging for Théo's early release from prison to take on the job. It is clear from the outset that Théo is a marginalized figure, and he gathers together a gang, including his son, Robin (Eric Brisebois), of similarly outcast figures under the pretense that this is a robbery for money, making no mention of the job for Meurseault.

While in *Pouvoir Intime* the ministry figures are francophone, there is a clear power differential between them and the socially marginalized gang members. In *Le Dernier Tunnel*, the distinction is made more explicit as a gang of criminals is assembled for the genre staple of "one last job." In this case, the heist is financed by an Anglo criminal, Smiley (Christopher

Heyerdahl), who exercises both monetary and social control over the gang. The class divide between the Anglo Smiley and the working-class Québécois gang is made explicit at their first meeting. Marcel Talon (Michel Côté) is fresh out of yet another stint in prison and is working to assemble a gang of past associates to tunnel into a bank vault. They first rendezvous with Smiley as he is leaving the "Orchestra's last concert of the season," a blatant mark of his social standing. The well-dressed, debonair Smiley contrasts with Marcel and his ally, Fred "Pops" Giguère (Jean Lapointe), both in manner and clothing. Language also plays an important role, as Smiley frequently switches from French to English, particularly at times where he wants to assert authority. This action reinforces a linguistic divide and a power relation that provides a reminder of Quebec's political situation as the sole French-dominated province within Canada. Smiley supports the heist plan, as it offers him a chance to recoup funds lost in previous failed heists. For the Québécois gang members, the potential "big score" represents a chance at a better life, exemplified by Marcel's girlfriend, Maggy (Marie-France Marcotte), and her desire to leave the city and start anew, which is pitched as aspiration to a middle-class life.

Smiley's indifference to marginalized lives is made apparent in his arranging for the killing of Marcel's parole officer, Annie Beaudoin (Céline Bonnier). Despite her toughness toward him, it is clear that Marcel respects Annie as hardworking and equally as someone struggling with aspects of her own life. She is going through marital difficulties and also trying to quit smoking. Like the gang members, she is a working-class Francophone, so her killing represents a further assertion of Smiley's Anglo power. That the killing is accepted by Annie's colleagues as a suicide suggests the same levels of administrative or judicial influence evident within the government ministry in *Pouvoir Intime*.

As noted, Marcel respects Annie's hard work, despite her interference with his plans. Her dogged pursuit of him, given her certainty that Marcel, a career criminal, will fall back into his old habits, is matched by Marcel's own efforts to fool Annie, including taking a purposeful shovel to the head to feign injury to explain a missed parole appointment. A similar work ethic is evident among the gang that Marcel has assembled. A substantial amount of film time is dedicated to depicting the work of digging the tunnel and preparing for the crime. Instead of fast-paced "elliptical montages," *Le Dernier Tunnel* devotes much more time to detailing the physical labor involved in the heist. In doing so, it aligns with another of the elements Lee ascribes to the heist genre: "The job must involve a risky operation that will reap great rewards; the plot 'concentrates' on a singular crime that occupies a significant portion of the diegesis and affective buildup of the story, ennobling the work, skilled labour and physical or mental effort of the crimes represented" (7). That this film puts even more emphasis on "ennobling the work" underscores the ways in which the Québécois working class is contrasted with the Anglo, Smiley, and the wider powers represented by the Mount Royal Bank (Mount Royal being the anglicization of Montréal).

As with so many films of the genre, this heist ends in disaster. As plans fall apart, members of the gang are killed, both by each other (Smiley and his own accomplice turn ruthlessly on Marcel and his friends) and by bank security officers. In the end, Smiley does escape with the money from the robbery. Marcel, who has the opportunity to stop Smiley, instead opts to stay and comfort the dying "Pops." He chooses class, and linguistic solidarity, while the Anglo power makes off with the money. The marginalized lives of the working class, and their subordinate position, even within their own province, becomes a quite blatant metaphor here.

The heist in *Pouvoir Intime* is also a failure, and indeed one that is quite spectacular in nature. Théo's plan involves using an "inside man" on the armored truck and staging a fake hostage taking as a distraction, allowing him and his gang to drive off with the truck in exchange for the "hostage." When the guard who is in on the plan suddenly takes ill and rushes into the restaurant in which the hostage taking is to take place, his colleague Martial (Robert Gravel) assumes his place on the truck. The mock hostage taking turns deadly when Robin panics and shoots and kills the other guards from the truck, while wounding Martial, who then barricades himself in the back of the truck as the gang drives off with it. Unlike other heist films where the heist is the denouement of the film, in *Pouvoir Intime* it leads to a lengthy standoff between the heisters and Martial. As Leach describes, "the forward momentum of the generic action is countered by a sense of claustrophobia that functions as a metaphor for Quebec's political situation" (87). In this film, all of the central characters, bar the shady political operatives, are marginalized, the gang for their class and criminality and Martial as both besieged hostage and gay. In an earlier scene, the lone female gang member, Roxane (Marie Tifo), has overseen a moment of intimacy between Martial and his boyfriend Janvier (Jacques Lussier), a server at the restaurant. Within the gang, Roxane herself is marginalized. She is the only female member, but her femininity is questioned by the gang. Théo suggests that the plan needs someone "more feminine" in the role of the hostage, "the secretary type." Even her boyfriend, Gilder

The abandoned church where the two surviving gang members meet to share the remains of the loot at the end of *Pouvoir Intime*.

(Pierre Curzi), says that he preferred her when they first met and her hair was longer.

By the end of the film, after the failure of the heist and a desperate escape attempt by Martial, all but two of the characters end up dead, including the shady politicos who have turned up to try to claim their bag. The survivors are perhaps the two most marginalized characters, Roxane and Janvier, who have formed an unlikely alliance based on Roxane's knowledge of Janvier's relationship with Martial. Neither conforms to society's expectations around femininity or masculinity and within the heist genre, and for the two of them to end up with the money is a telling shift. Thomas Waugh sums it up by pointing out that "only the butch Roxane and the cute widower Janvier survive, and even better, the two get away into the sunset with all the booty in their pockets, forming a new, triumphant social coalition among the sex/gender outlaws" (260). While it is not quite "into the sunset," and Roxane leaves alone in a car she gets from Janvier in exchange for a share of the loot, Waugh's point regarding a new social coalition holds true. For a film that spends much of its duration in dark, claustrophobic locales, the bright, open setting of the ending (a burned-out church set against a rural landscape) suggests a new start, for the surviving protagonists, but also possibly for Quebec society. And as Leach identifies, "the image also refers back to Quebec's rural and religious past, a history that seems to be irrelevant in the corrupt urban society that provides the film's generic action" (88). Perhaps, as Janvier's name suggests, this is a new beginning.

These Quebec examples are the most blatant in providing a social function to the use of the heist genre. The political dimensions of more than 250 years of oppression of French culture within a largely English Canada are addressed through a genre where, as Lee suggests, "the heist encodes in story form a particular desire to elude the oppressive aspects or limitations of contemporary mass society" (5). This is also evident in the other examples from English Canadian cinema, as each film provides elements of the social function and critique associated with the heist film. This eluding of the "oppressive aspects or limitations" is true of the losers who are able to outwit Interpol and gain their personal revenge in a globalized, postmodern world where giant plastic vaginas are "art"; the recent University graduates who can bring down an apparently uncatchable criminal mastermind; or a film that can use the elements of the heist to critique the hold that escapist Hollywood genre cinema can have on the cultural imagination. The heist film's appearance at different points in the development of a national cinema in Canada (or possibly, national cinemas) demonstrates the manner in which genre can be employed and reworked in distinct cultural contexts. The analysis here reveals how these films work culturally, while also underlining how that cultural meaning is embedded within the industrial context in which these films are produced and consumed.

Notes

1. Telefilm is a federal cultural agency for the development and promotion of audiovisual production by the Canadian private sector.

PART TWO

◊◊◊◊◊◊◊◊◊◊◊◊◊◊◊◊◊◊◊◊◊◊

Gender, Race, and Class in the Heist Film

Men, Women, and the Heist Film

◇◇◇◇◇◇◇◇◇◇◇◇◇◇◇◇◇◇◇◇◇◇◇◇

Gaylyn Studlar

As a crime-centered story form, heist films are often male-centered, if not male obsessed. The heist usually involves a group of men committed to a daring cooperative criminal scheme. Whether made up of professionals or amateurs or both, this criminal fraternity pulls together as a group to steal cash, gold, jewelry, or a priceless work of art. In the post–World War II period, the Hollywood heist film was crucial in the origination and consolidation of a popular genre that by the 1960s had spread internationally in terms of both production and popular appeal.

As important as stealing is to the heist film in its seventy-plus years of existence as a screen articulation of crime, the meticulously planned big heist tends to be about more than just loot, even in the less sophisticated entries in the genre. Heist films may seem to be popular culture at its most formulaic and suspenseful (or mindless), but they inevitably register aspects of the industrial and historical contexts in which they are made, and they are capable of something more, too—that is, of expressing broadly felt cultural anxieties and aspirations, fears and fantasies.

Heist films, typically marked by male activities, spaces, and values, are also highly gendered in their cultural implications. In this respect, they can reinforce, complicate, or sometimes call into question dominant discourses on the nature of masculinity and femininity and ideologies of gender and sexuality. The absence of women as heisters in films of the 1940s and 1950s is not uncommon, since females frequently were stereotyped, on-screen and off, as more moral and less criminally inclined than men, though the femmes fatales of film noir often upended those notions. Women also were often thought to be incapable of the basic qualities—skilled professionalism, cool rationality, and silence—that a heist demanded. Yet, as I will argue in the latter part of this essay, women's role in heist films changed noticeably in the 1960s, and even when their participation in the heist was limited, women still could play an important role in defining not only femininity but also masculinity, especially in relation to perceptions of American manhood in crisis.

Heisting to Recover Honorable Masculinity

Hollywood heist films offered a meditation on contemporaneous male identity in the mid-twentieth-century that shared much with US public discourse focused on the need for American men to respond to the imperilment of their manhood. The main threats to masculinity were identified as corporatism, conformity, and women. As early as 1942, Philip Wylie coined the term "momism" in his best-selling book *Generation of Vipers*. He argued that American men were being destroyed as independent individuals, first by their small-minded, power-hungry mothers, who encouraged blind fealty to all forms of authoritarianism, and then by their wives, who took over dominating them. As a result, women were causing the ruin of American society (186–94). Wylie called for men to "face the dynasty of the dames at once, deprive them of our pocketbooks . . . and take back our dreams which, without the perfidious materialism of mom, were shaping up a new and braver world" (205).

Following the war, a range of public commentary in the United States addressed the perceived crisis in masculinity. Continuing Wylie's hyperbolic view of women, a number of popular press commentators pointed to women having overturned male domination in postwar American culture and changed the tenor of masculinity itself. In an essay that first appeared in *LOOK* magazine, J. Robert Moskin claimed, "Scientists who study human behavior fear that the American male is now dominated by the American female . . . he has changed radically and dangerously . . . he is no longer the masculine, strong-minded man who pioneered the continent and built America's greatness" (3). Arthur Schlesinger Jr. wrote in 1958 in the men's magazine *Esquire*, "There are multiplying signs, indeed, that something has gone badly wrong with the American male's conception of himself" (64), but Schlesinger refused to jump on the bandwagon and lay the blame for beleaguered masculine identity on women and what Wylie, in the same year, called the "womanization" of culture ("Womanization" 51).

Like Schlesinger, more research-based reflections on postwar US culture looked elsewhere for reasons for this crisis. Perhaps most influential among these was David Riesman's *The Lonely Crowd: A Study of the Changing American Character* (1950). Sociologist Riesman argued that American character had changed from being "inner-directed" to being "other-directed," creating a nation moving toward being dominated by a social type that sought the approval of others rather than trusting an inner sense of right and wrong developed from tradition. Corporations, consumerism, and media were contributing to this change in American character. Riesman suggested that what was actually needed was the "autonomous" type, "capable of conforming to the behavioral norms of their society . . . but . . . free to choose whether to conform or not" (287). A few years later, William Whyte's best seller *The Organization Man* (1956) condemned the effects of corporate America that turned men into conformists who only wanted their lives to be pleasant and shared with others who were like them. In response to such disconcerting trends, George B. Leonard Jr. called for men to fight conformity and reclaim the traditional strengths of American manhood. Writing in *LOOK* magazine, he said: "The present age, as every other, demands dedication, daring and persistent individualism" (103–4).

Macho author Norman Mailer reasoned that, as women had become "more selfish, more greedy, less romantic, less warm, more lusty, and also more filled with hate," men were losing "faith in the notion of one's self as a man" (quoted in Kimmel 256). More sanguine observers might have noted that men were still firmly in control of government, finance, manufacturing and commerce, education, and just about everything else associated with the public sphere (Gilbert 74). Nevertheless, Mailer declared that the nation was suffering from a "built-in tendency to destroy masculinity in American men" (quoted in Kimmel 256).

American manhood was in peril because, as, Mailer bluntly stated, "masculinity is not something one is born with, but something one gains. And one gains it by winning small battles with honor . . . [and] there is very little honor left in American life" (quoted in Kimmel 256). Mailer's comments and those of numerous other observers of postwar identity in the United States resonate with film scholar Frank Krutnik's description of postwar films noirs, especially the tough suspense thrillers, and the attitude these films demonstrated: "'Tough,' controlled masculinity becomes an ideal which is lost or unattainable and which can only precariously be achieved: it is represented not as something which can be taken for granted . . . but as something which has to be achieved and consolidated through an awesome struggle" (131).

Originating as part of the film noir cycle and narrativizing a criminal plan of action, the heist film builds on the gendered character of men who engage in a collective adventure in stealing, reflecting an intention to defy both the law and the odds of successful completion. No surprise, then, that this daring "job" of theft, this struggle against the odds and the law, often is undertaken by men who are steeped in a homosocial world of gambling, whether they are career criminals or not. With a few exceptions, like George Peatty (Elisha Cook Jr.), the timid racetrack clerk in *The Killing* (Stanley Kubrick, 1956), this world tends to distance men from the twin evils of woman-dominated domestication and corporate conformity. Whether as pastime or profession, gambling encourages men to take risks, and the heist often is depicted as a higher level of risk taking, a ratcheting up of the norm. As Dave Burke (Ed Begley) says to Earle Slater (Robert Ryan) about his heist plan in *Odds Against Tomorrow* (Robert Wise, 1959), "One roll of the dice and then we're through forever." These men are not getting something for nothing. They are risking their futures, their freedom, and their lives.

Exemplary of this kind of world and the sense that it cuts across class lines is *The Asphalt Jungle* (John Huston, 1950), which served as a veritable blueprint for the genre. The opening scene introduces the film's chief protagonist, Dix Hanley (Sterling Hayden), traversing deserted city streets as he walks away from an early-morning stickup. He steals to live—and lives to play the horses. Once a Kentucky farm boy, he is now a small-time robber and deeply in debt to an illegal gambling joint visually represented as an urban hellhole, a noir maze of light and shadow. This depressing but all-male space will become ground zero for planning the heist. At the opposite end of the economic, social, and environmental spectrum, in *Seven Thieves* (Henry Hathaway, 1960) a Monte Carlo casino is the glittering site of a multi-million-franc heist executed by an unlikely ensemble of ex-cons and cabaret performers passing themselves off as high-society gamblers even though, like Dix, they are from the bottom of the social heap. In *Ocean's 11* (Lewis Milestone, 1960), Danny Ocean (Frank Sinatra), a World War II veteran and professional gambler, masterminds a plan to hit five big Las Vegas casinos simultaneously on New Year's Eve. After all, he tells his ex-GI comrades in recruiting them for the heist, "why waste all the tricks the army taught us?"

Unlike *The Asphalt Jungle*, with its subproletarian, corrupting urban environment, *Ocean's 11* allows the audience to enjoy the spectacle of Las Vegas casinos as a different cultural type of corrupting (or freeing) environment. As Elizabeth Fraterrigo says of Las Vegas in midcentury America: "Home to opulent casinos and hotels and saturated in sex, drinking, and gambling, this leisure destination suspended values of sobriety, self-restraint, and sexual conservatism" (151). The Rat Pack stars of

Ocean's 11—Frank Sinatra, Dean Martin, Peter Lawford, and Joey Bishop—formed the core of a group of high-living celebrity-entertainers well known for hard partying and relaxed musical performances in Las Vegas. Thus, their characters are automatically "at home" in such a place, in which they affirm their unconventional masculinity in male-defined (public) play rather than through woman-determined (domestic) responsibility. The focus on Las Vegas would continue to be exploited in heist films like *They Came to Rob Las Vegas* (Antonio Isasi-Isasmendi, 1968) and into the twenty-first century with Steven Soderbergh's *Ocean's Eleven* (2001).

Although the ambitious robbery that defines the narrative focus of the postwar Hollywood heist film is criminal and therefore morally and socially transgressive, paradoxically, it often also appears recuperative of traditional masculinity. The heist as a daring group-oriented process is envisioned as potentially transformational, changing the participating men's individual lives not just for the better but in ways fundamental to a reclamation of a dominant, independent, inner-directed, ideal male identity, or, as one heister says to another in *The Killing*: "After today, good Lord willing, you will be a new man." Is the act of daring to participate in the heist enough to restore normative masculinity or is the money acquired from the caper necessary?

Films may differ on their implied answer to that question, and certainly heist films in the postwar period are subject to a number of influences beyond a perceived cultural crisis in the construction of masculinity, but heisters' dreams of the big score were almost always frustrated in heist films made during the era of the Production Code Administration (which lasted from 1934 to 1968), complicating the screen fantasy of transgression and transformation. The PCA, as the American film industry's chief instrument of moral self-regulation, insisted on crime-does-not-pay endings to feature films. It also discouraged heist films from showing reproducible details of criminal planning and process that might inspire successful real-life imitation.

Protagonists typically die or are on the verge of arrest at the end of Hollywood heist films made in the 1940s and 1950s. Something inevitably dooms the big payoff, even if it doesn't doom the heisters to certain death: cheap luggage spills millions onto the airport tarmac (*The Killing*); an accident on a busy roadway reveals an automobile bumper to be made of heisted gold (*Plunder Road,* Hubert Cornfield, 1957); heisted casino money is marked, prompting its anonymous return by the thieves to save them from police pursuit (*Seven Thieves*). Even if the loot remains elusive during this period, the genre dramatizes how men attempt to defy the odds as well as the law to reclaim their masculinity in a criminalized version of the "daring" and "persistence" associated with past ideals of manliness. Distinctly male characteristics like these, it was noted in cultural commentary, would halt the confusion of gender roles and help restore traditional gender difference in the sexual realm (Pitzulo 29–34).

Daryl Lee has argued that the heist genre does not adhere to "a tidy timeline with discrete parts that line up teleologically and move towards some inevitable end" (75). This is no doubt true, but because of overdetermined cultural and industrial reasons, including major revision in moral self-regulation of US feature films, the heist film underwent noticeable changes, moving in the 1960s to less fatalistic and more "fantastic" crime-centered narratives. Heist films of the 1960s developed as so-called caper films, often with a satirical approach to the genre and ending in an ironic twist of fate that satisfied the crime-does-not-pay dictum. In *Ocean's 11*'s famous denouement, a heister's widow unwittingly allows the funeral home's cremation of eleven million dollars resting in her husband's coffin along with his body. In a scene that Quentin Tarantino paid homage to in his neo-retro heist film *Reservoir Dogs* (1992), the surviving heisters then leave the funeral home, slowly walking along the street in silence. The soundtrack offers Sammy Davis Jr. singing the film's theme song: "Show me a man without a dream and I'll show you a man that's dead—real dead"; the final movie credits are superimposed in small print over the scene, but the stars' names also appear in large letters on a Las Vegas marquee above them, capping the film's conflation of the fictional heisters with the star personas of the film's leading actors as Las Vegas celebrity entertainers "who made a spectacle of living by their own rules and thumbed their noses at middle-class propriety and its demands for responsible manhood" (Fraterrigo 151). In spite of the characters' failure to secure the loot, the audience can take pleasure in knowing that the "Rat Pack" stars will continue in their supercool rebellion against conformity—presumably in less illegal ways—beyond the screen fiction.

In contrast to the "flippant" and fantastically over-reaching heisters in *Ocean's 11* (Crowther, "'Ocean's 11'"), some heist films take the time to get closer to replicating postwar masculinity's struggle in everyday life, as discussed by Mailer. Moving away from the central drama of risky criminal adventure inscribed in the genre and cultivating a more serious tone than *Ocean's 11*, these moments of more ordinary masculine struggle are often important to establishing audience sympathy for characters who otherwise might seem undeserving of the audience's allegiance. For example, in *The*

Asphalt Jungle, Doc Riedenschneider (Sam Jaffe), a dapper career criminal who specializes in heists, gets out of prison and immediately begins work on realizing his plan to rob a jewelry store vault. He has been perfecting this plan behind bars, but years have passed and he is no longer familiar with the city. Doc must rely on the advice of a nervous local bookie, Cobby (Marc Lawrence), to find money and men. The money will pay the men needed to help him pull off the half-million-dollar theft: a "box man" (safe-cracker), a "top-notch driver," and a "hooligan" who is not afraid to use violence. Given the tendency of the last type of criminal to be drug addicted, Doc says he hopes for "a more or less reliable man." That man will be Dix Handley, who is earlier presented in the film as a criminal so intimidating that his menacing stare from a police lineup scares a robbery witness into refusing to identify Dix as the thief. Yet, when Cobby cuts off Dix's line of credit over his unpaid gambling debt in front of Doc, a stranger, Dix is visibly embarrassed and almost hysterical: "Don't bone me! Did I ever welch?" he protests. With the precinct swarming with police, it is too dangerous for him to try another robbery, so Dix borrows money to pay Cobby. He tells Gus (James Whitmore), the friend who makes him the loan: "You can't owe money to a guy like him, a little loudmouth who bones you even when he isn't trying to." Being humiliated in front of a stranger cannot pass without response in the social construct that figures in Dix's sense of male honor.

Dix Handley's insistence that he must pay what he owes is contrasted in the film with the high-society debtors who owe lawyer Lon Emmerich (Louis Calhern). Emmerich sends out a vicious private investigator to collect the $100,000 he is owed. Bob Brannon (Brad Dexter) threatens these debtors, but they refuse to pay. Brannon tells Emmerich, "You'll have to sue them." Emmerich is facing bankruptcy, but he has told Doc he will finance the heist via Cobby and then fence the jewels himself after he pays Doc off. Yet, from the very beginning he has intended to pull a double cross: he will take the heisted jewels from Doc on a mere promise of payment and flee the country.

Emmerich is as lacking in honor as those who refuse to pay him. In a world corrupted from top to bottom in which men cannot be trusted to keep their word, no wonder that when Doc observes Dix pay Cobby his debt he cannot help but be impressed and is moved to hire Dix as the heist's hooligan. When Doc and Dix show up at Emmerich's to complete the exchange after the heist, Emmerich admits he hasn't the money. Brannon pulls a weapon on Dix and Doc to force them to give up the jewels. A shoot-out ensues in which Brannon is killed. Emmerich stands crying, with his face

Dix (Sterling Hayden) confronts the inevitable double cross in *The Asphalt Jungle*.

cupped in his hands. A wounded Dix yells: "Are you a man or what? Trying to gyp and double-cross me with no guts for it. What's inside of you? What's keeping you alive?"

If the mythology of American manhood demands that men should connote strength, competence, and self-determined honor, the hooligan Dix, the lowest of the low by most social standards, is more of a man than the conniving, emotionally soft Emmerich, whose suave manners, luxurious lifestyle, and high social position disguise his failure to be a true man. In terms of postwar discourse on American masculinity, Emmerich registers "the decay of masculinity" (Schlesinger 66). He commits suicide rather than face disgrace and prison. Aided by a B-girl who loves him, Dix desperately attempts to get back home to rural Kentucky. He is successful in this, but his escape from the police and from the city life that has corrupted him will be a release into death. He staggers onto the farm that his family lost to hard times and collapses in a pasture, amidst grazing horses.

Focusing on men who "work" together as criminal outsiders, heist films like *The Asphalt Jungle* paradoxically suggest the recapturing of male individuality and autonomy through a collective criminal act. For the viewer, the heist may function as a fantasy of rebellion that recuperates the independent-minded, inner-directed, or autonomous masculinity of the country's forefathers, who were guided by their own instincts and intelligence instead of the herd mentality and group thinking that were cited as damaging gender-specific strengths of presumptively white US identity. The heist harnesses the varied skills of the male participants, returning them to a version (albeit criminal in intent) of the artisanal work that was nostalgically extolled in the postwar era. Although film heisters work as a group, their skills within the theft are individualized. In *Seven Thieves*, a former scientist and convicted thief, Theo Wilkins (Edward G. Robinson), masterminds the heist of a Monte Carlo casino as his "last experiment." He pays to fly in his most trusted ally, Paul Mason (Rod Steiger), to help him. Theo assures the skeptical Paul that the heist is not about money or living in luxury: "I have to accomplish something before I die. I want the world to gasp a little." The heist becomes the ultimate male outsider's attempt to regain his self-respect as a man even if it has nothing to do with restoring his reputation as an honest citizen.

Not only are skills individualized but so, too, are the stakes of the heist to the men involved. In more character-driven films, like *Ocean's 11*, the audience learns how each man nurtures a different hope or fantasy about what a successful heist will mean to his future. In the film, Anthony Bergdorf (Richard Conte) discovers that he has been released early from prison because he is dying; he decides to join the heist to pay for his son's college education; Jimmy Foster (Peter Lawford) seeks to relieve himself of the humiliation of living off his rich mother; and Vince Massler (Buddy Lester) needs money after he is fired as a bouncer at a Phoenix burlesque club. The lantern-jawed, middle-aged Vince attacks "paying customers" who get overly enthusiastic about his beautiful young wife—a stripper called "Honey Face." His situation is played for comedy. Admittedly, not all heist films construct their heisters as sympathetic characters seeking to reclaim a more secure hold on their masculine identity as father, independent adult, or husband, as these examples from *Ocean's 11* suggest. At the other end of the spectrum, heist films like *Armored Car Robbery* (Richard Fleischer, 1950), *Odds Against Tomorrow*, and a remarkably bizarre B picture, *Hell Bound* (William Hole, 1957), present heisters unsympathetically or emphasize dutiful policemen and efficient police procedure.

As the fifties closed, the crime-does-not-pay dramatic heist film gave way to a less depressing comedic focus on stylish heisters operating in appealing exotic locales, with the exemplary film being Jules Dassin's *Topkapi* (1964). Heist films expanded into international coproductions, often made by combining American and European money as well as talent. The conventions of the heist film, including the crime-does-not-pay ending were treated satirically. For example, in *Topkapi* the heisters are caught and serve time in a Turkish prison, but it is a cartoon version of a jail, a visual joke. Heister Elizabeth Lipp (Melina Mercouri) is amusingly reduced from high-fashion garb, sleek coiffure, and her sexy, come-hither smile to sack-like prison garb, hacked-off hair, and a dour pout. But the film quickly cuts to the last scene, in which Elizabeth and her fellow heisters are seen romping happily across an equally unrealistic snow-covered landscape as they make their way to the Kremlin to steal Czarist-era treasures. Crime may still not pay, but failure does not act as a deterrent to more criminal adventures.

As anticipated by *Ocean's 11*, a more "swinging" or "flippant" masculinity often was displayed in caper-as-fun films. This answer to the male identity crisis was derived in large part from *Playboy* magazine's modeling of a pleasure-centered, urban-based bachelor lifestyle as a response to the corporatized, domesticated, and suburbanized masculinity of the 1950s. The magazine defined its ideal of masculinity as a liberation from female-dominated domesticity, one best represented by a man who was "sophisticated, intelligent, urban—a young man-about-town, who enjoys good, gracious living" ("The Playboy Reader"). Films like the American-distributed and financed British film *The Italian Job* (Peter Collinson, 1969) invested in male heister identity as fashionably stylish and stylishly promiscuous (or "swinging"). Early in the film, Charlie Croker (Michael Caine) leaves prison. He makes stops by his tailor and his shirtmaker to be fitted for new clothes and then picks up his Aston Martin convertible from storage. When he arrives at a party hosted by his girlfriend, Lorna (Maggie Bly), he is the only man present in an expansive penthouse filled with scantily clad, beautiful young women. His girlfriend has prepared the gathering as a "coming out present" for Charlie: "Now what would you like?" she asks. "Everything," he replies, laughing, after looking the women over in a scene that resembles images of Hugh Hefner surrounded by "Bunnies" in his "Playboy Mansion." Immediately following, a shot shows Charlie exhausted, creeping out of the room and into the hallway.

As screen heisters like Charlie Croker show, the popular expression of a restoration of masculine potency and gendered power could be updated by drawing on contemporary trends like the so-called sexual revolution, associated with the 1960s but built on the foundation of the *Playboy* model of masculine sexual freedom without emotional entanglement that emerged in the 1950s. The poster for *The Italian Job* featured a bikini-clad young woman in a sitting pose and facing away from the camera with a mapped plan of the heist painted on her bare back; the poster features the tag line: "Introducing the plans for a new business venture." This is characteristic of how, in the 1960s, the heist as criminal adventure symbolically conflated sex and stealing as it continued to serve as a fantasy expression of men's escape from all those feminine dangers associated with their supposed emasculation in postwar life: nagging wives who sexually demeaned them at home, working women who challenged their public dominance, and deadening jobs that required them to conform and prevented them "from expressing their deep, now repressed, manhood" (Kimmel 257).

Nevertheless, by 1969, the heist film had grown too familiar to some. One genre-weary reviewer complained that *The Italian Job* was "the umpteenth film about the mechanics of a fantastic heist" ("The Italian Job"), and Vincent Canby dismissed it in the *New York Times* as the type of movie that had "been made before—very often and much better—by other people." As the formula wore thinner and thinner, the genre went into hiatus in the 1970s and 1980s, but it experienced a muted resurrection the 1990s with the success of *Reservoir Dogs*. A significant revival occurred in the twenty-first century based on remakes and variations on old themes, often reviving and mixing tonalities—drawing from both the tragic and comedic branches of the genre's family tree as well as nostalgic iconography (Lee 91).

As I will discuss in the next section, heist films have changed, but they continue to reproduce Hollywood's traditional ordering of the distinctions between the genders by channeling women into the roles of sexual spectacle or nurturing helpmate while securing the meaning of manliness through an inherited model. That model was associated with values of daring, rationality, skilled competence, steadiness of nerve, and, of course, compulsory heterosexuality. As I will argue, the self-conscious alteration of generic conventions trending toward the comedic and satirical radically rewrote the boundaries of the heist film beyond the "tragic" narrative of masculine failure and allowed women to become more central to heist films, but it did not necessarily redeem the heist film from sexism. In this respect, the Hollywood heist film has clung to some resilient gendered tropes. These tropes, as I will show, are especially pervasive when it comes to objectifying women as sexual beings and inscribing them as objects of love and lust in scenarios of male rivalry and revenge.

Beds, Broads, and Breathtaking Views

The role of women in the heist may not appear to be worth pursuing as a topic. Certainly, the homosocial group of men joined in criminal common cause seems "naturally" to exclude women. Actress Angie Dickinson's retrospective public comments on *The Tonight Show* (November 14, 1977) concerning her "starring" role in *Ocean's 11* could refer to the appearance of any number of actresses in many other heist films: "I was in it so very little because it was the men doing the robbery." As marginalized, maligned, or missing females may initially appear to be in many heist films, they do figure in important ways in the genre and even in a film like *Ocean's 11,* in which lounge singer Sam Harmon (Dean Martin) suggests to his heister mates that if he were running for political office, his platform would be based on taking the vote away from women and reducing them to slavery.

At the very least, the presence of women is necessary in heist films to allay the possibility of male homosexuality, which haunted the gangster film from the early 1930s and was evident also in the 1940s.[1] The faithful, nurturing, and sexually available woman is usually at the margins of the heist, unable to impact it. But even then, as in *The Asphalt Jungle, The Killing,* and *Plunder Road,* she may act as a counterforce to the threat of male homosexuality, a distinct possibility in the insular homosocial world of criminal conspirators. The possibility of heister homosexuality is made fun of in *Ocean's 11.* "What happened? I came in with a fellow," says Jimmy (Lawford) when Danny (Sinatra) abandons him at the elevator to talk to Bea (Angie Dickinson). "A fickle fellow," says Sam (Martin). "Stick with me, Lieutenant, I'm sincere," Sam remarks as he loops his arm in Jimmy's and leads him to his apartment. By way of contrast, Kubrick's *The Killing* makes homosexual attachment as explicit as Hollywood could allow it to be in a midcentury feature film. An older man, Marv (Jay C. Flippen) has embezzled to finance Johnny Clay's heist plan. Obviously in love with Johnny, on the morning of the racetrack heist Marv discourages Johnny from marrying and asks him to go away with him after the stealing is over. Marv is still in bed during their conversation. As he sits on the edge of the bed, Johnny tousles Marv's hair, as if he doesn't understand, in an act that desexualizes the older man, but the scene has put into play the classic location for the sexualized appearance of beautiful women in the heist film, including in earlier scenes in *The Killing.*

The woman in bed is a long-standing and much-used visual trope in heist films that secures the meaning of woman as fundamentally sexual. Its use dates to the strategic and highly eroticized appearance of Kitty Collins (Ava Gardner) on a bed in the initial meeting of the heisters in *The Killers* (Robert Siodmak, 1946). She is the girlfriend of Big Jim Colfax (Albert Dekker), but Ole "Swede" Anderson (Burt Lancaster) has gone to jail to

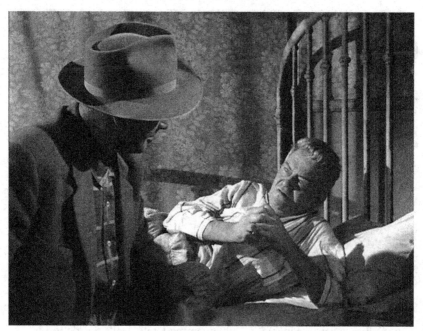

Marv (Jay C. Flippen) confesses his love for Johnny Clay (Sterling Hayden) in *The Killing*.

protect her. Before he answers the question of whether he will participate, Ole looks offscreen to her, and a reverse shot shows her looking at him. He's in. She has lured Ole into a double-crossing heist that will doom him.

Less subtle in her machinations than Kitty Collins, Sheri Peatty (Marie Windsor) lounges in bed in a sheer negligee in *The Killing*. She is anticipating not the joy of her husband George's return home from work but the satisfaction of mercilessly needling him. Sheri is inscribed in the film as one of the most verbally venomous of all femmes fatales, a character that could have been created by Philip Wylie as an exemplar of the modern married woman as emasculating harpy. When Sheri is discovered eavesdropping on the heisters' planning, Johnny Clay knocks her cold and dumps her on yet another bed. She tries to seduce him, but he condemns her as "a no good, nosy little tramp" and advises her "to play it smart and stay in character." She should wait and let husband George blow all the money he will soon have on her. Johnny's advice to Sheri falls on deaf ears. Her actions will be among the many that doom the heist.

In *Ocean's Twelve* (Steven Soderbergh, 2004), the audience's first view of international police agent Isabel Lahiri (Catherine Zeta-Jones) is of her

Kitty Collins (Ava Gardner), the sultry femme fatale, leads Swede to his destruction in *The Killers*.

sexily half-asleep in bed. Her body is languorously arranged for the view of the camera as her lover, Rusty (Brad Pitt), is shown returning to their apartment. She awakens and tells Rusty she is on the verge of a breakthrough in a theft case she is working on. Of course, viewers familiar with *Ocean's Eleven* know that Rusty is a thief, and his reactions clue us in that he is the perpetrator in the case she is investigating. He keeps up his conversation with her until the last shot of the scene, when Rusty adroitly slips out the bathroom window. Similarly, Charlize Theron's startlingly eroticized first appearance as Stella Bridger in *The Italian Job* remake (F. Gary Gray, 2003) shows her enticingly stretched out in bed. She is talking on the phone, and while the scene is visualized as if she might be having phone sex, she is actually talking to her father.

As these examples show, the eroticization of women, good and bad, was common in the heist film from its emergence in the postwar years. In the 1940s, the heist film shared with other films noirs a construction of the sexually alluring woman who functions as a dangerous incentive to male criminality. The heist genre often suggests that beautiful women, like the loot to be heisted, represent an object, a "something" dangerous and difficult to acquire safely. However, this trope did not arise out of thin air and owed a great deal to hard-boiled crime fiction. As an early film noir, *The Maltese Falcon* (John Huston, 1941), based on Dashiell Hammett's 1931 novel, stands as a model for the heist film's inscription of dangerous femininity. It is a film that is normally regarded as a private eye film. However, it is also a heist film. *The Maltese Falcon*'s narrative includes a heist in its final stages, when the heisters have fallen out and the possession of the heisted object is in flux. As is characteristic of hard-boiled detective fiction of the era, in this film the *femme fatale*, the alluring woman as heister, threatens to drag the private investigator onto the wrong side of the law. In this respect the film is important in anticipating a key trope of the postwar Hollywood heist film—the dangerous and duplicitous woman as a lure to male criminality.

At the beginning of *The Maltese Falcon*, private detective Sam Spade (Humphrey Bogart) is hired by "Miss Wonderly" (Mary Astor), a beautiful, refined woman. She says she is trying to find her younger sister, who has run off with a married man. Spade's partner, Miles Archer (Jerome Cowan), is shot dead on a dark street after he volunteers to take Miss Wonderly's case; Spade then learns this woman neither is who she says she is nor does she have a sister. Spade is only temporarily confounded by "Brigid O'Shaunessy." He intuits her double-crossing ways and then has his suspicions confirmed by three men, a queer gang that shows up to claim the Maltese falcon, a priceless, jewel-encrusted statue. Their leader, Kaspar Gutman (Sydney Greenstreet), relates to Spade how he hired Miss O'Shaunessy to assist in the Istanbul heist of this legendary relic, but she spirited it away with the help of a ship's captain and Floyd Thursby, an English gangster. Spade attempts to play the heisters against each other, and in one scene Brigid offers Spade her body: "What else is there I can buy you with?" she asks before he grabs her face and kisses her roughly. Though veiled by production code conventions, it is implied that Spade sleeps with her. Ultimately, the falcon is recovered by Spade but revealed as a fake. The heist is finished, the gang is "blowing town," but three men are dead (Archer, Thursby, and the ship's captain). Spade needs an accounting to keep from being accused of one or more of these murders. Brigid confesses under the pressure of his questioning that she did kill Archer. She declares her love for Spade, but he refuses to break his male code of honor. He says: "You'll never understand me, but I'll try once and then give it up." Does he expect her to be uncomprehending because she is a murderer, a thief, or a woman? He tells her: "When a man's partner is killed, you're supposed to do something about it. It doesn't make any difference what you thought of him. He's your partner and you're supposed to do something about it." Brigid tries to convince him to save her with one last kiss, but Spade hands her over to the police. In the final scene, the detective speaks wistfully of "the stuff that dreams are made of" as he cradles the worthless falcon. He walks into the hall, where he sees Brigid, whose tearstained face dominates a reverse medium close shot. She stares impassively from behind the prison-like bars of the elevator gate as the police take her away to pay for her crimes. By resisting the duplicitous woman as a sexual lure every bit as compelling as the financial lure of the fabled "black bird," Spade establishes his dominance over her and his fulfillment of an ideal of tough masculinity that lives by its own male code in a world of moral and sexual ambiguity characteristic of films noirs.

By adhering to his code, Spade, as the tough man of film noir described by Krutnik, escapes the fate of the weaker male protagonists in postwar films noirs like *The Killers*, *Criss Cross* (Robert Siodmak, 1949), and *Gun Crazy* (Joseph H. Lewis, 1950) who succumb to the woman's sexual allure. In these particular films, it is not the loot but the femme fatale who constitutes the true "stakes" of the heist to the doomed male protagonist, who is in her sexual thrall. The protagonist fails to resist his own transgressive desire for the beautiful but untrustworthy woman, who exploits his love and motivates his ill-fated participation in a heist.

Women such as these are coded primarily as eye candy in the heist film. They are beautiful and tempting but as unpredictable as the gambling wheel, a comparison made overtly at the beginning of *Seven Thieves* and also *Topkapi*. In *Seven Thieves*, the highly stylized opening credits (in black and white) show a roulette wheel from an overhead camera perspective. A scantily clad woman (Joan Collins) dancing barefoot to jazzy music appears superimposed in full figure over the roulette wheel. The audience will later learn that this woman is a heister, Melanie, who performs at a low-class nightclub on the French Riviera. She fascinates a highly placed employee of a Monte Carlo casino who comes to stare at her and may or may not be her lover (the film obscures this). In order to keep from losing her attention, the man, Raymond LeMay (Alexander Scourby), agrees to secure the heisters' access to the casino so they can steal millions from the upstairs vault. Melanie is highly sexualized in the opening and throughout, especially through costuming and dance movements. This is reinforced through the mesmerized looks of Raymond, but she is not a femme fatale. The film humanizes Melanie as dreaming of being better than she is although she has no illusions that money will somehow change her identity as someone who, as an infant, was abandoned and who, in her own words, dances "almost naked." In keeping with earlier heist films, *Seven Thieves* puts a great deal of emphasis on the woman as a sexual lure, either bringing male heisters to or keeping them in the caper, but Melanie is shown to be capable of nurturing domesticity as well as having those qualities demanded of male heisters, or, as Paul says, of "standing straight when the going gets tough." She and Paul fall in love in spite of his initial antagonism toward her as "a man trap" without a conscience.

In *Topkapi*, Melina Mercouri is also offered as a highly sexualized woman associated with the gambling wheel, in this case a Turkish carnival's wheel of fortune. At the beginning of the film, Mercouri appears as a vision in an emerald green dress and long gloves. She looks directly into the camera as she virtually floats in a kaleidoscope of colored lights. As one of the earliest cosmopolitan caper films stressing the fun of sex and stealing, the opening of *Topkapi* is itself a kind of seduction in which the viewer is enticed by a woman to join a fantastic, exotic adventure filled with likeable, if not loveable, characters. This woman (Mercouri) is certainly the mastermind of the heist, introducing its object—a sultan's emerald-encrusted dagger—as her personal obsession.

The opening is even more stylized than that of *Seven Thieves*, with eye-popping colors, distorting lenses and special effects, odd camera angles, and abrupt cutting. Mercouri's face is reproduced in various colors on the wheel of fortune along with card symbols, contributing to the sense that this is a fantasy about a big gamble. The film cuts to the carnival's wax figures, including Salome with the head of John the Baptist, Roosevelt and Stalin as they appeared at Yalta conference, and finally a sultan with a jeweled dagger. After these close shots, a high-angle long shot of the dark and deserted carnival shows Mercouri bidding Joseph, the carnival manager, adieu. She assures him that she will see him again and that he will become very rich. Then the audience is taken to the gardens of the Topkapi, where the woman, now in a stylish white suit, continues to talk directly to the audience, looking at the camera in close-up shots as she explains who is she is (her name, "Elizabeth Lipp," is an alias, she admits), where she is (Istanbul, Turkey), and what she is (a thief). Elizabeth strolls into the Topkapi museum and then leads the audience to the sultan's dagger. In close-up, she closes her eyes as she describes the dagger's emeralds, "the four greatest emeralds the world has ever known. Dazzling, flawless." She suddenly reanimates as if from a swoon and says to the camera/audience: "Forgive me! A strange thing happened to me . . . difficult to explain . . . I'm going to have it. It's going to be mine." The heist is on.

Like *Seven Thieves*, *Topkapi* involves the woman centrally in the heist, but in this instance she is more than a loyal and competent member of the team. She is the heist's instigator, its mastermind. The questing heist answers her desire and is coded in this opening scene as speaking to her fantasies and to an erotic compulsion rather than to the desire for mere money. Elizabeth flies to France. On a foggy Paris street, she enlists her former lover in her heist plans. Walter Harper (Maximilian Schell) finds her studio filled with designs. Elizabeth is already crafting a fake replacement for the priceless dagger they will pilfer from Topkapi.

This kind of inscription of the woman became characteristic of the comedic cosmopolitan caper version of the heist film that took off in the 1960s. Mercouri's character is very important to the heist plan in *Topkapi*, but she is also highly sexualized as an erotic lure to the audience to join the adventure. She also functions as a kind of sexualized den mother to the male heisters, encouraging them with kisses and flirtatious attention when their spirits flag or their efforts falter. In spite of her centrality to the film, her erotic presence may have inspired critic Bosley Crowther to dismiss her role in the film: "She is basically an indulgence and adornment, like those colored lights [of the opening scene]" ("Recruiting Jewel Thieves").

Yet, *Topkapi* can be seen as a breakthrough film establishing the box-office appeal of the cosmopolitan caper film that offered audiences a tourist gaze on stealing as exhilarating international adventure. It was equally important for presenting the female heister as an instigator rather than just a participant in the scheme, so that while she brings her beauty and sexuality to the caper, she also motivates the adventure as the culmination of *her* fantasy. However, we should not forget that there were other caper films in the 1960s in which the woman is represented as comically incompetent for much of the narrative. These include *How to Steal a Million* (William Wyler, 1966), *Gambit* (Ronald Neame, 1966), and the British caper film *Hot Millions* (Eric Till, 1968).

Finally, the woman in the heist film may also be a nurturing type, a nostalgic reminder of feelings and social values pointing beyond the typical economic goals of the criminal adventure. Angie Dickinson's Bea is this type in *Ocean's 11*. She is visually coded as very beautiful but quite modestly dressed. We first see her as she is delivering Christmas presents; her white-collared, high-necked navy sheath dress resembles a modernized nun's habit. Sam asserts that Danny and Bea are still in love, but Danny is sleeping with other women and does nothing to address Bea's dissatisfaction with him as a husband. In a particularly disturbing scene, the film has Bea defending him when a woman he has slept with calls her to report on his casual infidelity. The film portrays women, even those who nurture, as the chief danger to men's illicit fun in all its forms, and women as mother, wife, and sexual pickup create problems for the men in *Ocean's 11* from which not even a successful heist could hope to disentangle them.

Danny's heist plan in *Ocean's 11* seems to have nothing to do with Bea, in contrast to the remake *Ocean's Eleven*, which makes Julia Roberts's Tess, ex-wife to Danny Ocean (George Clooney), the motivation for Danny's heisting. The casino he plans to heist is owned by Tess's lover, Terry Benedict (Andy Garcia), a well-disciplined but notoriously "ruthless" man. Tess is coded as beautiful, classy, and cool (much like Bea in the original film version). Without knowing who she is, other than being Benedict's girlfriend, Linus (Matt Damon), a heister assigned to watch Benedict's comings and goings, points her out to Rusty: "Ah, there she is. This is just the best part of my day," he says while gazing at her longingly. A reverse shot of Tess shows her walking down the Bellagio staircase; accompanied by sexy music, she is a vision of elegance. Rusty reacts with worry, and he confronts Danny in the next scene: "Tell me this is not about her . . . tell me this is not about screwing the guy who is screwing your wife." Danny can only say, "It's not entirely about that," but during the heist Rusty has to relieve Danny of his duties because he puts the heist in danger with, first, his desire to avenge himself against Benedict and, second, his desire to regain Tess.

Unlike in the original version of the film, in the Soderbergh remake Danny is portrayed as a man who heists because of love, not in spite of it. In fact, the heist is a means of rescuing Tess from the equivalent of the fairytale dragon. Danny tells her that she may not love him anymore, and she can make a new life for herself, but not with Terry Benedict: "Not him." The audience, of course, is given ample opportunity to see why Danny does not want Tess to be with Benedict. She is obviously a well-educated woman (an art curator), but the film inscribes Tess as emotionally unobservant, a woman who cannot recognize a jerk when she sees (or sleeps with) one. It will take the heisters' surveillance video of Benedict admitting he values money over Tess for her to decisively break with him and return (literally running) to Danny as he is being scooped up for parole violation. An orchestrated version of Debussy's *Claire de lune* provides highly romantic soundtrack music to accompany this brief reunion. She reaches Danny and exclaims: "Wait. Wait. That's my husband." The police take him away.

The last scene of *Ocean's 11* suggests Tess must accept her man's larcenous ways for them to live happily ever after. Rusty meets Danny as he exits a prison. He tells him he has picked up his "personal effects." Tess, now wearing her wedding ring, sits in the back of a vintage convertible outside the prison. Danny (tuxedoed but in a state of dishabille) nonchalantly walks over and joins her in the backseat. They kiss tenderly. Rusty drives them away. Two casino hooligans trail them in what will no doubt be permanent surveillance. In spite of this, the film is a comedy, not only because Danny hurts no one (only Benedict's pocketbook suffers) and the heist succeeds but also because he rescues Tess from a bad man. Even if he cannot promise to be a law-abiding citizen, Danny does offer the promise of settling into blissful domesticity as a gentle, loving husband.

The *Ocean's* franchise, as well as *The Italian Job*, suggest that in the twenty-first-century neo-retro heist film, tough masculinity defending the boundaries of threatened masculinity is no longer necessary to the heist film. Rusty and Danny may have a stylish breeziness that resembles that of the Rat Pack stars of *Ocean's 11*, but the unrelenting misogyny and fear of women displayed in the earlier film is replaced by a new masculinity, sensitive and loving to the woman who is willing to accommodate herself to her man's need to steal. Such a strategy of delineating male-female relations and the construction of gender in twenty-first-century heist films suggests that all changes to the genre are not necessarily "progressive," even if they have the veneer of difference. Nevertheless, clear patterns emerge across the span of the over seventy years of heist films that suggest that gender and sexual identity are more important to the development, shape, and cultural meaningfulness of this traditionally male-centered genre than we might assume.

Notes

1. On the complexity of heterosexual dissatisfaction and implied homosexuality in classic gangster films, see Shadoian. On homosexuality in gangster films of the early 1940s, see Studlar 120–45.

Masculinity, Morality, and Action

Michael Mann and the Heist Movie

<><><><><><><><><><><><><><><>

Jonathan Rayner

> Since the late 1980s representations of white males as do-
> mesticated, feminised or paternal have featured prominently
> in numerous films in a range of genres including comedies,
> romances, action movies and thrillers; so much so that the
> cultish but mainstream gangster movie as revitalised by
> Quentin Tarantino is about the only mode in which macho
> masculinity remains intact. (Davies and Smith 19)

The above assertion of a restrictive and normative function in the representation of masculinity in contemporary Hollywood cinema suggests a
marked retrenchment of conservative values. Entertainment films, such as
Mrs Doubtfire (Chris Columbus, 1993) and *Jumanji* (Joe Johnston, 1995),
which champion familial attachment, emotional articulacy, and parental
responsibility for the American male, promote a return to the social principles of classical, Hays Code Hollywood. In some cases, studio-era productions serve as clear generic and ideological precedents: *The Family Man*
(Brett Ratner, 2000) embodies a fantastic and comedic reaffirmation of
domestic contentment reminiscent of *It's a Wonderful Life* (Frank Capra,
1946). Even the heroes of action movies have been defined in terms of the
motivating and redemptive fatherly role (*Con Air* [Simon West, 1997], *Collateral Damage* [Andrew Davis, 2002]). The distinction of Tarantino's stylized thrillers from this trend emphasizes the role of the crime film in the
exhibition of uncompromising and unaccommodating masculinity. However, where Tarantino's films offer an exaggerated and titillating portrayal of
a violent and autonomous masculinity unrestrained by conventional moral
or legal checks, the films of Michael Mann foreground rarefied, rather than

simply stylized, forms of male endeavor that consciously reject paternal and domestic roles. Professional and perfectionist criminality is explored and venerated in his work as a valid career choice, mutually exclusive with family life.

Mann has worked in both film and television as a producer, director, and writer since the early 1970s, with most of the movies and series to which he has contributed being concerned with crime. In both media, he has perpetuated and developed established genres and introduced innovation in texts that have influenced and defined their eras. His films *Thief* (1981), *L.A. Takedown* (1989), and *Heat* (1995) combine and extend the characteristics of gangster films and heist movies, while his series *Miami Vice* (1984–89) and *Crime Story* (1986) and the film *Manhunter* (1986) represent the amalgamation of the director's emphasis on contemporary popular cultural forms and artifacts and the 1980s obsessions with surface style and consumerism. In the characterization of his protagonists and the exploration of their dilemmas, Mann foregrounds crises in and the erosion of conventional, societal values, as criminality emerges as a superior alternative to law-abiding, domestic existence. Mann's visual style, characterized by imbalanced widescreen compositions, location shooting in modern cityscapes, and single, overriding colors dominating the mise-en-scène, articulates the isolation of his individualistic males and the incompatibility of the professional and domestic spheres. In Mann's oeuvre, the work of crime for criminals and police officers alike requires a professional and emotional detachment from societal standards of morality and conjugality. This alienation is at once sought, lauded, regretted, and yet maintained, and leads to the subversion of the conservative ideology of law and order generally ascribed to the representation of crime in popular entertainment. For Mann's men, professionalism on either side of the law is preferable to deference to the values of conventional society, even where criminal activity is chosen as the route to the acquisition of a stable domesticity, and where law enforcement activity is putatively supportive of consensual social values:

> *Heat* is a film about work and its increasing personal costs. For the characters in *Heat*, work provides excitement and challenge, but it ultimately excludes any emotional life outside the demands of the job . . . their work—what it is, how they go about it, how they like it, what distracts them, and, especially, what they have to sacrifice to keep doing it—takes centre stage in the film and in the lives of the characters. (Lindstrom 21–22)

The nature and implications of this choice in lifestyle are reflected in their meticulously planned actions and are verbalized in infrequent and idiosyncratic speech. Through the physical performance of individually determined roles (both the criminal "act" and its attempted prevention), Mann's characters redefine, qualify, and deny moral and behavioral norms and evade domestication.

Genre Conventions, Character Traits

Thief, L.A. Takedown, and *Heat* are heist movies, the subgenre of crime films that concentrates on the planning, execution, and repercussions of robberies, or "capers." Although there are numerous discernible precedents and influences, *The Asphalt Jungle* (John Huston, 1950) and *The Killing* (Stanley Kubrick, 1956) can be used for comparative purposes in order to highlight the vexed morality of Mann's films. The prominence of heist movies from the 1950s onward reflects the decline of the Hays Code restrictions of the classical era, which hitherto had prohibited the detailed representation of criminal practices (Maltby 239).

The Asphalt Jungle follows the preparation and undertaking of a safe-cracking operation, a project nurtured by a recently released and aging criminal mastermind but financed by a gambling operator and a corrupt businessman. The gang assembled for the heist consists of a safecracker (who wishes to support his growing family with his take) and a gunman (who wishes to leave the urban environment and buy a farm in order to return to the rural idyll of his childhood). The film's narrative inspires compassion for the gang: the robbery is portrayed as an essentially victimless crime, and the individual goals stated by the gang are uncontroversial. Also, the robbery represents a last offense and a last chance for escape and happiness for all of its members. However, the gang's planning and expertise are undone by mischance during the heist and by treachery when the stolen goods are taken to their backers. The leader is recaptured and both the safecracker and the gunman are fatally wounded, the latter dying in a meadow after a futile attempt at escape into the country.

The apparent sympathy for the criminals in this narrative resides in their conventional motives for financial gain (the erasing of debts, support of family, and escape from urban corruption to rural innocence). However, the tragic denial of these objectives in death and imprisonment is inseparable from an inherent judgment of criminality. By contrast, the corrupt businessman is allowed the dignity of suicide. In the words of the investigating police officer, the jungle of the title is not a corrupting environment responsible for the downfall of the gang but a contested space, marked by minority antisocial behavior that the police fight to contain. The conservatism of the police chief's closing speech, which punctuates the scenes of the gunman's death, justifies the gang's dissolution as both tragedy and punishment. A similar pattern of scrupulous preparation overtaken by fate and individual weakness is present in *The Killing*, albeit with a more dispassionate, observational stance toward the ignominious ends of the gang members. The latter film's complication of the plot's linear progression, in juxtaposing disparate but simultaneous events, can be seen as an influence on the self-conscious structuring of Tarantino's films, but Kubrick's clinical and impartial analysis of a crime differs from Tarantino's provocatively nonjudgmental stance. The sense of tragedy alloyed with inevitable and justified punishment in the heist movie persists into later and non-American examples (e.g., *The Criminal*, Joseph Losey, 1960), but undergoes a gradual alteration in later decades. While expertise in crime remains paramount, it can be appropriated by noncriminals as a form of satire (*Fun with Dick and Jane*, Ted Kotcheff, 1976) or as a symbol of wealth and virility (*The Thomas Crown Affair*, Norman Jewison, 1968/John McTiernan, 1999). However, the representation of ineptitude in the heist movie also becomes associated with overt social and political commentary. Desperate protagonists are seen to be driven to criminal extremes by social and racial inequalities but find these injustices reaffirmed by the punishments meted out by the establishment (e.g., *Dog Day Afternoon*, Sidney Lumet, 1975; *Dead Presidents*, The Hughes Brothers, 1995). In such examples, sympathy and active support for the criminal are expressed within the text (by a vocal general public in Lumet's film), with the result that criminal activity assumes a revolutionary zeal.

The heist movie's abiding concentration on proficiency and unity of action in pursuit of a specified goal is central to Mann's crime films. The enhancement of professional expertise is foregrounded not as one characteristic but as the dominant and defining element of character. The realization of personal (masculine) identity is accomplished through vocational activity, and this refinement of action (in the protagonists' evaluation) peripheralizes or discounts moral and legal distinctions:

> The heist film frequently depicts ambition, work ethic, and the use of skills by the criminals that would be valued in the legal world of work, but these qualities are used instead in the service of crime. The effort to develop a detailed plan, gathering of workers with specific

and diverse talents, search for financing, meticulous preparation, trial runs, and concentration and precision-timing required for the heist itself—all these sound much like legitimate work. (Lindstrom 25)

What distinguishes the criminal groups in Mann's films is their continuity. The crews are not assembled for specific tasks but work together routinely and repeatedly. These groups exist as focal points of association that outweigh the conventional family in importance. Prison experience, as both a common frame of reference and a collegiate base of acquaintance and loyalty (Letkemann 38, 123–5), is stressed in *Heat*, where four of the gang members are identified as former inmates of Folsom State Prison. The character Neil McCauley's (Robert De Niro) prison record, known and respected by policeman Vincent Hanna (Al Pacino) just as Neil is aware of the detective's career, is also the first topic of conversation during their meeting in the coffee shop.

Mann's protagonists seek personal goals that are similar in their idealism to those of the gang in *The Asphalt Jungle*. Frank (James Caan), the "self-employed" safecracker in *Thief*, operates with his own group of independent specialists in Chicago. He strives to assemble a fortune and a family in line with a plan laid out graphically in a collage of photos he carries in his wallet. This composite image contains a house, a wife, a child, and his surrogate father and mentor, an aging safecracker who is dying in prison. His criminal activities are intended to facilitate rather than impede the rapid acquisition of a conventional and respectable middle-class life. The Chicago detectives who pursue Frank respect his professionalism, but only insofar as they expect and demand their own payoff from his crimes in order to allow him to operate in peace. Appropriately, Frank's contempt for them arises from their indolence rather than their corruption: "Did it ever occur to you to work for a living? Take down your own scores." A more serious hindrance to Frank's life plan comes in the form of a crime "family," an Italianate boss and his gang who seek to exploit Frank's expertise. The offer of speeding up his financial gain with robberies planned and financed by Leo (Robert Prosky) and his gang is undercut by the loss of autonomy. Leo makes Frank a "father," overcoming his problems in adopting a child by literally purchasing one for him, but as a result comes to see himself as Frank's father and the owner of "the paper" on his life.

Neil McCauley in *Heat* wishes to take his accumulated fortune to New Zealand, a specific pastoral idyll very distant from the urban environment of Los Angeles. Essentially he plans for an early retirement supported by the wealth amassed through his work. The motives for the other members of

Neil's "crew" vary subtly. Chris Shiherlis (Val Kilmer) is a gambler who loses most of the earnings from their jobs and who needs a big score on the last robbery to sustain his marriage. Michael Cheritto (Tom Sizemore) has a substantial fortune but continues with the gang's activities for the thrill rather than the financial gain involved. Trejo (Danny Trejo), the driver, is relatively undeveloped, but Donald Breedan (Dennis Hayshort), his replacement on the crew's last venture, is characterized as the reformed recidivist unable to thrive in a vindictive society. His incautious return to crime on Neil's spontaneous offer appears at once tragic and inevitable and justifiably provoked. The singularity of this "tight crew" is its multi-ethnic composition (encompassing Black, Italian, Hispanic, and Anglo-Saxon American males) and its apparent commitment to domestic stability. All except Neil are connected to partners or spouses, and both Chris and Michael have children.

The group supporting Vincent Hanna, the leader of the robbery homicide squad, is superficially similar. The squad is variegated in racial and generational terms, including young, middle-aged, black, and Native American members. However, important distinctions emerge as both groups become more fully delineated. Where the film juxtaposes social outings by the two groups taking place on the same night, the apparent rowdiness of the cops in a bar contrasts with the restraint of the crew's behavior in a restaurant with their families. Children are present at the crew's table, where it is obvious that some of the cops have "dates" rather than long-term partners. In large measure, the two groups become defined in relation to their atypical leaders. Vincent's failed marriages are inseparable from his obsession with his work, but he coordinates the efforts of his subordinates, a group of similarly dedicated single men. Vincent's irascibility jars against Neil's self-control, and yet Neil's solitariness alienates him from his companions. His rigorous, businesslike approach hides a comparable desire for stability and a partner, which is potentially satisfied through his meeting with Eady (Amy Brenneman). Ironically, both leaders assume a pastoral, counseling function in offering emotional support to others in the "work" environment (Vincent gives solace to the victims of crime and Neil intervenes in Chris's and Charlene's [Ashley Judd] marital problems) while their own emotional connections (to wives, partners, and stepchildren) are compromised. Remarkably, Hanna upbraids his stepdaughter Lauren's unreliable father in the midst of an argument with his wife, Justine (Diane Venora), about his own absences. Similarly, when Lauren (Natalie Portman) chooses Vincent's hotel room for her suicide attempt, he is freed to respond to her professionally, treating her as a victim rather than a relative.

In balancing the heist movie's analysis of criminal technique with the police procedural drama's exhaustive cataloguing of detective work, *Heat* juxtaposes a film genre with an antithetical television narrative framework (Rubin 244, 249). The connection and equation of each group's activities contribute to the film's erosion of legal and moral distinctions between them. However, the linkage of criminal and cop in Mann's work is at variance with the undercover investigator's pretense of kinship. In *T-Men* (Anthony Mann, 1947) and *White Heat* (Raoul Walsh, 1949), the cop's infiltration of a gang never undermines his professional and moral identity. More recent films (*Deep Cover* [Bill Duke, 1992], *Donnie Brasco* [Mike Newell, 1997]) have suggested the seductiveness of the criminal life, as much because of the apparent ineffectuality or corruption of the law enforcement establishment as due to the conducive society of the gang. By comparison, Mann's elevation of the individualistic criminal above cops and gang bosses in *Thief*, and the equalization of legal and illegal professionalism in *Heat*, serve different and less conventional ends. Having suggested the motivations and goals for each elite group, both *Thief* and *Heat* lead inexorably toward a series of related losses and defeats. This nesting of comparable and concomitant tragedies within the principal, individual conflicts underlines the films' pervasive and subversive engagement with the ideology of crime genres in popular entertainment, and their questioning of the protagonists', antagonists', and audience's values.

Action and Execution

In Mann's films, the sequences that detail the robberies and burglaries receive emphasis as generic set pieces and as embodiments of the protagonists' codes and principles. The opening sequence of *Thief*, depicting Frank's drilling of a safe containing diamonds, is exemplary of this economy of characterization and narrative. The three group members (Joseph [William La-Valley], the driver, scanning police radio frequencies; Barry [James Belushi], disabling alarm systems; and Frank, drilling the vault) are linked by cuts between their locations, but they work without need of verbal communication. The leaching of color from the night shooting and the absence of establishing shots for this sequence (beyond a shot of the getaway car in an alley) act as a further isolation of their individual, albeit interdependent, actions. The drilling of the safe is seen in a series of close-ups that center on Frank's manipulation of the machinery and the painstaking movement of the bit into the door. An extreme close-up traces the drill's path through the door to reveal the exposed workings of the lock mechanism. Once the door is opened, Frank discards cash and jewels and selects only a collection of anonymous white paper packets from the safe's contents. The exit and escape, involving several exchanges of vehicle before the group disperses, are also accomplished wordlessly.

The definition of Frank's character through the enacting of this first heist is reinforced by the extended preparation for and execution of the burglary that occupies the main plot. The identification of countermeasures to the next vault's alarm systems and the construction of a thermic lance to cut through its doors are shown in detail as Frank assembles his team and equipment. However, this second heist, which is also completed perfectly and without incident, does not represent the climax or conclusion of the film's narrative. The climactic and destructive action of the film's conclusion centers instead on the incompatibility of Frank's professionalism with the demands of mafia-based organized crime and with his domestic objective of home, wife, and family.

The plot of *Heat* is also punctuated by the enactment of the crew's "scores": an armored car holdup, a safe-breaking operation, and a bank robbery. In each case, preemptive and collaborative action is seen in preparation and execution. The anonymous purchase of explosives, the monitoring of the armored car's progress and radio communication, the disabling of police pursuit vehicles, and the crippling of alarm systems at the bank and precious metals depository all serve to illustrate the crew's excellence and apparent unassailability. An additional action sequence follows a setup and counterambush at a drive-in movie theater, precipitated by a plan (suggested by Neil's fence, Nate [Jon Voight]) to sell bearer bonds stolen during the armored car raid back to their owner, Roger Van Zant (William Fichtner), a corrupt investment banker. This transaction, based on profiting from defrauded insurance, should be a logical move if Van Zant is the "businessman" Nate assumes him to be, but Van Zant's pride provokes him to instigate the ambush by his henchmen. The crew's evasion of the trap is again marked by pre-planning and interdependence as Neil, Chris, and Michael cooperate to wipe out their would-be assassins. However, despite the crew's apparent mastery of each criminal act and its repercussions, the consummation of each heist is interrupted by an eruption of chaos. The sudden ascendancy of disorder within the orderly conduct of crime threatens the completion of the individual score, but also previews the eventual dissolution and death of the crew and its members.

Although the criminal planning and execution progress perfectly for Frank, the project that his crimes are supposed to finance (the assemblage of home and family) actually proves deleterious to his career. Between the two pristine burglaries, Frank begins his association with Jessie. In outlining to her the delays imposed upon his objective by prison terms, he insists that nothing can prevent him from conjuring his dream family (depicted on his photo collage) into being. In a manner redolent of his aspiration, he does not accept her refusal to be part of his life, and counters her admission that she cannot have children with an instantaneous decision to adopt. Notably, Frank approaches Jessie after his meeting with Leo and after his acceptance of assurances that with the crime family's scores he can amass his fortune and assemble *his* family more quickly. Unfortunately, Leo's motive for the procurement of Frank's house and son is restraint rather than reward. Once installed, Frank's wife and son function as instruments of control, since the "family" boss assumes that threats to their safety will force Frank to conform. The irony of Leo's use of Frank's family in business is extended by Frank's businesslike response to Leo's fatherly equivocation ("Where is gratitude?"—"Where is my end? I see my money is still in your pocket, which is from the yield of my labor"). Illegality (the reclamation of the leased child and home, and the threatened prostitution of Jessie) endangers Frank's ersatz family. However, Frank's resolve to destroy the boss who seeks to control him also entails the ruin of the newly established family. He hands his savings to Jessie before expelling her from the house with their son. He then burns down his legitimate domestic and business premises (their home and his secondhand car lot) and throws away his "life" picture. After his shootout with the crime family in which Leo and his henchmen are killed, Frank walks away into the night, now apparently bereft of all domestic and criminal attachments. His solitude, in professionalism and individualistic terms, is reaffirmed as a defeat for domestication and a Pyrrhic victory for personal principles. Without any other goal or association, he is again defined solely by vocation, delimited by the film's monosyllabic title. The perfection of Frank's work, his "magic act," ultimately requires its and his removal from the criminal as well as the domestic milieu.

Where the forces that eventually destroy Frank's domestic project are connected to "organized" crime, the chaos that threatens to overwhelm Neil's crew is characterized as an undisciplined and profitless form of criminality. Van Zant's preferment of reputation above business sense is matched by, and later comes to be allied with, the uncontrolled violence of Waingro (Kevin Gage). Waingro is not part of the "tight crew" before or after the armored car holdup, and the need for his inclusion is unspecified. That he is considered to be less experienced or reliable is suggested by his being armed with an inferior weapon during the holdup: a pistol rather than the automatic weapons of the rest of the crew (Letkemann 113). Aside from his disruption of the robbery, Waingro's other criminal acts (serial rape and murder) are portrayed as violently antisocial and pointlessly destructive. His unnecessary killing of one guard when the robbery has been completed dictates the execution of the others. Michael obeys Neil's logical command, interpreted by Vincent at the scene later, in order not to "leave a living witness." In similar fashion, the logic of self-preservation compels the crew to abandon the burglary at the precious metals depository (where a lack of professionalism from the police reveals their planned ambush), to kill Van Zant's henchmen, and to shoot their way out of the bank heist when the police are tipped off.

In each incident, when the chaos of the unplanned, the irrational, or the motiveless intercedes, the crew strive to reimpose order. Although abandoning the precious metals burglary represents a prudent avoidance of conflict, during the armored car robbery, the ambush with Van Zant's men, and the aftermath of the bank robbery, the attempt to reassert the crew's sense of order is based on an escalation of violence: the killing of the other guards and the ambushers and the extended gun battle in downtown Los Angeles, which envelops police and pedestrians alike. A comparable but markedly unsympathetic escalation of violence characterizes the successive bank raids undertaken by the initially attractive, countercultural group of surfer–bank robbers in *Point Break* (Kathryn Bigelow, 1991). The effect of this shift is to emphasize, as in Mann's films, a personal bond between the FBI agent who infiltrates the gang and its enigmatic leader, while reinstating, unlike Mann, a conservative stance toward crime. Similarly, the actions and expertise of the gang assembled for a complex robbery in *Ronin* (John Frankenheimer, 1998) are codified as the preserve of an elite warrior caste. Set-piece sequences in Paris and Arles (at the Roman gladiatorial arena) emphasize the distinction of the group and their adversaries from the general populace, but in each case their activities result in an escalation of violence and its infliction on innocent bystanders. The portrayal of such disregard (when one of the gang members is in reality an undercover or renegade CIA agent intent on foiling a terrorist plot) highlights the mismatch between disruptive violence and conservative ideology in action cinema, when compared to the ambivalent, self-conscious, and self-destructive nature of violence in Mann's work.

The crew's reaction is in marked contrast to the premeditated, controlled, and suppressive violence used at the outset of the armored car and bank robberies (Letkemann, 100, 110). As the bank's occupants are herded together, Neil appeals to them rationally and emotionally in order to *avoid* the use of violence: "We're here for the bank's money . . . you're not going to lose a dime. . . . Think of your families." Neil's entreaty is all the more ironic, given that the immediate repercussions of the robbery, including and provoked by the crew's violent response to the disordering of their plans, overwhelm and destroy several family units. Like other crime thrillers, such as *Bullitt* (Peter Yates, 1968) and *The French Connection* (William Friedkin, 1971), which can be defined by their controlled or chaotic chase sequences (Rubin 250), the central theme of *Heat* is distilled by the reactive violence and endangerment of domesticity apparent in its heist sequences. The survival of the crew members' families and domestic environments is sacrificed to the professional cause at the same time as their logical, professional, but escalatory response to crises in action endangers the law-abiding public.

Action and Value

After the bank robbery, the deliberate decision to compromise the domestic sphere (previewed in Michael's admission of enjoyment of the "juice" ahead of the financial reward) is marked by the actions of each member of the crew. The presence and influence of stable domestic and family environments have been recognized as significant checks upon the initiation of criminal behavior (Felson 23–26). By contrast, the intercutting between the crew members' homes or partners, which introduces the bank sequence (a shot of Eady packing to leave with Neil after the robbery, followed by one of Charlene Shiherlis at home with her son), underlines the lives and values placed in jeopardy. As a result, a similar pairing of shots (of Elaine Cheritto [Susan Traylor] watching news of the gun battle at home, and of Breedan's partner, Lily [Kim Staunton], seeing a report of his death in a bar) emphasizes the pervasiveness and inevitability of loss. The juxtaposition of actions and environments articulates a choice rather than a competition of values. The most poignant and conclusive incident in the sequence, which encapsulates this choice, is Michael's instantaneous and pragmatic decision to take a child hostage to facilitate his escape. Any parental sentiment is secondary to the practical course of action. (As such, Michael's act prefigures Neil's abandonment of Eady.) Similarly, after his killing of Michael, Vincent's comforting of the child hostage (anticipating his rescue of Lauren) appears to be as much a professional as a pastoral response.

Michael's preference for action, as stated in the decisive meeting before the bank robbery, precipitates his subsequent actions and his death. By comparison, Chris's decision to undertake the bank raid is motivated by the desire to restore his domestic relationships. Chris is the first to open fire when the police appear outside the bank. After Chris is wounded, Neil instructs Nate to keep him safe until their escape route from the country is secured, but Chris decides instead to seek out Charlene, despite the risk of imprisonment. This sets in motion a second series of pragmatic decisions, ironically antipathetic to the maintenance of domesticity. When the police bring Charlene to a safe house in order to lure out Chris, Sergeant Drucker tells her that her only option to avoid imprisonment along with her husband, and the resultant institutionalization of her son Dominic, is to betray Chris and facilitate his capture. (Drucker's outline of Dominic's likely future after being raised by the state mirrors Frank's recollection of his own childhood in *Thief*, which he seeks to redress through his own adoption of a child in state care). When Chris appears, her coded warning allows him to escape and allows her to avoid the repercussions for her own and her son's future, but the family unit is splintered irretrievably. Her action can be construed as equally selfless and self-serving (she protects her son and manages to maintain her own and her husband's freedom at the cost of their unity), but Chris's choice to leave embodies a final resignation from the family group.

Chris's dislocation from his family is compared with Neil's lack of similar commitments from the aftermath of the armored car holdup onward. The argument between Chris and Charlene over his gambling debts results in his violent departure from their home and his spending the night on Neil's floor. The comparison of living spaces is indicative of the characters' status: Chris smashes various ornaments before he leaves his home, but in Neil's house the only articles in view are strictly functional (a telephone, his keys, his handgun, and a coffeemaker). When he is seen alone in his house, Neil is isolated in extreme close-up at the farthest right edge of the frame, with the rest of the composition made up of the glass windows and the sea beyond. The single blue-grey color and the racking of focus from the interior to the waves outside are indicative of Neil's alienation and of the focus of his life existing beyond his dwelling. On waking up, Chris asks Neil two apparently long-standing and inseparable questions ("When are you going to get some furniture? . . . When are you going to get an old lady?"), to which Neil makes identical replies ("When I get round to it"). In one home, the eruption of violence is directed against the trappings of domesticity and illustrates the imperiled state of the family itself; in the other, there is no physical or material presence beyond the artifacts associated with work against which to react. It is noticeable that Neil's closest associates are also seen to be contained by work-oriented or neutral social spaces. His meetings with Nate take place in cars and car parks, and he encounters Eady in the bookstore where she works and later in a café. More revealingly, both Kelso (Tom Noonan) (who gathers information electronically to set up the bank robbery) and Eady (who is pursuing her preferred career as a freelance graphic designer) are seen to work from home, converting the domestic space into business premises. In addition to these compromised spaces, we see Van Zant's office being used as a living area when he fears Neil's revenge, but when he returns to his home it appears to be as underfurnished and unoccupied as Neil's. With the contamination of both Michael's and Trejo's home spaces (with the television report of the robbery watched by Elaine and the torture and death of Trejo and his wife at the hands of Waingro), no purely domestic environment remains unaffected by consequences of the crew's activities.

Of the policemen, only Vincent's domestic space is seen within the film, but this area is a site of unremitting conflict. Vincent is seen either rushing to leave, as on the morning of the armored car holdup, or returning late, on several evenings during his investigation. In any case, the house is not his but Justine's, forming part of her divorce settlement. The only possession Vincent seems to value in the house is his television, which he watches in preference to talking to Justine and which he insists on removing when he discovers her infidelity. This episode is remarkable in itself since it is the only occasion on which a meal is seen to be made in any of the homes, and yet even this food, prepared by Justine for her lover Ralph (Xander Berkeley), is left uneaten. Vincent's withdrawal to the anonymity of a hotel room is succeeded by his discovery of Lauren in the bathtub. The suggestion of a familial bond between the policeman and his stepdaughter, intimated in her choice of his room for her suicide attempt, is undermined by the neutrality of this space and the professionalism of his response.

Vincent's preference for nonaligned or professional spaces is different but comparable to Neil's desire for but failure to create his own home environment. The coffee shop scene, in which cop and criminal meet and converse for the first time, exemplifies their denial of attachments and considerations outside of professional commitments. The sequence is introduced by Vincent's return home to find a sink full of unwashed dishes and Justine dressed to go out. Unwilling to engage with marital or domestic concerns, he returns to work and instigates the meeting with Neil on the freeway.[1] The seeking of this contact, immediately succeeding the avoidance of familial interaction, represents the crystallization of Vincent's choice, in line with Neil's, Michael's, Chris's, and Charlene's. The resolution to meet with Neil, prompted by their mutual, professional admiration, encapsulates the

Vincent (Al Pacino) and Neil (Robert De Niro) meet face-to-face in a café in *Heat*.

immersion of both characters in their intensive and exclusive activities, described by the director as a "morphine groove of self-confidence and decisiveness" (Mann 17).

The exchange between Vincent and Neil replaces the candid conversation between Frank and Jessie in *Thief*, in which a life plan financed by and eventually divorced from crime is mooted as an achievable goal. However, the earlier film ends with a loss, or more precisely a renunciation, of this stated objective, and with the hero's return to a solitary existence. In the coffee shop, Neil and Vincent note the similarity and, in their opinion, inevitability of their activities and choices, and consolidate the recognition and respect their mutual surveillance has inspired up to this point. When police incompetence reveals the police stakeout at the precious metals repository, Neil and Vincent appear to stare at each other via surveillance cameras. The centrality of their faces in the frame in intercut shots, and the appearance of Neil's face as a monochrome, negative image, illustrates graphically their equality in perception and judgment.

Their distance from a "normal type life," which they recognize and nominally desire but ultimately abjure, is marked in the coffee shop by the presence of ordinary families around them: "people living normal lives who have never used guns, never experienced physical violence, never been stolen from and never steal. Surrounded on all sides by this flow of normalcy" (Mann 15). During the conversation, Neil repeats the maxim he stated earlier to Chris: "Allow nothing to be in your life that you cannot walk out on in thirty seconds flat if you spot the heat around the corner." When Neil asserts the primacy of this "discipline" (which will eventually require his abandonment of Eady), Vincent describes this creed as "pretty

After their gun battle at the Los Angeles airport, Neil grasps Vincent's hand as he lies dying at the end of *Heat*.

vacant," apparently unconscious of the irony in his own abandonment of Justine in order to establish contact with Neil. Neil's next remark, that "it is what it is," encapsulates the unarguable, self-evidential nature of both men's professional principles. While the coffee shop scene notes visually and verbally an alternative to the paths the two characters have chosen, it ends with a recognition, and championing, of their difference and exclusivity. Each assures the other that their kinship will not prevent them from attempting to kill their adversary if their professional judgment demands it. Their final meeting confirms this necessity.

Conclusion: A Mutuality of Condition

Mann's heist films examine the intricacies of criminal activity and policing with an attention to detail that ultimately renders moral distinctions relative. The antisocial nature of criminal acts is defused by the promotion of expertise and discipline required for their successful enactment. The inclusion of comprehensible and sympathetic motivations for criminal behavior (the constitution and support of families, the desire for self-realization and escape) might appear as an excuse for the crew's undertakings, and the loss of life and destruction of domesticity that attend the heists are certainly stressed as both personal tragedy and waste. However, these losses frequently appear ambiguous or one-sided. Michael's decision to go on the bank robbery, his hostage-taking, and his own death are logical, albeit self-centered, selections that he does not survive to regret. Similarly, Eady's consternation at Neil's abandonment is based on her ignorance (compared to the viewer's knowledge) of his maxim. His earlier verbal commitment to her ("There's no point in me going anywhere any more if it's alone, without you") is, like Frank's contract with Jessie, ultimately incompatible with individual principles and professional conduct. Charlene's warning to Chris and Justine's resigned releasing of Vincent at the hospital before his final confrontation with Neil represent an informed female accession to the males' vocational demands.

Despite the inclusion of the domestic domain in Mann's films as a fact, goal, or ideal to be supported or defended by criminals and policemen alike, alternative systems of value and existential meaning and behavior predominate for the male protagonists. Only in *Manhunter*, in which the FBI agent's investigations into the serial murder of families imperil his own household, is the hero allowed to complete his task, revoke his profession, and return to the home. The annihilating "givens" of adult life identified within existential psychotherapy—the inevitability of death, our inalienable free will, our fundamental solitude, and the absence of meaning in life (Yalom, *Love's Executioner* 4–5)—are countered by personal strategies of comfort, containment, and denial. Family connections at once represent a source of support and the potential for further stress, as separations and deaths reaffirm solitude and mortality. While families, and by implication legal and conventional lives, exist in *Thief* and *Heat*, they do not represent the favored repository of meaning for the male protagonists. Self-realization and meaning in life is achieved through the attainment of excellence and the observance of self-imposed rules in work. The family is reduced to "a tool, a defense against isolation" (Yalom, "Existential Psychotherapy" 362) that is discarded nonetheless, since it cannot defuse the crisis of meaning as effectively as the work of discipline, and the discipline of work. Criminal and police work are as equally invalid and antisocial in domestic terms as they become valid and admirable within their exclusive groups, and for the viewer.

The codification of dress, behavior, and expression in Mann's work goes beyond the simple elevation of visual style over narrative substance, as criticized in series like *Miami Vice*. It also assumes a greater significance in social and contextual terms, as it combines generic and moral debates with the discussion of pertinent, work-based "lifestyle issues of the mid-1990s" (Lindstrom 21). By comparison, the stylization of conduct and dress in contemporary Tarantino films such as *Reservoir Dogs* (1992) actually works to undermine their reverence for violent, individualistic manifestations of masculinity from within: "the defining contradiction is between the symbolic signification of the sharp suits (conventional masculinity) and the frailty they expose, as for most of the film they are roughed up and drenched in blood" (Bruzzi 89). Noticeably, Tarantino's emphasis on the compromised power of the criminal male rarely includes any representation of domesticity, even as a deselected alternative.

In *Heat*, Neil's spotless business suit is tarnished only by his own blood, when he is fatally wounded by Vincent in their final shoot-out. The affluence and composure embodied in the suit mark his professionalism and become points of attraction for both Eady, when she watches him in the bookstore, and Vincent, whose own suit is frequently disheveled. In a reversal of practice in mainstream cinema, *Heat* proposes Neil as an object for the gaze of both Vincent and Eady, instead of foregrounding the female as an erotic spectacle. In the bookstore scenes, Eady appears as a small and indistinct figure in the background as she watches Neil, who, by contrast, dominates the foreground and center of the frame. Consequently, she is not allowed to assume or retain the status of an erotic, desired object, as Neil's principles (the insistence on killing Waingro and on abandoning her) remove her from the gaze and quash a conventional, heterosexual conclusion to the narrative. Instead, the two central males exchange narcissistic gazes derived from respect and desire, even as the film proposes them to the viewer as equals, adversaries, and objects for admiration:

> Battles, fights and duels of all kinds are concerned with struggles of 'will and strength', 'victory and defeat', between individual men and/or groups of men. All of which implies that male figures on the screen are subject to voyeuristic looking, both on the part of the spectator and on the part of other male characters. (Neale 16)

The reciprocal surveillance of the cop and the criminal, and their respective engineering and acceptance of the coffee shop meeting, articulate their literal and metaphorical regard for each other. They mirror and complement each other up to the point of death (Vincent sees and shoots Neil only when he is betrayed by his shadow), and in so doing provide the viewer with twinned points of voyeuristic identification without a correspondingly secure moral, legal, or conventional perspective. We are forced to confront the vagaries and ambiguities of social constructs of criminality, legality, and domesticity, just as the law-breaking and law-enforcing protagonists are forced to acknowledge "the mutuality of their condition" (Mann 18). Mann's work within the crime genre stands as the apologia for the classical gangster film, and the apotheosis of the heist movie, in its articulation of insoluble social and moral ambiguities.

Notes

1. In the previous incarnation of this narrative as *L.A. Takedown*, this encounter takes place by accident, lessening its impact as a conscious and enlightening meeting of kindred, solitary professionals.

Hollywood and the Black Stickup

Race and the Meaning of the Heist on the Big White Screen

◇◇◇◇◇◇◇◇◇◇◇◇◇◇◇◇◇◇◇◇

Jonathan Munby

What is a heist? It's a robbery, a stickup, but to be successful it is necessarily premeditated, planned and carried out by criminals with a sophisticated understanding of money. Thus a high level of organizational skill and notions of individual initiative and group coordination go hand in hand with the notion of the heist. Until the civil rights movement impacted on Hollywood in the 1950s, however, the legacy of white racist assumptions about the capacities of African Americans (as "primitive," "natural," and uncontaminated by capitalist progress) militated against their inclusion in the heist formula. Even in the cycle of films most critical of American modernity, film noir, African Americans had almost no representation. The black/noir combination, ironically, came together only in the last of the film noir cycle, *Odds Against Tomorrow* (Robert Wise, 1959), precisely as a way to frame the perversity of racism. This chapter will examine how subsequently the heist in a number of black-themed films opened up creative ways to contest white control of what "black" signifies on the big screen.

Critically, the heist in African American–oriented films has often featured as a means to put a lie to the racial indifference of capitalism. What follows examines the blueprint for a black-themed American heist film, *Odds Against Tomorrow*, before analyzing how and why the heist scenario has proved particularly productive in mediating heightened periods of interracial tension, first in the context of Martin Luther King's assassination and then in the light of Rodney King and the impact of deindustrialization on African American communities.

Odds Against Tomorrow: The Black-Themed Heist Film Setup

In *Odds Against Tomorrow*, an upstate New York First National Bank is targeted by three heisters. The mastermind is a disgraced cop, Dave Burke (Ed Begley), who solicits the services of two men desperate enough to take on a job they have never tried before. One is an African American nightclub entertainer, Johnny Ingram (Harry Belafonte), who is in debt to the mob and must pay them off or he, his estranged wife, and his young daughter will be killed. The other is a white unemployed war veteran, Earle Slater (Robert Ryan), who feels deeply ashamed of relying on his doting girlfriend for financial support. He is also a white racist bigot.

Burke's initial challenge is to persuade both Ingram and Slater to take on the caper. Once this is achieved, he then has to broker the interracial tension between Slater and Ingram that threatens to undermine a heist that demands group trust and an integration of interests. In the context of 1959, the concept of "integration" had obvious connections to the wider world of civil rights activism. In the end, although the three execute the robbery and steal the $50,000 payroll, the attempt to get away from the scene is jinxed by mistrust based on racial prejudice. Slater breaks with the original plan that Ingram take the car keys and get the getaway vehicle. Instead he insists Burke do this. Burke takes the keys and leaves the bank but is spotted by a cop, who approaches him. Slater sees this and shoots at the policeman. In the ensuing shoot-out Burke is fatally wounded. Ingram and Slater have found cover but cannot escape without the car keys in Burke's possession. Burke resorts to shooting himself so that the police will not be able to make him name his accomplices. Ingram flies into a rage at Slater, blaming the "screwup" on his racism. They then take shots at each other while taking flight on foot. The film climaxes with the two atop gas storage tanks, taking aim at one another. They are surrounded by cops, but their pursuers are of no interest, reduced as they are to being an audience to an apocalyptic denouement. Slater and Ingram shoot at each other, and the gas tanks explode. When the ambulance men come to collect their immolated bodies, no one can tell black from white. This final scene reflects tellingly on how racism undermines the possibility of class solidarity between two dispossessed Americans.

One of the key original attributes of *Odds Against Tomorrow* is the unsentimental stance it took on interracial brotherhood. While we are given good reason to empathize with all the characters (even the racist bigot is seen to be an affectionate lover, and we are given several contexts through

Burke (Ed Begley) tries to keep the peace between Johnny (Harry Belafonte) and Earle (Robert Ryan) in *Odds Against Tomorrow*.

which to understand how his bigotry is primarily a function of economic impoverishment), the film's message is distinctly dark. The title itself is redolent of the nihilistic character of film noir. In this film, the odds are stacked precisely against integration, which sets it up against the grain of Hollywood films mediating a more tolerant interracial future. As the film's director, Robert Wise, stated, "We were too close on the heels of *The Defiant Ones* [Stanley Kramer, 1958], where the two came together at the end. I didn't think we could make a film about the same racial problem, and have the same resolution where they get together. . . . It seemed to be too pat" (Polonsky 157).

The Defiant Ones was a Sidney Poitier vehicle in which his African American protagonist, Noah, is a prisoner on the run handcuffed to a white racist cracker. The film resolves itself and the issue of interracial tension by having Noah sacrifice his chance of freedom. Instead of jumping a freight train, he elects to stay with his injured white partner and wait for the police hunt to catch up with them. Belafonte (as both star and head of the film's production company, HarBel) envisaged *Odds Against Tomorrow* as bringing a more realistic depiction of "tomorrow" to the screen: "Take my good friend Sidney Poitier; he always plays the role of the good and patient fellow who finally wins the understanding of his white brothers. Well, I think audiences are ready to go beyond even films like *The Defiant Ones*. I think they would be terrifically relieved to see on the screen the Negro as he really is and not as one side of a black-and-white sociological argument where brotherhood always wins at the end" (quoted in Nason).

Odds Against Tomorrow's divisive image of race hate was designed to question the platitudes informing Hollywood mediations of race and racism up to 1959. As a film made in the middle of a civil rights campaign that would secure de jure changes in racial discrimination, it is significant for the way it underscored the de facto continuity of white racism. When Ingram protests to his ex-wife, Ruth (Kim Hamilton), that she is fooling herself if she thinks anything will improve by working with her "ofay" (white) friends, he poses awkward questions about the terms of antiracist politics and the kind of film that deals with such matters. The pessimistic tone of the film connected it to the moment in Hollywood history when something like a cycle of black-themed heist films emerged, namely in the aftermath of the assassination of Martin Luther King.

After King: Post-1968 Black-Themed Heist Films and Black Power Politics

The late 1960s and the 1970s gave increased screen space and time to African Americans in heist films. Some key examples include: *The Split* (Gordon Flemying, 1968), which exploited the super sports star status of Jim Brown, who masterminds the heist of gate money during a football game at the Los Angeles Coliseum; *Cool Breeze* (Barry Pollack, 1972), a reboot of *The Asphalt Jungle* (John Huston, 1950) featuring a jewel heist with black perpetrators donning Richard Nixon and George Wallace masks; and *Blue Collar* (Paul Schrader, 1978), which dramatizes the coming together and falling out of three assembly-line automobile factory workers, one white and two black, when they try to hold their union to ransom, having stolen a ledger revealing the union's links to the mob. While all of these films bear some relationship to the world of black political choices, this is not their central narrative concern. The focus here will be on those heist films that took up directly the problem of antiracist political entropy resulting from divisions between those espousing an integrationist platform based on nonviolent civil disobedience, on one hand, and a militant, separatist Black Power doctrine of armed self-defense, on the other.

In 1968, Paramount released *Uptight*, directed by Jules Dassin, who had come to prominence with his seminal heist film, *Rififi* (*Du Rififi chez les hommes*, 1955). A victim of Hollywood's anticommunist blacklist, Dassin was in European exile when *Rififi* was made. *Uptight* constituted a Hollywood comeback film for Dassin, who chose to team up with African American artist-activists Ruby Dee and Julian Mayfield in cowriting a screenplay dramatizing dissent and disloyalty among black political activists based on Liam O'Flaherty's 1925 novel (and 1935 film) about betrayal in the Irish Republican Army, *The Informer*. *Uptight* offered Dassin a chance to comment acerbically on the culture of informing that had forced him into exile (Munby, *Under a Bad Sign*; Sieving). It also proffered the opportunity to use the heist as a scenario that precipitated not only the disintegration of faith in integration (the legacy of *Odds Against Tomorrow*) but the rise of a new ideology to replace it.

After the opening credits, the film is introduced with a title, "Martin Luther King was assassinated on April 4, 1968, in Memphis, Tennessee," overlaying extended documentary footage of King's funeral cortege and thousands of mourners marching and gathering outside the Ebenezer Baptist Church in Atlanta. In Cleveland, African Americans are watching the same footage on television, this time with the voice-over of King incanting his "I Have a Dream" speech. Things on the street are uptight. A state official in a police squad car and on the radio pleads for peace in the black neighborhood. A van with three young African American activists embarking on an arms warehouse heist pulls up outside a house to pick up their comrade, Tank (Julian Mayfield). He declines to join them, however, asking them to call the robbery off, as it's "the wrong night." Tank is drunk and depressed following the assassination of King. Johnny (Max Julien), the group's leader, tries to sober him up. For Johnny, King's demise is not a reason to call off the heist; rather, it is precisely a call to arms: "Listen to me. He was a big man . . . but he was holding us back. And Memphis proves the answer is guns, more guns. Tonight's on."

Despite Johnny's insistence that Tank come along, as the plan depends on his participation, he refuses. Johnny departs, accusing Tank of letting them down. A man down, the robbery is compromised. Although the breaking and entry are executed with consummate skill and speed, it takes too long to carry the heavy boxes of guns, and the perpetrators are discovered by a security guard. In the chaos of the attempt to get away, Johnny fatally shoots the guard and forgets his shirt, which he had taken off in order to do extra heavy lifting in the absence of Tank. The shirt is labeled with his name and makes him the focus of an ensuing police manhunt.

The heist's complication becomes an allegory for the wider problems confronting African American political organization in the wake of King's murder. The difference of opinion between an undecided old school Tank and an adamant revolutionary Johnny compromises the effectiveness of the team. The consequent narrative focuses on a split between integrationist nonviolent resistors and Black Power organizers (the "Movement Committee"), who reject cooperation with white activists and believe in armed self-defense. Tank is expelled from the ranks of the committee, and the film chronicles his downward spiral into betraying Johnny and finally being killed by committee goons.

Uptight's nihilistic treatment of the political choices confronting those fighting white racism following the assassination of King is taken further in *The Lost Man* (Robert Aurthur, 1969). As a vehicle for Sidney Poitier, *The Lost Man* was part of a strategy to remake Poitier's image in line with an increasingly militant black political culture. By the late 1960s, Poitier's almost saintly screen persona as a black man who dies for white sins was increasingly derided as a form of Uncle Tomism by black militants, especially in the aftermath of King's death. Poitier was subject to being called a "million dollar shoeshine boy" by radical Black Arts Movement leader Larry Neal, for example (quoted in Neal). Perhaps as a way to redeem his image, Poitier committed to a story featuring a black political activist, Jason Higgs, a US Army veteran who has lost patience with older nonviolent integrationist ideals. Symptomatically, he is trying to break up with his white lover, Cathy (Joanna Shimkus), and has taken up arms and planned a factory payroll robbery to fund a black radical group, "The Organization," which is committed to helping support the families of incarcerated revolutionary brothers.

Higgs's militancy is framed by the use of location shooting in some of the poorest parts of Philadelphia, which look like a war zone replete with dilapidated buildings and detritus piled up blocking roads. Higgs decries how money is ultimately "all that it has ever been about." His determination to commit armed robbery and do some wealth redistribution is pitted against his friend Dennis's (Al Freeman's) continued adherence to more moderate nonviolent civil disobedience. The first scene features Poitier looking on at a peaceful civil rights demonstration, which is subsequently subjected to unwarranted police brutality. Impassively, Higgs drives away from the scene. He will later ask Dennis to organize a picket and stage a protest in front of the Affiliated Labor Council in order to divert police attention while he conducts the heist.

The heist itself involves Higgs and three associates posing as members of the "Community Action Committee" (responsible for improving industry-community relations) attending a meeting at the executive office of a big corporation's personnel department. Part of the ruse depends on how they, as black people subject to a white racist gaze, can pass because the white front office has never really taken notice of the real members' identities, reduced as they are to being ciphers for worthy black leaders, such as a doctor and a preacher. The heisters steal the $200,000 payroll, but things go awry on trying to get away. One of the white hostages tries to break free, resulting in a gunfight. Higgs is wounded and separated from the others, all of whom are eventually killed. Although he manages to get the money to The Organization, he is shot down with his white lover in a form of suicide pact.

The no-exit premise of *The Lost Man* underscores a key impression: that meaningful collective action is achievable only in the planning and execution of the heist. The world before and beyond this is fatally divisive, crippling black agency. For these heisters there is no post-robbery sanctuary. The police shooting of Higgs and Cathy symbolizes the killing off of the integrationist dream. Other possibilities of racial solidarity are also stymied when two of the other perpetrators wanted by the cops are betrayed by the reward-seeking black madam of a brothel in which they have sought refuge.

The nihilistic notions of militancy that inform both *Uptight* and *The Lost Man* are also integral to *The Spook Who Sat by the Door* (Ivan Dixon, 1973). Yet, in this film there is a clearer sense that the utopian political possibility of black enfranchisement that informs the planning and execution of a heist can spark a real uprising. The informing ruse in *The Spook Who Sat by the Door* is to use white racism to your advantage. The CIA is under pressure to integrate and conducts an excessively hard recruiting program to find a token black agent. Dan Freeman is the successful black candidate. In recognition of his intellectual acumen and physical prowess, he is given the responsibility of looking after the agency photocopier in the basement. For the next five years, however, he conforms to being a compliant token African American and learns from his training the art of guerrilla warfare, how to organize insurrection, and how to use guns and explosives. In conforming to white racist assumptions, Dan, who is actually a revolutionary black nationalist, can hide in plain sight of the enemy.

After five years, Freeman resigns, saying he wants to use his experience to help Chicago's social services. Using this as a front, Freeman sets about training and building black revolutionary cells. Cell members hide in plain sight through the manipulation of white racist stereotypes: they masquerade as criminal gang members and junkies all over the country. Key to arming the insurrection is an armory heist. The impressive way the freedom fighters execute the heist demonstrates the effectiveness of Freeman's training. His comrades ask if they should go into hiding from CIA and FBI investigators afterward. Consistent with his understanding of the white racist gaze, Freeman replies, "No. They'll be looking for everybody except us. You see this took brains and guts, which we don't have, right?" He also organizes a bank robbery worth $300,000 using lighter-skinned African Americans who are mistaken for Caucasians. Ultimately, the real heist here is how the black revolutionary steals all the knowledge one needs for an armed uprising from an unsuspecting CIA. The film climaxes with the cells going to battle with the National Guard in multiple cities across the United States. The fate of Freeman is suspended. We know he has been badly wounded but the film finishes with a freeze-frame of him still upright and alive. Even if our mastermind protagonist may die inevitably, the film's ending suggests that the revolutionary activity he has set in motion cannot be halted.

While *The Spook Who Sat by the Door* made the most of the revolutionary potential inherent to a black-themed heist, *Detroit 9000* (Arthur Marks, 1973) reflected a more cynical understanding of the caper as the basis for political opportunism. The heist in *Detroit 9000* is the locus of racial tension, an event that is exploited by an ambitious African American politician, Congressman Aubrey Hale Clayton (Rudy Challenger), who is running for governor of Michigan. Almost everyone in this film is a form of hustler perceived to be on the take. As the film's tagline put it: "It's the murder capital of the world. And the biggest black rip-off of the decade." Politicians and preachers are revealed to be no different (indeed possibly worse) than pimps, whores, and armed robbers. The film's lack of resolution at the end over whether one of the main protagonists, white detective Danny Bassett (Alex Rocco), was the best of cops or the worst of cops only compounds this idea.

The film starts with a Hail Our Heroes ball at the Hilton designed to celebrate the achievements of some of Detroit's African American community. In effect, the event is hijacked by Congressman Clayton, who uses the gathering to announce his candidacy for state governor and asks those gathered to contribute generously to his campaign launch. Cajoled by a charismatic preacher, Reverend Markham (Scatman Crothers), the good and the worthy of the black community throw substantial amounts of jewelry and money into a collection basket. Intercut with this scene is the arrival of a van at the back of the hotel that deposits a gang of masked men who then proceed to rob the gathering, asking all present to add everything of value to the basket. They make off with the loot, their racial identities hidden by their balaclavas.

Congressman Clayton takes to the media and plays the race card, accusing the cops of negligence in terms of lack of protection and presence at the ball, stating that if this had been a white event things would have been different. This situation and the accusations of white racism that attend it fuel already heated racial tension in the city. Not only are the cops accused of not caring for African Americans but rumors abound about whether the heisters were politically motivated in trying to jeopardize the congressman's campaign.

Unlike other heist films that deal with race and racism, *Detroit 9000* does not make much of the caper itself as a site of contradictory racial interaction. We are left to guess the identities of the heisters, which is part of the film's deliberate play with audience assumptions. The main arena in which race and racism play a role is in the relationship between the two detectives assigned to resolve the case, white Lieutenant Danny Bassett and black Sergeant Jesse Williams (Hari Rhodes).

What gets between the two men is the notion for Danny that Jesse has exploited the race card to advance his police career and the suspicion on Jesse's part that Danny is somehow crooked and on the lookout for one last payoff before retirement. In many ways, the film never disabuses either party of his assumptions about the other. Jesse follows Danny, who has the loot and is killed trying to deliver it to the fence. Jesse remains unsure about whether Danny was intending to solve the case or trying to profit himself from the heist. While Congressman Clayton celebrates the resolution of the case as an example of interracial brotherhood, we know that these are insincere words delivered by an unethical political opportunist.

The film leaves us with a cynical understanding about racial integration. It is seen to be empty rhetoric when it comes to improving policing, both in terms of protecting and serving the community and in terms of the internal relations between cops of different races. And it is only ironic and Pyrrhic in meaning when it is discovered that the heisters, successful in executing the caper but nearly all killed subsequently, were a mix of races. As one black detective comments ironically, "All dead. A very *integrated* operation."

Hip-Hop's Heist: The Ghettocentric Postindustrial Caper

When one of the bank robbers in *Set It Off* (F. Gary Gray, 1996), Frankie (Vivica Fox), a recently fired bank clerk, justifies the heist to her partners in crime by saying, "We just taking away from the system that's fuckin' us already," the words of Bertolt Brecht from his gangland musical theater work,

The Threepenny Opera, come to mind: "What is the robbery of a bank compared to the founding of a bank?" (Brecht 267).

This question has had different ramifications for different communities at different times in history. As we have chronicled, the late 1960s and 1970s black-themed crime film necessarily engaged the wider issue of the civil rights struggle with its language of integration and black nationalist militancy. Even in blaxploitation films such as *The Split* and *Cool Breeze* that could be seen as being cynical or indifferent toward progressive "rights" politics, the world of crusades and causes remained an informing context for understanding the heist as a way to fight "the Man." In the postindustrial context of the 1990s, however, the word "urban" constituted a different reality. The so-called 'hood cycle that emerged post–Rodney King exploited the themes and aesthetics associated with hardcore gangsta rap, a ghettocentric subcultural movement that was skeptical at best about the prospects of a political movement that could serve African American urban interests (Massood; Munby, "From Gangsta" and *Under a Bad Sign*; Watkins).

Witnessing the video footage of the beating of a black driver by white cops was just the prelude to seeing the perpetrators being acquitted of committing any crime. The incident triggered the Los Angeles urban uprising as nonwhite denizens of the abandoned inner city expressed their outrage. The apparent collusion between the law and police brutality had only confirmed a shared sense among African Americans of being redundant in a white racist world. A ghettocentric perspective on the reality of being black in white America gained increasing authority, with its black nationalist precepts also gaining credibility and assuming a form of "common sense." As Kara Keeling argues, "The shift to ghettocentricism for some of those who operate according to common sense black nationalism hinges on a recognition of a new reality—the post-industrial city's ghettos—that sets it apart from the experiences of ghetto life that precede it" (121).

In looking at three black-themed 1990s hip-hop heist films, *Dead Presidents* (The Hughes Brothers, 1995), *Set It Off*, and *Three Kings* (David O. Russell, 1999), we can see how the caper scenario mediates a worrying sense of continuity with the problems of the past, while also opening up the conditions of possibility for the heist as a way to address new or overlooked issues to do with the victims of white racism.

Dead Presidents bears the ghettocentric imprimatur of its directors, the Hughes Brothers. They had built a reputation for an unflinchingly violent representation of the black inner city, both through their music video work

The money goes up in flames at the end of the heist in *Dead Presidents*.

for gangsta rapper Tupac Shakur and for their 'hood film, *Menace II Society* (1993). *Dead Presidents* was consistent with the Hughes Brothers' mantra of "keeping it real," based as it was on the true story of a disenchanted black Vietnam war veteran, Haywood Kirkland, who conducted the heist of money destined to be taken out of circulation by the federal bank.

Given its setting in the 1970s, *Dead Presidents* links the concerns of that time to those of the 1990s, reminding its audiences that not much has changed. The film's tagline, "the only color that counts is green," constitutes a satirical jibe at the expense of a history of failed attempts to care about the fate of African Americans. The personal history that informs the undertaking of the heist has everything to do with the hypocrisy of sending young black men to fight a war in the name of democracy abroad for a country that treats them unequally at home. Moreover, as a Vietnam veteran, there was the added issue of having fought in a deeply unpopular war. Veterans were not likely to be greeted as sacrificial heroes. And for a *black* veteran, domestic disdain was compounded by the perception that you had colluded in a white man's war against nonwhite people.

The film's main protagonist, Anthony (Larenz Tate), loses his self-esteem through shame at the atrocities he committed abroad, his inability to secure a steady job at home, and having to stomach seeing his girlfriend and daughter being given financial support from a sexual rival. As with many 'hood films, black disenfranchisement is cast in patriarchal and misogynist terms as a form of emasculation. Resorting to a heist constitutes a way to recover one's manhood. And conducting a heist that targets money that is surplus to requirement invites troubling parallels with the main protagonist's own sense of redundancy as a black man in white America.

Both similar and different, *Set It Off* engages the issue of socioeconomic redundancy for urban black Americans from the perspective of four women. It was the second film for African American director F. Gary Gray, whose reputation had been established through making music videos for major hip-hop figures. Indeed, *Set It Off* might be considered an extension of Gray's video work with Ice Cube on "It Was a Good Day" (1993) and with Queen Latifah on "Black Hand Side" (1993). "It Was a Good Day" features South Central Los Angeles location shooting replete with Cube cruising in his customized "drop top" automobile, sharing time with other black youths trying to avoid "static" from the cops, attending a brother's funeral, indulging in "chronic" alcohol and casual sex. The quotidian mood of the video is underscored by the laid-back and chilled-out cadence of the music. But the underlying nihilistic sense that a "good day" is exceptional in the 'hood erupts violently at the end as Cube returns quietly home at 2:33 a.m. only to find himself surrounded by LAPD squad cars and helicopters, a scene repeated toward the end of *Set It Off*.

Equally, *Set It Off* elaborates on Queen Latifah's "Black Hand Side," which is driven by an "us versus the cops" narrative in which white policemen fail to find an underground party of African Americans dancing to Queen Latifah's rap. Her lyrics celebrate close community solidarity ("Tell me who got my back?") and feature the command to "Set it off" (do something crazy or start a fight) as the main chorus line. Giving a rapper like Queen Latifah star billing was important to giving the film its urban authority, repeating a strategy that underpinned the success of earlier entries in the 1990s 'hood cycle, such as *New Jack City* (Mario Van Peebles, 1991, with Ice-T), *Boyz N the Hood* (John Singleton, 1991, with Ice Cube), and *Juice* (Ernest Dickerson, 1992, with Tupac Shakur). Moreover, Queen Latifah brought with her a set of extradiegetic womanist associations that helped mark *Set It Off* as a distinctive entry in the otherwise male-dominated and frequently misogynist 'hood cycle.

Queen Latifah had cultivated an androgynous tomboy image to accompany her assertive relaying of issues germane to black women. Topics such as sexual harassment, domestic violence, and female independence made her stand out as "representing" (hip-hop argot for speaking up or setting a good example for) African American women. In a film whose originality lay in making its heisters black women, casting Queen Latifah as a gun-wielding butch lesbian helped broaden the meaning of a heist sisterhood. Substituting male with female protagonists opened up the heist as a vehicle through which the patriarchal conditions that delimit black female agency could be exposed.

In *Set It Off* the victim of a heist becomes a heister herself. Frankie, a bank clerk who has been recently promoted, finds herself at the wrong end of a gun held by someone she knows from her own South Central Los Angeles project. Her knowledge of the robber-murderer provides the white bank manager with an alibi to fire her. As he puts it: "The fact that you knew the perpetrator doesn't sit well with us. . . . How do we know you're not in collusion?" Despite the fact that she has a record of being an entirely trustworthy model of diligence and responsibility, she finds herself not only unemployed but under surveillance by a white cop, Strode (John McGinley), who gave the bank manager reason to mistrust her. Strode's belief in racial profiling will also lead him to kill the brother of one of Frankie's close female friends, Stoney (Jada Pinkett Smith), in a case of mistaken identity. And it is Strode's sense of remorse that makes him turn a blind eye to Stoney at the end of the film when she is on a bus leaving for Mexico.

Between the opening heist and Stoney's escape at the end of the film, we witness a story of four African American women friends who, in response to the double burden of being demeaned on the basis of both race and gender, pool their meager resources to carry out a couple of heists. All four women have poorly paid jobs working for an exploitative African American janitorial company owner, Luther. The motivation to rob a bank is different for each of them but is driven by a shared understanding of socioeconomic subordination. Frankie is out for revenge against the banking world that has made her redundant. Stoney, having assumed a maternal responsibility for her brother, Stevie, in the aftermath of their parents' death, is devastated when Stevie is wrongly killed by the police. T.T. (Kimberly Elise), a single mother, needs money to pay for child care so she can retrieve her toddler son from social services. And Cleo (Queen Latifah), knowing herself to be additionally marginalized on the basis of her sexuality, lives only for the moment and sees in the heist a thrilling chance to help her sisters.

The women successfully carry out the first caper, having secured weaponry from a dealer, Black Sam, played by gangsta rapper Dr. Dre. Television news reports that the heist of a South Los Angeles Savings and Loan bank was "a first" because the perpetrators were women. Although the women had stolen $12,000, the bank announced that $90,000 had been taken. The perpetrators all know that this is the bank's way of conducting an insurance scam. Brecht's comments about the lack of difference between bank robbers and bank owners are reinforced.

The money soon runs out. They plan a bigger heist in order not to live a life where heists are necessary anymore. They rob the Balboa Savings and

Loan bank, which yields $75,000 dollars each. The money, however, is stolen by Luther. The women hunt him down to a motel where he is having sex with a white woman. Before they can glean the whereabouts of the money, T.T. kills him when he draws a gun on Cleo. The women are left broke and without an employer. They decide on one last caper, this time as big as possible. They target the downtown Federal.

The heist is interrupted by Strode. During the getaway, T.T., Cleo, and Frankie are all killed. Stoney witnesses Frankie's death from her seat in a Mexico-bound bus. Although Strode spots Stoney in the bus, he lets her go, and she makes it to Baja California to start a new life. This deus ex machina ending, however, is out of character with the film's fatalistic depiction of urban African American women's lives.

Set It Off's innovations, then, are not associated with trying to align the 'hood film's hegemonic work with a recognizably affirmative black "rights" program. Rather, in focusing on women's experience, *Set It Off* augments the 'hood film's brutal "common sense" depiction of black ghettoization. Like *Dead Presidents*, this film renders the heist as a space of autonomous black collective action by those with the least agency—on one hand, unwanted black Vietnam veterans, doubly redundant both as black and as soldiers who fought a despised war, and oppressed black women, on the other. In doing so, these films make explicit the way the postindustrial urban world functions to make black folks redundant.

If *Dead Presidents* and *Set It Off* dramatized the damaging impact of domestic white racism, *Three Kings* expanded the scale and scope of the hip-hop heist as a means to critiquing the global ramifications of American race prejudice. Set at the end of the Gulf War, the film tells the story of a group of US soldiers who plan and execute the theft of Kuwaiti gold stolen by Saddam Hussein and hidden in one of his bunkers in the Iraqi desert. The execution of this colonial caper not only brings a group of disparate American characters together but also makes them interact directly with an alien people normally seen only through the crosshairs of a rifle. In doing so, the film revivified the heist film's political potential as a mediator of racism and its consequences.

In setting up the gold heist, mastermind Major Archie Gates (George Clooney) goes into partnership with Sergeant Troy Barlow (Mark Wahlberg), Private Conrad Vig (Spike Jonze), and Staff Sergeant "Chief" Elgin (Ice Cube). Characters otherwise separated by race and rank form an oddball family. In turn, these characters are taken outside their comfort zones as "victors" living in hermetic US military bases. In the process of hunting down the gold, the heist perpetrators are forced to revise their view of the people beyond the camp. As soldiers without any understanding of the Iraqis, the heisters are exposed to their own colonizing prejudices. As the story unfolds they become increasingly involved with the fate of Iraqi rebels who are being suppressed and tortured by Saddam's army while the US forces withhold any protection of their rights. In the end, the intruding American heisters gain a conscience and redistribute the wealth of Kuwaiti royalty among the Iraqi dispossessed and help them find refuge over the border in Iran.

The journey to this conclusion starts with a satirical debate about the appropriate racial epithets to be used about the enemy. Vig, a southern cracker, is confused about why he has been castigated for using terms such as "dune coons" and "sand niggers" for the enemy. In the presence of black Chief Elgin, who sees the war as "a four-month paid vacation from Detroit," they discuss how these terms are too closely related to racist ones denigrating black Americans. However, "camel jockey" and "towelhead" are deemed fine. This inability to reflect critically on how domestic racism might be linked to colonial ways of seeing is eventually overcome when the colonizing heisters have to deal directly with indigenous Arabs.

In their search for the gold, the heisters burst into one bunker to find it crowded with US consumer goods. The Iraqi soldiers guarding the loot are listening to Eddie Murphy on a boom box and watching the Rodney King beating on a television. Ironic connections between racism at home and US foreign policy are taken one step further in a later scene. Here Troy Barlow is being subjected to torture, having been captured. His captor, Said (Said Taghmaoui), asks him about what Michael Jackson has done to his face and hair. Barlow cannot answer. Said explains, "Michael Jackson is pop king of your sick fucking country. . . . It's so obvious. A black man makes the hair straight and skin white and you know why? Your sick fucking country make the black man hate himself just like the Arab children you bomb over here."

The Gulf War itself is set up to be exposed as an act of colonial hypocrisy. Here the nihilistic path that the "best laid plans" forges is the war itself. US involvement in Iraq is reconceived as a foreign policy heist with no postwar plan. From the beginning we see that the soldiers don't really know what the war is all about. "What did we do here?" is Archie Gates's early refrain. And ultimately what guarantees this unethical and morally bankrupt situation is racism. While this racism is overcome through the heist and its aftermath for a small group of soldiers, it sets in relief the larger way racism underpins the colonial interests that maintain the world order.

Who Is the Suspect? The Post-2008 Black-Themed Heist and Racial Profiling

The economic meltdown of 2008 compounded problems confronting urban black American communities. Ongoing socioeconomic immiseration has fed racist understandings of the plight of black inner-city denizens. That such racism informs legal and political procedures in dealing with crime that arises from poverty has been exposed by justice groups working with census data, such as the Vera Institute of Justice, and concerned activist-academics, such as Michelle Alexander, who has called this the era of "New Jim Crow" (see also Munby, "Art in the Age of New Jim Crow"). Perhaps the most controversial practice associated with so-called New Jim Crow is the police use of racial profiling. This is what one of the most recent black-themed heist films takes as its prime narrative interest.

The Suspect (Stuart Connelly, 2013) could be seen as a reworking of *The Spook Who Sat by the Door*'s subterfuge that a smart, seditious black man can hide in plain sight by exploiting white racist understanding of African American capabilities. But the game in 2013 is given a different spin. Here the heist is not about taking from the Man or using the loot to arm black revolutionaries. Rather the setup is designed to reveal the extent to which we all indulge in racial profiling, which infects even our film-reading practices.

Early in the narrative we are witness to a classic visual trope. We see a handcuffed young black male cowering under the gaze and domineering presence of a white cop in a police cell. There are no names for the black heisters. They are simply called the Suspect (Mehki Phifer) and the Other Suspect (Sterling Brown), reduced as they are to being types onto which we and the cops project our assumptions. The suspect is being interrogated about a small-town bank robbery because he stands out as a black man in a white town.

The big con is that the black robbers turn out to be university psychologists conducting a sociological experiment designed to display how racial profiling is endemic to law enforcement. Although the use of the heist could have been limited to this critique of profiling by the police, the film contains a further twist. The suspect is actually using the pretense of a legitimate and progressive sociological experiment to replace stolen money from the heist with counterfeit currency, which is then returned to the banks he and his accomplice rob. The motivation for this is provided only in fragments and flashback glimpses, which constitute a partially seen parallel narrative—a

The suspect (Mekhi Phifer) undergoes interrogation in *The Suspect*.

different story that is rendered incomprehensible because of the way assumptions about race underpin narrative continuity.

Critically, for example, the opening scene seems far removed from the rest of the diegesis. A mailman delivers a letter to a white woman. She opens the envelope and we get a brief glimpse of a check, a name, an amount. Fade to black. Fade in to a long shot of a bucolic farm landscape. The small-town look is corroborated by the soundtrack, featuring the languid tones of an acoustic guitar and a radio voice inviting folks to a varsity scrimmage. As the radio then reports on news about a bank robbery, the film cuts away to a white cop in his patrol vehicle. The whiteness of the scene and the information on the heist set us up for finding a suspect. And the suspect will be black.

In the end we discover that the heist is part of the suspect's quest to finance the medical treatment needed to save his daughter's life. That his wife is white and his kid is mixed race is significant. The fact or sight of the color difference between the suspect and his partner initially hinders any narratively logical connection between them. That is, we as an audience are confronted with the way we have been complicit with racial profiling through the search for coherent story.

The Suspect is a film made and released during a time that may well come to be defined by a depressing list of deaths that could be attributed to racial profiling. Its use of the heist is significant for how it reveals what should otherwise remain hidden as a condition for a social order's legitimacy. As such, *The Suspect* honors the legacy of the black-themed heist film in the way it poses profoundly awkward questions about the conditions of possibility for a future free from racism.

In his critical appraisal of *Odds Against Tomorrow*, John Schultheiss argues that "the failed robbery is a metaphor for a stalled society, impeded in its progress by bigotry" (in Polonsky 273). The film's uncredited screenwriter, Abraham Polonsky, stated that the story was "based on a situation that can have no other conclusion except destruction" (192). And when one reflects on the history of the American black-themed heist film since 1959, we observe a repeatedly nihilistic engagement with the relationship between capitalism and prejudice. As heist films that focus on the predicament of African Americans (or of racialized others abroad), the movies discussed here exploit the moral determinism central to most stories of failed robbery in a specific way. The motivation to rob is invariably associated with disenfranchisement. The heist itself is proffered as a moment of utopian possibility for enfranchisement. Its inevitable failure becomes an indictment of a putatively democratic socioeconomic order that has failed to deliver on its promise. And in revealing the perversity of what is done in the name of that promise, the black-themed heist film exposes not so much the inconsistency between racism and the law but how bigotry actually constitutes the legal order.

The Inevitability of Failure

The Small-Time Criminal and the Heist Film

<><><><><><><><><><><><><><><><><><><>

Fran Mason

The heist film is a genre populated by the dispossessed underclass, its criminals comprising misfits and outcasts who emerge from "society's fringes"
(Telotte 163) to create within the ranks of the heist gang "an ephemeral or
pseudo-collectivity," as Munby (*Public Enemies*, 138) describes the gang of
The Asphalt Jungle (John Huston, 1950). Characters in heist films are also
often on the edges of the milieu of organized crime, either because they are
freelancers unwilling to bond with a gang, because their felonious talents
are trivial, or because there is no demand for the skills they might supply
to the underworld's pool of illicit labor. Whereas some freelance criminals
can be underworld celebrities, such as the flaneur figure Bob in *Bob the
Gambler/Bob le flambeur* (Jean-Pierre Melville, 1956) or Max and Riton in
Touchez pas au grisbi (Jacques Becker, 1954), whose gold heist allows them
to pose as wealthy men about town, the disconnection of most heist criminals from the organized criminal economy establishes their irrelevance as
small-timers outside of the world to which they seemingly belong. Even
in caper films (which have a lightly comedic tone, greater cohesion in the
gang, and often an ideological justification for the heist), such as Steven
Soderbergh's remake of *Ocean's Eleven* (2001), the members of the gang
are outsiders drifting on the margins of the underworld before the heist,
forced into small-time activities for want of a purpose. Their marginality is
made evident in the way they squander their "impressive skills and talents"
(deWaard and Tait 135), either on meaningless activities or in their collabo-
ration with losers and incompetents they consider beneath them, like the
inept criminals and wannabe gamblers with whom Don Cheadle's Basher
and Brad Pitt's Rusty, respectively, associate. The gang members are, however, little different from these small-timers until their successful heist and

thus serve as the epitome of the heist gang as a collection of petty crooks who have so far failed to prosper in either official or criminal society.

In this context, a specific focus on small-time heist criminals highlights important traits that are shared with criminals of classic noir heist films, among which is an alienation from society so profound that nothing can resolve the criminals' condition of disempowerment or prevent the inevitable failure of the gamble of the heist as it enacts the struggle to overcome a state of economic lack. An examination of the small-time criminal in films such as *Big Deal on Madonna Street/I soliti ignoti* (Mario Monicelli, 1958), *Palookaville* (Alan Taylor, 1995), *Welcome to Collinwood* (Antony Russo, Joe Russo, 2002), *Killing Them Softly* (Andrew Dominik, 2012), and *Victoria* (Sebastian Schipper, 2015), which forms the focus of discussion here, also draws attention to the litany of flaws that mark the criminals of the noir heist film as comparable losers or failures. While the classic noir criminals may possess professional skills that the small-time heist criminals lack, they are frequently excessively violent (Dix Handley in *The Asphalt Jungle*), unreliable (Cobby in the same film), treacherous (Dave Purvis in *Armored Car Robbery* [Richard Fleischer, 1950]), has-beens (Tony Le Stéphanois in *Rififi/Du Rififi chez les hommes* [Jules Dassin, 1955]), underachievers (Rusty in *Ocean's Eleven*), weak-willed cowards (George in *The Killing* [Stanley Kubrick, 1956]), or alienated misfits (Gus in *The Asphalt Jungle*). The key difference is that heist films involving small-time or loser criminals emphasize the origins of their protagonists in everyday life in which their failings are the shortcomings of ordinary people, whether these are self-inflicted, such as ineptitude, mediocrity, impetuosity, and disharmony, or the product of circumstance, such as bad timing or blind chance. The small-time heist film can best be defined as an exaggerated or parodic version of the heist genre that centers on members of the underclass and their small-scale ambitions to overcome marginalization through criminal endeavor, in which the heist is less a criminal act than a displaced metonymy of the struggle experienced by the dispossessed within capitalism's subsistence economy. Because its protagonists are ordinary, the small-time heist film emphasizes the amateurish actions of small-timers poorly qualified for crime while also drawing on the fatalism of noir versions in framing the inevitable failure of the heist. There are, however, different styles of small-time heist film, including the noir-inflected fatalism of the postrecession films *Killing Them Softly* and *Victoria*, comedy heist hybrids that leaven fatalism with slapstick humor, in *Big Deal on Madonna Street* and *Welcome to Collinwood*, and tragicomic versions such as *Palookaville*, where the emphasis is on the comedy of failure and incompetence, albeit using such tropes to high-light the desperation of everyday troubles and the inability to find respite from them.

Despite concerns with the desperation of economic privation, the heist film is nevertheless a genre of dreaming with a basis in "aspiration and long-ing" (Rafter 58), within which the heist is an uncertain and nerve-racking gamble by which characters, outside of the world of money and with no other way out of their predicament, seek to empower themselves by taking control of capital. Heist films often meditate on money-as-power in capital-ism, on the dreams and desires that accessing capital will fulfill, on the eco-nomic and social failures of the criminals, on the "lack" for which they seek to compensate through the heist, and on the rewards the robbery promises. Heist narratives are premised on a logic of lack and desire within economic parameters that can be understood in Lacanian discourses through the fram-ing of the heist as the *objet petit a*, where the object of desire (the robbery as a life-changing moment of personal and financial empowerment) is "never found in the position of the aim of desire" (Lacan 186), because it necessarily precedes and causes the condition of desire that motivates the movement toward the object in the first place. As a subject within the desiring relations produced by capitalism, whether this is the classic form of capital acquisition (*The Asphalt Jungle*) or consumer capitalism (*Rififi*), the heist criminal is em-bedded within a system in which lack and desire are constituted within eco-nomic relations that also drive social and power structures. This logic of lack and desire is a drive toward "completion" within which the heist functions as both completion through fullness, by creating the possibility of a fulfilled selfhood in the motivation of desire toward economic ends, as in successful caper movies, and completion through negation, in containing the risk of a return to the preexisting state of lack and failure, as is the case with Johnny Clay in *The Killing*, or worse if death is the "completion" of the heist, as in *Rififi* and *Odds Against Tomorrow* (Robert Wise, 1959).

The heist film's telos (the causative principle framed by the end toward which the narrative trajectory is directed) is only the heist, therefore, in so far as the heist signifies the "all or nothing" gamble that defines the fine line between success and failure. For the misfits and outsiders of the heist gang who seek to transform their lives through a major robbery, there are no half measures or partial successes. Even if small-time heist films might occa-sionally offer compensations (the money found in a cookie jar in *Welcome to Collinwood* or the medals for civic duty in *Palookaville*), these neverthe-less still signify failure. The gamble of the heist, as a solution to personal, social, and economic lack, is therefore premised on an overreaching desire on the part of criminals who dream beyond both their capabilities and their social and economic situation. This is signified narratively by the impossibility of achieving the robbery through individual action because the "logistical and technical difficulties of a crime and its execution" (K. Thompson 43) demand either numerous actants performing tasks at precise moments (both versions of *Ocean's Eleven*) or different kinds of criminal specialism (*Rififi* or *The Killing*). In social and economic terms, such dreaming entails characters who think beyond their current condition of "lack" as disempowered and overlooked members of the underclass whose agency is nominal or unrecognized. Dix Handley (Sterling Hayden) in *The Asphalt Jungle* helps originate this trope and serves as its paradigm in both his state of lack, as he scrapes by, committing petty crimes on the periphery of the criminal underworld, and in his dream of transcending this condition by buying back the family farm lost by his father. Despite his goal, however, Dix also lives in the apparently desireless state that typifies the preheist small-time criminal because he drifts on the edges of society until the possibility of the heist provides the opportunity to enact his fantasy.

Besides its narrative necessity, the heist also has a key function in offering the gang a condition of possibility through the occupation of a "utopian" time and space separated from social and economic factors for a short period in which, despite being subject to temporal exigencies and spatial confinement (a jewelry store in *The Asphalt Jungle* and *Rififi* or a casino vault in *Ocean's Eleven*), the protagonists can create a "life-world" that allows the potential to achieve personal fulfillment through the operation of their abilities. Here, they are able to briefly reinvent themselves as purposeful agents by leaving behind the problems, failures, and inadequacies associated with their prior selves in the mobilization of professional skills that realize the "fullness" of their abilities as individuals in the accomplishment of the heist. Although the small-time heist and classic heist criminal share the same condition of disempowerment, it is the absence of professionalism and the utopian moment that most fully signals the differences between the two. The lack of cohesion and the concomitant failure to achieve agency in the heist derives from the inability of small-time criminals to separate themselves from their ordinariness as bunglers unable to manage within everyday life, crystallizing their status as paradigms of failure within the genre through their lack of professional or criminal skills, their ineptitude, the futility of their dreaming, and the inevitability of their return to a life of disappointment.

The differences between the small-time criminal in the classic heist and in the small-time heist movie, along with their continuities, can be outlined by comparing the paradigm of criminal professionalism in *Rififi* with the incompetent criminal amateurs of *Palookaville*. Although *Palookaville*'s tragicomic treatment of the small-time criminal mirrors aspects of *Rififi*'s noir-inflected heist film, the latter "elegises manual and creative labour" as part of its "progressive social message" to romanticize the criminal working class (Lee 42). *Rififi*, however, also focuses on the economic lack of the working class from its first scene, in which Tony Le Stéphanois (Jean Servais), a small-time crook just out of prison, is rescued from a losing streak at cards by Jo the Swede (Carl Möhner), who gives him a handout and introduces him to Mario (Robert Manuel), the man with a plan for a smash-and-grab raid on a jeweler's. Tony refuses to get involved initially, but agrees to take part when he discovers that an ex-lover, Mado, has taken up with an underworld linchpin, Pierre Grutter, who has provided her with a fur coat and jewelry. Tony changes the plan to a heist on the store's safe, which requires a safecracker (César, played by Dassin), but which will accrue greater wealth, in a bid to transform himself from loser to big shot so that he can supplant Grutter in Mado's affections. Tony's role as the driver, however, makes him peripheral to the heist until, during the planning, he solves the problem of disabling the jeweler's burglar alarm by using foam from a fire extinguisher to clog up its mechanism.

Much has been written about *Rififi*'s heist sequence, particularly its depiction of "crime as work and the role of skill and cooperation in transforming labour into art" (Rolls and Walker 154) and the way "the skills on display are specifically located in working-class consciousness" (Hayes 73–74). In these accounts, the heist sequence expresses the craftsmanship and professionalism of labor as the means by which the subordinated working class can fight back against capitalist control of production. Although the labor involved in *Rififi*'s heist is monotonous and repetitive work (such as the slow hammering away of plaster in the ceiling and its repeated retrieval from an upturned umbrella), which would be alienating under factory conditions, it nevertheless allows all of the gang members to make effective personal contributions within the collective action. Equally, because the members of the gang are in control of their labor and, at least for the moment of the heist, believe that they control the profits of their enterprise, the labor is nonalienated, thereby offering a utopian moment comprising both a sense of willed purpose and an apparent control over time and space. This utopian moment is, however, a false utopia because the outside world presses in on the gang during the heist, not only in the threat of interruption by the forces of the law but also because the gang must return to the social world from which they are temporarily abstracted. When they leave the jeweler's, therefore, they come under threat, as Grutter tries to seize the takings by kidnapping Jo's son and is thwarted only because the heist has allowed Tony to become an effective willed agent able to track down his quarry, release Jo's son, and dispose of Grutter, even if he is fatally wounded in the process.

The heist gang's fragile situation derives from the need to reenter the outside world, and this is frequently expressed by the unforeseen events that interrupt their actions both during and after the robbery, such as the friendly parking attendant in *The Killing* who threatens to disrupt the assassin's shot at a racehorse, designed to provide the disturbance that will allow the heist to occur, the appearance of a watchman just as the gang make their exit in *The Asphalt Jungle*, or the discovery of the getaway car by two police officers in *Rififi*. Although the latter event has no real consequence, because the car is far enough away from the scene of the crime that it is immaterial whether the gang use it for their getaway or find other means, its accidental discovery nevertheless represents the intervention of blind chance. Mark Bould identifies the motif of chance as part of the heist film's "complex determinism" (88), which describes the way the heist fails because of the gang's inability to anticipate the unpredictable intersections of the paths of others with their own planned movements. The necessity of engaging with or returning to the complexities of social reality means that the heist provides only a temporary escape from the cares, failures, and frustrations that the gang members experience in everyday life, not least because it is mundanity itself that very often foils the robbery. Thus, Bould argues that the heist in *The Killing* is thwarted by an unanticipated chain of trivial events that lead to the gang's leader, Johnny Clay, being "undone by airline regulations, a suitcase with a faulty lock, and a yappy little dog" (89). The frequency of the appearance of metaphorical "yappy little dogs" in the small-time crime incarnation of the heist film is an important motif that helps establish its difference from the classic heist movie. Small-time criminals are more often afflicted by complexities, frustrations, annoyances, and unexpected turns of chance that occur on an everyday basis to transform apparently simple matters into challenging or insoluble problems. Specific examples of these frustrations include the bickering old men who interrupt the observation of the armored car during the preparations for the second heist in *Palookaville* or the couple having an argument beneath the gang as they make their way across a glass roof in *Big Deal on Madonna Street*.

However, the misfortune of "complex determinism" is most often caused by the personal failings that small-time criminals carry with them, which produce numerous self-inflicted difficulties that hinder their plans. This is the case in the robbery sequence that opens *Palookaville*, which emphasizes the preexisting frustrations and failures that affect the gang as they attempt to break into a jewelry store. Undertaken by Russell (Vincent Gallo), Sid (William Forsythe), and Jerry (Adam Trese), three unemployed men living in a run-down area of New Jersey, the heist establishes the amateurish incompetence of the criminals despite their apparent control of circumstances. Initially shown walking past the unprotected window of a jeweler's, the gang forgo the easy smash-and-grab option by making their way around to the back of the store, where they noisily smash the lock off a door and the light above it, jimmy their way in, and then hammer away to demolish an inside wall. A light jazz soundtrack with repeated piano refrain and lightly brushed cymbals produces suspense while also suggesting that the gang's heedless production of noise is merely a minor effect of the purposefulness indicated by their direct and swift actions. The misleading motivation of these effects is made clear, however, with the revelation of the gang's cluelessness when they break through the wall and start kicking pans around because they have broken into the bakery next door to the jeweler's. While Russell is furious over the error and raids the cash register, Jerry responds calmly by helping himself to the cakes on display, but his seemingly admirable composure becomes folly when sirens are heard and he delays his escape to stuff pastries into his pockets, leaving him trapped in the bakery as the police search the premises. In contrast, the urgency of Sid and Russell seems sensible as they scramble to the getaway car, but the blind panic of their flight further signifies the gang's incompetence.

The heist sequence illustrates both the gang's amateurism and their inability to control "complex determinism," not only because they fail to plan for the most likely of events (the arrival of the police) but also because Jerry's delayed escape as he continues eating is a sign that they are not even in command of the predictability of their own actions. The gang's failure is further underscored by the fact they have made one simple but major mistake in breaking into the wrong place. This means there is no utopian moment through which they can achieve fulfilled agency in the execution of their abilities, like Tony in *Rififi*, because the only fulfillment they attain is the awareness of their own futility. There is still a utopian moment, but only in its comedic displacement onto the consumption of baked goods by Jerry, who finds the same "parallel world of utopian desire" in the luxury of eating that Bolongaro (6) identifies in "Theft in a Cake Shop," one of three stories by Italo Calvino used in the film to underline the characters' frustrated existence in a state of personal and economic lack. The pleasure with which Jerry consumes the cakes in the bakery therefore reflects on the state of lack associated with small-time criminals as well as the low-level desires of the gang and their inability to dream beyond their subsistence condition except through small pleasures that provide a temporary and, in this case, unexpected release.

The basic failings displayed by the gang are also typical of criminals in the small-time heist film because, in a genre that privileges expertise and organization, small-time criminals are incompetents whose ineptitude in planning and execution leads to errors such as breaking into a bakery or, in *Big Deal on Madonna Street* and *Welcome to Collinwood*, the wrong room. Even when the robbery is successful, as in *Killing Them Softly*, it is the result of amateurs gaining the element of surprise (because no one in the mob gambling den subject to the heist can believe the criminals are so stupid as to be unaware of the consequences of their actions) and then being guided through the robbery by one of the victims. The fantasy of agency in the exercise of professionalism is therefore unavailable to the small-time criminal in the way that the heist in *Rififi*, *The Killing*, and *Odds Against Tomorrow* at least extends the possibility for losers to transform themselves into purposeful individuals through both the application of their abilities and the future prospects its financial rewards offer. Characters on the margins of the underworld in the noir heist or caper movie, such as Tony in *Rififi* and Dix Handley in *The Asphalt Jungle*, can surround themselves with professional criminals whose presence within the gang allows them to exercise abilities or knowledge that prove indispensable in contributing meaningfully to the work of the heist. The small-time crooks of *Palookaville* have no such skills because they have no relationship to either criminal or legitimate forms of labor. When they try to earn money honestly by setting up a car service to drive senior citizens home from the supermarket (albeit as a front for observing the route of the armored truck they intend to rob), their enterprise is fraught with difficulties even before the licensed taxi drivers sabotage their competition by slashing the tires of the car, an act that fully registers the criminals' marginalized status because they lack the capital to make the necessary repairs.

The representation of such a condition of lack frames the small-time criminal more generally as a paradigm of the dispossessed heist criminal as a loser, outsider, or outcast who has nothing except the bare means to survive. In *Palookaville*, the lack of employment prospects means that Russell, Jerry, and Sid are stripped of both hope and desire. Denied access to capital through labor, and to the means, therefore, to be part of a desiring economy directed to the material rewards of consumption, they think the heist will allow them to survive in capitalism's world of dispossession. For Russell, Sid, and Jerry, crime represents undirected longing for a change to their condition, which, because they have no other options within the limited parameters that constrain their lives and desires, transforms them from ordinary, good-natured people into small-time criminals. Even so, they are effectively desireless in being content with "a momentary shift in lifestyles, a little itty-bitty alteration," as Russell describes the trivial ambition of a further planned heist when he pays out the negligible proceeds from the bakery till. They might want to escape the present, but they lack a meaningful sense of future possibilities, even if Russell's expression of this condition, when he hands Jerry his money and says, "There, big shot, go buy a donut," implies an understanding of the small-time nature of their criminal aspirations. The resignation of the crooks to their low-level aspirations also implies that any dreams will be broken dreams, that desire itself is a folly leading only to further failure, and that avoidance of desire is therefore a way of avoiding disappointment. Accordingly, Jerry just wants a job while Sid seems to have no desires beyond scrounging sufficient food for himself and his dogs. Only Russell displays any kind of yearning for something more, but his dreams of escaping the dissatisfaction of living with his family by leaving for Los Angeles with his girlfriend, Laurie, are revealed to be fantasy when she leaves him behind, having realized that he is never going to act on his stated desires.

Such frustrations preclude the possibility of a utopian moment in the heist because the gang take their "lack" with them, particularly the understanding that they return to the same disempowered condition, should they fail. The anxiety caused by the knowledge of "before" and "after" is too powerfully present within the heist situation for the small-time criminals to cohere into a functioning and purposeful unit. This is the case in the second failed heist of *Palookaville*, in which the gang's fractious relations are merely the continuation of prior bickering caused by their economic failure, such as an argument over a few cents' payment for coffee and pastry the night before the job. Their lack of criminal proficiency arising from their ordinariness also hinders them, and their ineptitude is depicted during both the planning and the heist of the armored car, including advertising their intentions by talking loudly about the scheme in the public space of a diner, accidentally killing a guard dog when sabotaging the armored car, or taking notes for the heist by watching *Armored Car Robbery* on television, during which Russell and Sid are joined by Russell's mother (who brings popcorn), his sister, and his police officer brother-in-law, Ed the Cop, who luckily is as bungling as the gang. The heist itself involves a series of metaphorical "yappy little dogs," including the appearance of a suspicious Ed, the failure of the armored car to overheat where intended, and a collision with the back of the truck, after which the gang confirm their inadequacy when they are unable to overcome the two guards despite the fact that they are old men. The heist ultimately fails, however, because of the gang's common decency as ordinary people, which has already been established during the shadowing of the armored car in the planning stage, when the geriatric guard has a cardiac arrest and the men forgo the opportunity to raid the truck, after displaying uncharacteristic efficiency in very quickly breaking into it to save his life. This good nature recurs during the heist when Russell, having substituted a real gun for a toy gun, finds he is unable to fire at the guard fleeing with the money.

The gang's lack of affinity for crime is a common trope among on-screen small-time criminals. The dysfunctionality of small-time criminals is not, therefore, the criminal dysfunction that characterizes the film gangster's ruthless will to power through violence or the obsessive professionalism of the individual heist criminal. Their motives in turning to crime may develop out of the same impulse to overcome the lack of opportunities available to the underclass in capitalism, but their criminal tendencies serve more as a displaced sign of the dysfunction of their everyday life of economic and social lack, whether this is Sid's utter penury, Jerry's domestic difficulties, Russell's self-loathing, or their shared experience of unemployment. These personal failures and difficulties also derive in *Palookaville* from the diminution of masculine power crystallized in Jerry's situation: he is supported by his wife, Betty, who works at a supermarket until she is fired after Jerry assaults the manager he discovers sexually harassing her. His assertion of masculinity is undermined, however, when, after an argument with Betty over his inability to provide her with basic domestic goods, he is forced to return to the supermarket to apologize so that Betty can return to the position of family wage earner. He refuses to go through with the apology, which would both confirm his failure to provide for his family and refute his previous assertion of power, and his ensuing decision to join the heist conveys his desire to reempower himself through the robbery. The fantasy of agency through crime fails to follow, however, and it is only the civic awards given to the gang for saving the life of the geriatric guard that provide the gang with a social value, albeit as an ironic sign of their failure in everything else.

Despite their incompetence, the persistence of *Palookaville*'s gang in seeking to overcome their disempowerment in the face of continued disappointments makes them lovable losers. This trope is common to the comedy heist film, which deploys humor, frequently absurd or slapstick, to judge its characters for their ineptitude rather than their criminality, while allowing sympathy for both their desperate straits and their status as underdogs. *Welcome to Collinwood* is a remake of *Big Deal on Madonna Street* involving a seemingly foolproof plan or "Bellini," as it is referred to, that will set up the gang financially through the heist of the safe of a family business. In both *Big Deal on Madonna Street* and *Welcome to Collinwood*, the idea is appropriated from the criminal who has planned it by two gangs of losers on the edge of the criminal underworld whose desperate circumstances cause them to grasp at any hope. The films differ, however, because the gang of *Big Deal on Madonna Street* has a closer relationship with the world of crime, whereas in *Welcome to Collinwood* the criminals are an underclass of unemployed drifters and petty crooks without connections to the underworld, all in possession of an unfulfilled "Bellini," but otherwise similar to the ordinary, dysfunctional characters of *Palookaville*. Their failure to act on their "Bellinis" suggests the same desireless condition of economic subsistence, but also indicates that they inhabit a world of endless delusions where they only dream of changes to their lives, signified most obviously by Leon (Isaiah Washington), an idler who dresses in smoking jackets and cravats, and Pero (Sam Rockwell), a boxer who is quickly disabused of his fantasy of becoming a champion.

Another difference between the two films derives from *Big Deal on Madonna Street*'s setting during the 1950s Italian economic miracle of expanding employment and consumption (Di Carmine 463), within which, however, the criminals desire to access consumerism (such as the Donald Duck aprons one of them buys in a market) without engaging in honest work. The economy of consumption even extends into the underworld, where the gang buy equipment from a criminal who stocks them up with an excess of thieves' tools for which they have to sign a receipt as warranty in mimicry of the official economy of consumerism they hope to enter by criminal means. The failure of the heist in *Big Deal on Madonna Street* is used, however, to offer a moral that there is no easy money through the ideological affirmation of labor within capitalism when, in its final scene, one of the criminals hides in a queue of workers to evade the police and then accepts his lot as an honest laborer when he is bull-rushed into a work site. There is no such moral in *Welcome to Collinwood*, where it is desperation rather than aversion to work that forms the motivation for the heist, as Pero recognizes when, at the funeral of the criminal who devised the plan, he questions each member of the gang on how they will live if they fail to go through with the robbery, beginning with Riley (William H. Macy), whose wife is in jail: "What's your son gonna eat? Your guilt?" before telling the decrepit Toto (Michael Jeter) "You're the poorest man I ever seen," and then asking Basil (Andrew Davoli) "And you? What? Are you going to stay a bum all your life?"

The film has, however, already established that the criminals' attempt to overcome their plight is a failure in its opening shot of Pero, Leon, Riley, and Toto standing on a sidewalk after the broken dream of the heist, disconsolate and with their clothes in tatters, staring straight ahead but noticing nothing as a truck and a car go by. This image signifies their return to the condition of losers that Pero describes at the funeral, and their small-time credentials are established soon after when the search for a "Mullinski," a no-hoper who has so little he will serve someone else's prison sentence for money, brings together a gang of people who are included because they are needy rather than because they have any expertise or professional skill (Browning 130). They are so marginalized that the nuns from whom they borrow the money to hire Jerzy Antwerp (George Clooney), an inept safecracker, have more access to capital, and seemingly stronger connections to the underworld, than the gang. They are a sub-underworld underclass, so irrelevant that they go unnoticed by the police until they make contact with Jerzy, an act that emphasizes their haplessness because of the self-inflicted surveillance it precipitates. The heist itself is characterized by the fractiousness that has attended the gang all the way as they continually argue and shout at each other when one error or piece of bad fortune follows another, thereby preventing them from reaching the coherence of a utopian moment despite a simulation of such during a pause in which they take satisfaction in their imminent success by discussing what they intend to do with the money. On discovering that they have spent several hours breaking through into the wrong room, they begin bickering until Toto finds $1,000 in a cookie jar as compensation, but the job then becomes a disaster when they accidentally ignite a stove and cause an explosion. Like *Palookaville*, *Welcome to Collinwood* is a directorial first feature that draws on influences from Italian sources and independent film comedy (Levy 280–81). In both films, these resonances not only generate episodic and meandering narratives charting the unmotivated lives of the characters' wageless existence but also invoke a sensibility that withholds judgment on their shortcomings and criminality by framing their actions as the inevitable result of the lack of possibility available to the disempowered underclass.

In these comedy heist films, small-time criminals are a source of humor, which they are not in the recent postrecession heist films, *Killing Them Softly* and *Victoria*, whose contexts highlight the misery of economic hardship, the impossibility of ever escaping the underclass, and the futility of desire under such conditions. *Killing Them Softly*, an adaptation of George V. Higgins's 1974 novel *Cogan's Trade* that shifts the action from Boston to New Orleans during the 2008 presidential election, maps the underworld onto contemporary capitalism to depict the organized mob as a corporation, its hirelings as middle management, and its many petty criminals as an underclass drifting or scraping by in a recession-hit society. The film opens with Frankie (Scoot McNairy), who later takes part in the heist on a mob gambling house, walking out of a tunnel into an empty urban wasteland where he is assailed by a blizzard of discarded paper. Fragments of Barack Obama's acceptance speech play on the soundtrack announcing the renewal of the "American promise," before a medium close-up shows Frankie grimacing as he holds back tears, confirming that Obama's promise of opportunity fails to extend into the world of the underclass, where it is the desperation of restricted possibilities that drives Frankie and his partner, Russell (Ben Mendelsohn), to take part in the heist. Frankie is just out of prison after taking the fall for Squirrel, a small businessman who organizes the job, but unable to receive unemployment because he lacks a car, while Russell's limited world is signified by his aspirations to become a slightly less small-time criminal through earning enough money from dognapping to set himself up as a drug dealer. Russell and Frankie are not, however, the only small-time losers in the film because the film's underworld is almost entirely composed of chiselers, chancers, and dumb lugs. Markie Trattman (Ray Liotta), whose game is the target of the heist, lives in a house so small it surprises a thug hired to beat him up; Mickey (James Gandolfini), an out-of-town hitman, is a has-been interested only in sex and alcohol; and Kenny, Russell's dognapping partner, manages to run himself over when he ignites the gas tank of a car.

The heist in *Killing Them Softly* goes surprisingly smoothly despite the lack of planning and the antagonisms between the criminals caused by Russell's belligerent attitude to Squirrel and by arguments over the wisdom

Killing Them Softly: Russell (Ben Mendelsohn) and Frankie (Scoot McNairy) plan a heist amidst an urban wasteland.

of heisting a mob-run gambling house. Frankie and Russell nevertheless disprove Squirrel's claim that heisting a mob game makes them "smart guys" (on the basis that retribution will fall on Markie because he robbed his own game in the past) by turning up for the heist equipped with kitchen gloves and a sawn-off shotgun cut so low that it could only ever inflict damage on its user. They also lack a clear plan, which means that they have to be guided through the robbery by Markie. Their ineptitude is made obvious when, during the drug-fueled celebration of their apparent success, Russell informs Frankie that there is already a contract out on them, which, as the next scene reveals in a conversation between Cogan (Brad Pitt), the hitman brought in to find and punish the heist gang, and his mob contact, Driver (Richard Jenkins), is the result of Russell's stupidity in telling Kenny, who is also Cogan's henchman, all about their involvement in the heist during the trip to sell the kidnapped dogs. Cogan, whose expertise is contrasted to the incompetence of the heist gang, comments that Russell and Frankie are so small-time it is as if they want to go to jail, and this is soon proven when Russell is shown to lack any grasp of reality as he stumbles and slouches to the locker where he has stashed his drugs, completely oblivious to the DEA agents who are there to arrest him. Russell at least survives, whereas Squirrel is killed by Cogan with the aid of Frankie, who can only be viewed as a dumb lug for not having left town (thereby allowing Cogan to find him), for justifying why he took a six-year rap for Squirrel (when Cogan questions his continued loyalty to someone who exploited it for his own ends), and for believing that betraying Squirrel to the man so obviously appointed to kill him will save his life. Frankie's inevitable death signals the radical marginalization of small-time criminals, not least because the casual nature of

Victoria: In a dark underground garage, Andi (André M. Hennicke) (*right*), uses threats and bribes to intimidate the gang into undertaking the heist.

his murder suggests that Frankie is simply a social irrelevance whom no one will miss.

The insignificance of the unseen underclass is also the subject of *Victoria*, a meditation on the hopelessness of the deracinated working class in contemporary Germany recording the experiences of characters so inconsequential that they barely even register on the social map. The film's narrative traces, in one continuous shot, the experiences of the eponymous heroine (Laia Costa), a Spanish woman working in Berlin, during the early morning hours after she hooks up with Sonne, Boxer, Blinker, and Fuß, four unemployed men she encounters on leaving a nightclub to which they have been denied entry because they cannot afford the admission fee. Thereafter, she drifts with them through the night, engaging in petty theft and spending time simply sitting on a roof talking until, joined by Sonne (Frederick Lau), with whom she establishes a bond, she leaves to open the café where she works. Here, Boxer finds them and draws his friends into an opportunistic heist to return a debt for the protection extended to him by a gangster, Andi (André Hennicke), while he was in prison. With Fuß too drunk to take part, Victoria joins the others as the driver in a makeshift gang when Andi uses their desperation and fear to force them into robbing a private bank, intimidating the young men through a brief but tense practice run before plying them with cocaine to reduce their will and dispatching them to perform the robbery.

Before the heist, the men are shown as marginalized drifters with no economic power, wandering the night because they have no apparent home to which to return. They are at the bottom of society, with nothing to fill their lives except continual desultory talk expressing both their empty existence and the absence of future prospects, which are highlighted in Sonne's obvious lies to Victoria about owning a shop and being a pianist. This is a life of "lack" without purpose, desire, or agency, in which the young men's disempowerment and lack of social function are most evident in their co-ercion into becoming a gang by Andi, who threatens to keep Victoria as "collateral" for Boxer's debt and who treats them like the dregs of society to transform them from drifters into heist criminals as if they were mere in-struments or bodies to perform a task. This denial of agency is symptomatic of their will-less state and accentuates the desireless condition expressed in their lack of any thoughts beyond the present moment because there are no meaningful possibilities toward which they can orient themselves and there is seemingly no *objet petit a* to engender desire, except perhaps Sonne's im-pulsive attraction to Victoria. Originating in the old East German district of Mitte, the young men are rootless working-class Berliners without employ-ment and with no ties or place in social structures except as distrusted out-siders, drawing only the brief attention of suspicious police officers cruising by as they wander the streets with Victoria. They are seemingly outside of desire, therefore, not least because desire is socially constituted as desire for social meaning and they have none, nor do they seem to want it, except in their unspoken bonds of community based on class and marginalization.

The heist is no kind of release from their condition, and its occurrence offscreen also withholds, through the denial of representation, a utopian moment of escape from their own powerlessness, because they are only ever shown as panicky amateurs. The robbery, indeed, underlines their meaninglessness and lack of purpose because the release from marginal-ity that the heist signifies in *Rififi* is replaced in *Victoria* by the displaced post-heist embrace of immediate gratification when the gang return to the club from which they were previously excluded to heedlessly celebrate their success in an act of abandonment. In a show of defiance that flaunts their newly found economic power, Blinker and Boxer strip naked to dance in celebration while Victoria and Sonne laugh at their antics in between hug-ging each other, although these acts also convey their lack of responsibility in forgetting that the robbery will have repercussions. This is neverthe-less their utopian moment, during which they live in a present of pleasure without apparent consequences because their lives have been so restricted and aimless beforehand that they must grasp a moment of freedom in the "now" of their success before returning to their prior condition. This occurs sooner than they think when they are ejected from the club and find that the getaway car where they have left Fuß has already been discovered by the police. There follows a pursuit and a gunfight in which Sonne is fatally wounded and Blinker and Boxer are killed, the latter choosing to die, in an act that is ambiguously either self-conscious heroism or nihilism, because there is no hint of hope for anything better than purposeless drifting in a world in which he and the others are going nowhere except to death, either now or after a lifetime of nothingness.

Blinker's negation of self expresses more generally the condition of small-time criminals in the heist film. They are ordinary people doomed to failure, and no amount of struggle against their disempowerment, as signified by the metonymy of the heist, will alter the socially driven inevitability of their return to marginality. In this context, desire becomes meaningless because nothing seems worthwhile. The life of the small-time criminal in film is often, therefore, a state of lifelessness characterized by lethargy and aimless drifting. Although some small-time criminals survive the heist, as in *Palookaville*, *Big Deal on Madonna Street*, and *Welcome to Collinwood*, this is not in itself any kind of compensation for their failure to exceed their dispossessed existence because they are effectively as dead as the small-time criminals of *Killing Them Softly* and *Victoria*. Thus, although Victoria survives and walks away with the money from the robbery, and despite her bravado and self-confidence in trying to help Sonne survive after the heist, it is implied that her fate is a magnified version of the lonely alienation she experienced before she met the gang. This is a condition shared more widely by members of the underclass who become small-time criminals to survive but who discover that the heist gang provides only precarious community and temporary release from the alienation and redundancy that characterize their general condition in the heist film's rendering of capitalism's operations, to which they must return, if they survive, to continue as failures in a society that ignores or derides them as losers.

PART THREE

The Aesthetics
and Ideology
of the Heist Film

Economic Sentiments in Kubrick's *The Killing* and Furukawa's *Cruel Gun Story*

◇◇◇◇◇◇◇◇◇◇◇◇◇◇◇◇◇◇◇◇◇◇

Homer B. Pettey

Civilizing factor and untamed natural force at the same time: by operating with this oxymoron, repeated by countless authors, this discourse manages to simultaneously integrate speculation into the natural and social order, to bring together the rational and irrational into one overarching view, and to rank speculation with respect to other domains of human activity. While the civilizing side is characterized by hard work, attention, observation—all qualities intrinsic to speculation as a privileged form of knowledge—the wild, adventurous side means taking risks, developing emotions, being caught in the ardor of the game as a means of escaping the boredom and dullness of ordinary life. (Preda 179)

Stanley Kubrick's *The Killing* (1956) and Takumi Furukawa's *Cruel Gun Story/Kenjû zankoku monogatari* (1964) mirror each other by relying upon intricate heists of horse-racing profits as allegories for postwar economic sentiments. Hope for stability in domestic life provides the initial impetus for the protagonists' determination to execute the heists. Greed, unfortunately, motivates the other principal players in the heists. Altruism, loyalty, and sacrifice lose out to self-interest and betrayal, as both protagonists consciously give themselves over to vicissitudes of fate. Both heist films focus their narratives on uncompromising, self-assured, and doomed petty criminals—Johnny Clay (Sterling Hayden) in *The Killing* and Togawa (Joe Shishido) in *Cruel Gun Story*—who mastermind complicated schemes to steal money from racetracks, ultimately for a chance to escape their miserable lives. In the two highly stylized noir films Kubrick and Furukawa work out the heists in meticulous detail, both in the planning stages and during the time-dependent actual robberies. Risk taking and beating the odds dominate the films' plots, which aptly correspond to horse-racing's pari-mutuel betting structure, which forms a market within a compressed time scale that produces payoffs that are always contingent upon the house take. The mechanics of horse-race gambling often adumbrate the psychological expectations of individual bettors, who, like heist crooks, research, plan, and work out scenarios for ultimate success only to fail in the end. Both films critique postwar economic conditions by employing the processes of gaming and robbery as visual metaphors for a world in which time is literally money. Profit seeking, however, exceeds the law of diminishing returns as the films allegorize postwar attrition and futility as the negative results of a system far beyond the zero-sum game of winner-loser economics.

The Killing, based on Lionel White's novel *Clean Break* (1955), was the first screenplay by noir crime fiction writer Jim Thompson (Pezzotta 18). *The Killing* represents Kubrick's first major film, one that incorporates elements of his noir photographic style and neorealist documentary work. Kubrick's use of an offscreen narrator began with *Day of the Fight* (1951) and continued with his first feature-length film, *Fear and Desire* (1953), which provided a filmic authority that reinforces Kubrick's own "early, quixotic quest for thematic and narrative clarity" (Sperb 28). While working for *Look* magazine in the late 1940s, Kubrick developed more and more cinematic techniques in his photo-essays, which exist between documentary realism and fiction film structure. The layout of a photo-essay often resembles both the preproduction organization for shooting a film and the postproduction editing for narrative content. Most influential for Kubrick was his summer of 1947 assignment to shoot behind-the-scene photos of the production of Jules Dassin's film noir *The Naked City*, whose "title and subject matter were borrowed from the famous photojournalist Weegee's book 'Naked City,' published in 1945, which focused on night-time crime scenes in New York" (Mather 183).[1] These film noir techniques find their way into *Killer's Kiss* (1955) and *The Killing*, both of which employ gaming—boxing and horse racing—as commentaries on American modernity.

Hollis Alpert, in "The Inexpensive Look," praised *The Killing* for its "astonishing air of reality," costing one-fourth of de Mille's *The Ten Commandments* (1956), and for its adherence to expressive filmmaking: "It should be noted, however, that movies are still appearing in which black-and-white photography is substituted for color, for which the screen is reduced to its pre-CinemaScope size, which use one track instead of multi-channel sound, and which manage to tell their stories in ninety minutes or less" (Alpert 32). In an annual review of films, *The Saturday Review* (January 5, 1957) referred to *The Killing* as "the sleeper of the year" for its "tight pace" and "ingenious story" that surpass the French caper *Rififi/Du Rififi chez les hommes*, Jules Dassin (1955) ("Looking Backward" 27). Kubrick's international influence on film noir would be evident in the use of long tracking shots, intense and obscure lighting, and doomed protagonists of Nikkatsu Corporation's 1960s noirs, particularly *Cruel Gun Story*.

Cruel Gun Story derives its title from a subgenre of Japanese film in the late 1950s and 1960s, the "cruel story" or *zankoku monogatari*, known for its graphic violence, doomed anti-heroes, and critiques of society—in short, a Japanese version of film noir. In 1959, Nanjo Norio published a collection of stories, *Cruel Stories/zankoku monogatari*, which may well have set off this subgenre of Japanese postwar cinema (Standish 359 n.11). *Jidai-geki*, or samurai period dramas, of the 1960s, such as Tadashi Imai's *Tales of Bushido Cruelty/Bushido zankoku monogatari* (1963) and Tai Kato's *Cruel Tale of the Shogunate's Downfall/Bakamatsu zankoku monogatari* (1964), displayed a violent, nihilistic ethos in Japanese culture. The *kaidan,* or ghost narrative, also followed the cruel story line of escalating violence, as in the now-obscure *Cruel Ghost Legend/Kaidan zankoku monogatari* (1968), which featured blood-filled moments of death and suicide. Junya Sato's *Story of Military Cruelty/Rikugun zangyaku monogatari* (1963) condemned the horrors that recruits faced in World War II with its promotional film poster showing a close-up of a recruit with a large bayonet in his throat.

Most famous of the *zankoku* films remains Nagisa Oshima's *Cruel Story of Youth/Seishun zankoku monogatari* (1960), which was produced and distributed during the political uproar over the United States–Japan Security Treaty being renewed. The film combines political disenfranchisement, criminal extortion for money, violence, and a fatalistic sense of hopelessness in the relationship between a disaffected college student, Kiyoshi (Yusuke Kawazu), and a sexually active high school girl, Makoto (Miyuki Kuwano). They become predators and victims, caught up in exposing the ethical duplicity of society while simultaneously exploiting sexuality for economic gain. The scheme of relieving perverted businessmen of money ultimately turns against the couple, who can no longer express affection without some form of emotional degradation. In the end, they do not commit seppuku in a lover's pact but die separately, alienated from themselves and the modern world. In *Cruel Story of Youth,* contemporary politics play an allusive and ambiguous role in the film, even with the opening credit sequence of newspaper headlines, newsreel footage of South Korean student demonstrations, and connections to current Japanese turmoil over the treaty's renewal. Like *Cruel Gun Story*, this film links the powers of politics, economics, and criminality in a "bleak view of modern society, where money irreversibly destroys the fabric of human relationships" (Yoshimoto 176).

Both *The Killing* and *Cruel Gun Story* take cinematic risks, especially in the temporal construction of their narratives. Kubrick's fragmented, overlapping narrative of the heist shifts the time structure in patterns that almost reflect point-of-view accounts of the action, focusing upon each criminal's role during the heist. Similarly, Furukawa's repetition of the heist as imagined and the heist in actuality splits the narrative. He imposes, in the first instance, the desired outcome of the heist plan and, in the second, the dashed hopes, the scheme gone awry, with the armored vehicle guards not acting as Togawa had anticipated. Kubrick also includes flawed, unforeseen moments that undermine the gamble on a heist as a series of unpredictable events to conclude the film: the shoot-out in the apartment belonging to Marvin (Jay C. Flippen), the acquisition of a suitcase for the loot that has no locks, the inexplicable toy poodle running onto the tarmac and causing an accident, the suitcase bursting, and the money whipped through the air by the plane's propellers. Furukawa also sets up a series of mischances and miscalculations through which the gang moves from failure to failure.

In general, gambling entails decision making under some condition of risk. For horse racing, as Richard A. Epstein has revealed, the pari-mutuel system, developed in Paris in 1865 by Pierre Oller, works out two systems of potential profits simultaneously: a fixed profit for the track and a variable profit for the successful bettor. For the track, the profit is consistent and risk-neutral, but for the risk-seeking single bettor, the profit has been determined by consensus of an aggregate of bettors, "thus constituting a weakly efficient market within a compressed time scale" (296). According to Epstein's calculations of payoff probabilities, for the average gambler, horse racing is a very unlikely method for successful investment, especially with the track garnering 15 percent or more: "Overcoming the highly negative mathematical expectation of horse racing poses virtually insurmountable obstacles in terms of acquiring the requisite knowledge, constructing an appropriate model, and performing the attendant computations . . . for all methods are based solely on subjective evaluations" (303). A heist of a racetrack involves similarly limited subjective evaluations that happen within a compressed time scale of high risk. Both *The Killing* and *Cruel Gun Story* rely upon precision timing to commence the heist, but the plans fail due to unpredictable emotions and uncertainty.

A racetrack arouses a range of emotions that correspond to a social drama: "Between periods of high drama, aimless, bored roaming, socializing, and observing between races are activities common to all and add to the theatre of the site, as these periods emphasize the cyclical drama of the day" (Allen 190). Gambling offers a dual emotional appeal between hope and despair within a theater or culture that is liminal, not rational, and that reinforces middle-class values of success and merit as products of work toward a reward, even though this reward is determined entirely by risk. Goffman describes the *action* of gambling as an affective state: "It is here that the individual releases himself to the passing moment, wagering his future estate on what transpires precariously in the seconds to come. At such moments a special affective state is likely to be aroused, emerging transformed into excitement" (246). Such, too, is the emotional anticipation for future benefits from gambling on the precarious heist.

Betting markets, with "decision-making under uncertainty," provide economists with examples that pertain to complex financial markets (Peirson and Blackburn 30). Walls and Busche empirically examined thirteen thousand races at Japanese racetracks and discovered that "bettors at tracks with low bet turnover show risk aversion," which is consistent with "the hypothesis that they trade off mean returns for more highly skewed returns" (61–62). The efficient markets hypothesis looks at information efficiency in relation to capital markets and, in general, depicts "the aggregate tendency to over-bet runners with low objective win probabilities, and to under-bet those with relatively high objective win probabilities" (Smith 67). In general, economic studies look at outsiders, those with past knowledge of performances, and insiders, those associated with the track and the horse owners and handlers. In *The Killing*, this dual structure can be observed with the distribution of the heist gang's expertise, literally positioned inside and outside the track. In *Cruel Gun Story*, the same duality exists, but there remains a third element, as in Kubrick's film, an external group of thieves willing to kill to obtain the heist gang's loot. The plots for both noirs rely upon the planners, Johnny Clay and Togawa, who wish to eliminate risk, and thieves, Sherry Peatty's lover, Val Cannon (Vince Edwards), and mob boss Matsumoto (Hiroshi Nihonanagi), who seek risk through a counterplan of heisting by killing off the heist gang.

In an economic theory of greed, the organization of the small group that operates on a reciprocal model applies to the heist gang dynamics of *The*

Killing and *Cruel Gun Story*, from which arise "the role of social norms as mediators of violence; the role of risk-sharing and appropriation as underlying motives to form groups; the importance of within-group monitoring to sustain cooperative outcomes; and the role of norms about overall aggression and group loyalty in maintaining either a parasitical or a cooperation equilibrium" (Frijters and Foster 372). If these conditions explain tribal and conquering groups, they also apply to the general economic ethos of heist gangs, who must maintain incentives so that their combined risk taking and risk sharing will produce a collective profit. Violence will arise only if hostile individuals within the heist gang violate assumed loyalty, renege upon promised allegiance, and seek greater claim to the accumulated profits. Of course, what had been collective risk sharing becomes a far more risky proposition with a renegade individual. In both *The Killing* and *Cruel Gun Story*, one factor for the collapse of the heist's plan can be attributed to the manipulation and disloyalty from within the gang, usually attributed to a motive outside the group's construction.

With such a risky enterprise as a heist, ironically often the idea men are quite risk averse, preferring to limit the execution of their plan to a time-benefits ratio that yields the most profit with the least amount of risk. In this equation, then, the heist film plays out a rather conservative economic strategy within a highly dubious criminal plan. In this way, certain heist films mimic investments in bonds and stocks in the market and even sure-thing horse betting at the track. As paradoxical as it may seem, the heist planner often follows the procedures of *homo economicus*, as the rational economic man who holds to principles of self-interest when judging potential risk-reward outcomes. Rationality hardly fits these heist films, which, as allegories of modern capitalism, reveal the extent that irrationality and chance pervade markets. This categorical assumption of rationality in economic theory has had detractors. Deirdre McCloskey, for example, has challenged the metaphorical underpinnings of Lester Thurow's zero-sum economics for being as invariably and inescapably rhetorical as any economist's language, particularly phrases that couch humans as "calculating machines and rational choosers" (McCloskey 223).[2] Thurow, however, does elicit relevant points about such a zero-sum metaphor by describing the process of economics itself: "Economic construction is based on economic destruction" (22). Joseph Schumpeter modeled his entrepreneur in terms of qualitative innovations to the marketplace, particularly the dynamics of "creative destruction," "because the new destroys and invigorates existing industrial structures" (Vaggi and Groenewegen 267). Both *The Killing* and

Cruel Gun Story critique any zero-sum model of "creative destruction" for economics, for in their final moments no winners are left, all the money is lost, and the protagonists have no future. In short, heist economics is a less-than-zero game.

Two theories for cooperation promote alternative views of economic action. As Dan M. Kahan explains the two theories, the incentive approach assumes that rewards or punishments induce the alignment of individual interests with the collective action, whereas trust outcome theory relies upon reciprocity of "face-to-face assurance-giving" that "promotes trust, which in turn generates reciprocal cooperation" (343). Kahan goes on to challenge the assumption that "material incentives invariably diminish trust," because incentives may well produce "a self-sustaining form of reciprocal cooperation" that obviates more coercive and invasive tactics (344). In the case of heist films, however, neither system appears to work, since material incentive not only remains the goal of the heist but also produces diminished trust, and face-to-face assurances hardly solve the disloyalty prevalent in such operations based upon greed. In this respect, economic endeavors offer little beyond the theoretical state for either the incentive or the trust outcome benefit analysis for social organization. Too many counterexamples to these theories occur. The heist film, then, may well serve as a more pertinent and reliable model of economic behavior than hypothetical, abstract models. As demonstrated in 2008, the gambles of the subprime housing market revealed that risk trumps incentive and trust at every turn.

Mark Osteen divides the structural elements of noir heist films into Fordist principles of employing specific tasks to reduce risk and Taylorist management principles of precise execution, measurement, and optimizing time and motion performances. For Osteen, *The Killing* demonstrates essential Taylorist elements: "fragmenting jobs to minimize skill requirements; separating execution from planning; dividing direct labor (the amateurs) from indirect labor (the pros); conducting time and motion studies to ensure optimum performance; paying according to result" (182). Such reliance upon the corporate organizing principles of Ford and Taylor in capitalism David Harvey believes to be overstated. Both systems met with considerable resistance in the labor market, as opposed to the more influential Henri Fayol's *Administration industrielle et générale* (1916): "With its emphasis upon organizational structures and hierarchical ordering of authority and information flow, it gave rise to a rather different version of rationalized management compared to Taylor's preoccupation with simplifying the horizontal flow of production processes" (Harvey 128). The differences in management relate to the planning, enforcement, control, and execution of not only the heist in *The Killing* and *Cruel Gun Story* but also the films' narratives. Spatial-temporal designations of horizontal movement (Fordism and Taylorism) account for story-unit movement in constructing the films' plots; vertical (Fayolism) authority accounts for Johnny Clay's and Togawa's dispensing information, calculating order, and providing temporal details for executing stages of the operation for the heist. Both films adapt economic models in order to subvert them in the end.

Ultimately, in both films, the heists are failures, a fact that is reinforced by a fragmented narrative structure. For *The Killing*, overlapping narrative perspectives in flashbacks are brought to a current temporal moment for different members of the heist gang, but it would be misleading to assume that the voice-over narrator's obsessive time details relate to a kind of mechanical precision in the execution of the crime. Kubrick was not concerned about the fragmented temporal structure of *The Killing*'s narrative; in fact, as Philip Kuberski points out, several scenes have clock faces that are completely blank, an image that "throws the film's time consciousness into doubt," as it does the dependency on absolute linearity of time (45). As James Naremore explains, temporal complexities of the plot, while accentuating rationality and contingency, transform "a hyper-rational plan for a robbery into a splintered montage of lurid details or local situations" (10). For *Cruel Gun Story*, the flash-forward imagined execution of the heist has a mechanical precision that the actual heist fails to achieve. In both films, the narratives are fragmented rather than strictly linear. As in economics, it is a matter of scale. The macronarratives appear to be linear, as in the planning of the heists, while the micronarratives—those moments of missteps, accidents, unexpected actions, interruptions, delays—point to irregularity, chance, and randomness. The relationship between the two narrative models corresponds to economics in general, whereby the desire for predictability of a normal state of equilibrium ignores or overrides the vicissitudes of chance, which tend to be far more significant and disturbing factors in market outcomes, as they are for heists. In his "Introduction" to *Fractals and Scaling in Finance*, Mandelbrot explains the problem of randomness for scientific and economic predictions: "Randomness is an intrinsically difficult idea that seems to clash with powerful facts and intuitions. In physics, it clashes with determinism, and in finance it clashes with instances of clear causality, economic rationality and perhaps even free-will" (14). In *The Killing* and *Cruel Gun Story*, the global deterministic desire of the heist plan becomes disrupted by localized incidents of unforeseen randomness, which prove to be utterly catastrophic.

What these two heists play with is the expected utility theory: Risk-averse individuals rank desirable, probable future outcomes; that is, the ordering of payoffs correlates to their utility. Expected utility implies rational decision making that points to one choice over another only if the expected outcome of one exceeds that of another. Maurice Allais's famous paradox relates to how complementary choices are in fact contingent upon one another, which means that expected utility predictions are not always applicable.[3] In the case of *The Killing* or *Cruel Gun Story*, the rationale for the big payoff, then, is based upon a series of contingent choices along the way. These choices are not calculable in mathematical terms, like expected utility or the Allais paradox, but rather remain psychological and emotional at their core. In short, the "killing" in theory turns out to be no sure thing in reality. Similarly, in *Cruel Gun Story*, Togawa rationally assumes that killing the motorcycle policemen escorting the armored truck will induce the two guards to exit the vehicle, either out of compassion for their fallen comrades or for self-preservation. Of course, they do not do either, and Togawa's plan spirals out of control. As with gambling on the ponies, the sure thing cannot always be counted on to occur. As with economics in general, imprecision and unpredictability are products of human behavioral uncertainty.

Risk, then, is not a rational economic decision process in the face of uncertainty; instead, unpredictable emotional reactions produce and compound risk. *The Killing* and *Cruel Gun Story* critique simple nonhuman, paradigmatic, and statistical economics in favor of human affect, which accords with recent studies of how choice and responses under uncertainty occur:

> The risk-as-feeling hypothesis suggests that feelings play a much more prominent role in risky decision making than they are given credit for. . . . Thus, feelings may be more than just an important input into decision making under uncertainty; they may be necessary and, to a large degree, mediate the connection between cognitive evaluations of risk and risk-related behavior. (Loewenstein, Weber, Hsee, and Welch 583)

In heist films, the cool mind often has emotional attachments that invariably lead to disaster. In *The Killing*, Sterling Hayden plays Johnny Clay as restrained, but even the mechanical and stoical Johnny does reveal moments of affection for his naively devoted girlfriend, Faye (Colleen Gray), and his overly sentimental financial backer, Marvin (Jay C. Flippen). Faye and Marvin represent Johnny's domestic life as common-law wife and surrogate father. Johnny's romantic attachment to Faye and filial loyalty to Marvin will prove to be his undoing, a point not usually acknowledged by Kubrick scholars. At the chess club, Maurice (Kola Kwariani), the ex-wrestler whom Johnny enlists to start a one-man bar brawl at the racetrack, agrees to the proposition but offers Johnny sage advice about the hazards of dealing with the emotions of others: "Individuality is a monster and it must be strangled in its cradle to make our friends feel comfortable. You know, I often thought that the gangster and the artist are the same in the eyes of the masses. They're admired and hero-worshipped, but there is always an underlying wish to see them destroyed at the peak of their glory." For heist protagonists, their positions are continually undercut by the emotional discord, envy, and hatred of the gang members. In *Cruel Gun Story*, Togawa's lack of affect belies his feelings of guilt toward the paralyzed condition of his sister Rie (Chieko Matsubara), for which he blames himself. So tormented is he by this guilt that Togawa wants to die at one point after the failed heist. To compensate, Togawa kidnaps the son of the underworld boss, Matsumoto (Hiroshi Nihonyanagi), in order to shift emotional distress and risk onto his betrayer. This plan, too, fails, even after Togawa robs and kills Matsumoto. Like Johnny's sentiments, Togawa's affection for his sister will ultimately cause his demise.

Another economic issue that both films reflect is moral hazard that provides little incentive to reduce risk. The concept of moral hazard "refers to the fact that insurance coverage drives a wedge between the net benefit to the individual and the net benefit to the society when the individual acts to reduce risk" (Campbell 180). In the case of *The Killing*, the post-heist laxity counters all preventative measures both before and during the heist. Val's attack on the gang is as unforeseen as any accident that might befall uninsured property: in this case, the loot, which is ironically not with the gang at the time. Caution could have been taken, as George Peatty (Elijah Cook Jr.) worriedly expresses, because Johnny Clay is taking too much time: "Everything else runs on a time table, until it comes to paying us our shares." Here, temporal delay evolves into an unforeseen force, a randomness that proves disastrous for the gang and, consequently, for Johnny himself. In the case of *Cruel Gun Story*, the moral hazard is not so immediately apparent, since the gang's infighting poses a number of possible catastrophic outcomes. Additionally, the betrayal by the Yakuza bosses, their ambush of the gang's hideout and the ensuing gun battle, and their attempted assassination of

Togawa and Shirai, who have sought an escape route through the sewers—
all of these unforeseen, untimely acts of subterfuge, betrayal, and reneging
on the heist contract occur as forces majeures.

Lionel White's 1955 novel *Clean Break* (later republished under the film's
title) serves as the basis for Kubrick's views on economics in American culture. Risk plays a fundamental role in all heist films, but no more so than in
The Killing. White begins his novel, very much like the divisions of action
and temporal shifts in Kubrick's film, with a series of character portrayals of
the various members of the heist crew, all based upon economics. Marvin
Unger, Johnny Clay's backer in the heist scheme, has worked as a court ste-
nographer for a decade and a half and that experience "had given him frequent opportunity to see what usually happened when men place their faith
in luck in opposition to definitely established mathematical odds" (1). At the
beginning of *The Killing*, Marvin has placed bets that are entirely meaningless to him, since their tickets serve only as a means of communication with
George Peatty about the time and place for the heist planning. Marvin's piece
of the action comes from his bankroll and not from his participation in the
heist, which Johnny knows to be an uncertainty when he tells him to stay
away from the track during the heist.

As frugal and seemingly financially conservative as Unger appears in
White's novel, especially by eschewing racetrack odds, he nonetheless plays
the other American gambling pastime—the stock market. White describes
Unger sitting down in a cafeteria with a paper containing both "the final
stock market quotations and the race results" (30). Unger, unlike almost
every other amateur in the rising market, was a perpetual loser:

> He invested the slender savings in stocks, but unfortunately, he never
> had the courage to hang on to a stock once he had bought it. As a
> result he was constantly buying and selling and, with each flurry of
> the market, he changed stocks and took losses on his brokerage fees.
> He also had an almost uncanny ability to select the very few stocks
> which went down soon after he bought them. On the several thou-
> sand dollars he had managed to scrimp and put away from his small
> salary over the years, he had almost nothing left. (30)

In this admirable passage, White connects the process of horse racing with
the stock exchange, whereby brokerage fees equate to the house take at the
track and whereby the multiplicity of investors, like multiple bettors, produces a game of unstable and unpredictable successes and losses. Unger's

risk aversion also plays out ironically as a form of risk taking; in an attempt to avoid loss, Unger wagers on other stocks that uncannily lose value almost instantly, very much like betting on horses whose odds depreciate at the moment of the first wagers. Unger's plight of gambling on the stock market serves as a paradigm for America's postwar almost blind optimism about the future stability of an unsure market. In the film, that optimism in Johnny's abilities is undone when, unpredictably, a drunken Marvin arrives at the racetrack during the heist, a foreshadowing of an unsuccessful plan.

Bartender at the track, Big Mike dreams of a big score to take his tramp of a daughter, Patti, out of the corruption of a life of poverty, which had resulted from his being "an inveterate gambler" who consistently lost half of his paycheck on betting the ponies but "still had a great deal of difficulty knowing just where he stood at the close of the last race," owing to the fact that he had "no mind for figures at all" (8). As with Unger, Big Mike's dilemma remains an economics of risk aversion that results in more risk taking, but the twist for White occurs with his inability to comprehend his position vis-à-vis the market in which he enters. Both Unger and Big Mike serve as examples of the irrational man, the real *homo economicus*, who confronts risk not with rationality but with contradictory feelings of apprehension and attraction. They exemplify the actual status of investors' dreams, and only dreams, of future profits in the American marketplace. In *The Killing*, Kubrick replaces the corrupted daughter with the invalid wife to whom Mike O'Reilly (Joe Sawyer) devotes himself. Kubrick's shift emphasizes a pattern of male impotency in domestic relationships, as evidenced by George Peatty's impuissance before and emotional dependence upon his demanding, meretricious wife, Sherry (Marie Windsor).

While Unger and Big Mike devise ill-conceived systems for financial success, the other members of the heist crew view the world in terms of chance, luck, and fate. George Peatty, the racetrack cashier whose wife, Sherry, will be the uncontrollable risk factor in Johnny Clay's plan, views his mismatched marriage and his life in general in terms of a lost coin toss with luck on one side and happiness on the other. In particular, Peatty blames his predicament on chance:

In the hard core of his mind, he blamed the thing not on himself and certainly not on Sherry. He blamed it on luck and on fate. A fate which limited his earning capacity to what he could make as a cashier at the track. A fate which had made Sherry the sort of woman she was—a woman who wanted everything and everything the best. (13)

George (Elijah Cook Jr.) and Sherry (Marie Windsor) discuss money and marriage in *The Killing*.

White's focus upon luck and fate in terms of the Peattys becomes the linchpin to the entire operation, particularly Sherry's adulterous affair with Val, who will attempt to rob the heist crew of their loot. Kubrick plays out the Peattys' ill-fated marriage in monetary and materialist terms:

GEORGE: You used to love me. You said you did, anyway.

SHERRY: I seem to recall you made a memorable statement, too. Something about hitting it rich, having an apartment on Park Avenue and a different car for every day of the week. Not that I care about such things, understand, as long as I have a big, handsome, intelligent brute like you.

George: It would make a difference, wouldn't it? If I had money, I mean.

SHERRY: How would you define money, George? Now, if you're thinking about giving me your collection of Roosevelt dimes . . .

GEORGE: I mean big money. Hundreds of thousands of dollars.

At this point, George's emotional state gets the better of his sense and he tells his rapacious, manipulative wife what will be the heist target.

Police officer Randy Kennan (Ted De Corsia) arrives at a sleazy lounge for "personal business," as the narrator claims. In truth, Kennan owes money to a loan shark, Leo Steiner (Jay Adler), to the tune of $3,000 with the accumulated interest for extensions. In the novel, Kennan views a moment of coincidence of running into Johnny Clay as his break in life, the opposite of George Peatty's take on the world: "It was luck, real luck" (18). Johnny Clay, after serving four years in prison and all the while outlining this heist, understands that a heist needs to balance risk seeking with outcome: "Any time you take a chance on going to jail, you got to be sure that the rewards are worth the risk" (22). Moreover, as Johnny explains to his girlfriend, Fay, his plan has none of the traps and loose ends of the usual criminal heist, because he has made sure of his confederates from the outset:

> "The others," she said, "they all seem sort of queer."
> "That's the beauty of the thing," Johnny told her. "I'm avoiding the one mistake most thieves make. They always tie up with other thieves. These men, the ones who are in on the deal with me—none of them are professional crooks. They all have jobs, they all live seemingly decent, normal lives. But they all have money problems and they all have larceny in them. No, you don't have to worry. This thing is going to be foolproof." (23)

Here, White has normalized the crew so that his commentary on American economics resists devolving into criminal activity and instead rests with normal men who confront the marketplace with foreboding and a measure of contempt. Their larceny derives from their pathetic economic conditions. Sterling Hayden repeats this speech almost verbatim in one of Kubrick's most famous tracking shots, as he moves through the railroad apartment, beer in hand, all the while foreground objects occasionally obscuring him, as he states the main problem of the film: "If you take a chance, be sure the reward's worth the risk." Key to the irony of this scene is Lucien Ballard's cinematography, especially the noir signs of entrapment with furnishings and blinds producing barred shadows on the ceiling and walls.

In White's narrative, for the heist to succeed, Johnny requires three other men to perform specific tasks on the day of the Canarsie Stakes for a total outlay of ten thousand dollars: Nikki must use a silencer on his 30.06 rifle to shoot Black Lightning as the horse rounds the last turn of the track for five thousand; Tex, a drunken boxer, must start a melee in the track bar in order to draw the Pinkertons away from the cash reserves for twenty-five hundred; and Maurice Cohen, a former football player, must block any interference to Johnny's postrobbery escape for the remaining twenty-five hundred. Heist games, like stock games, require substantial investments in order to garner returns. Johnny informs the other members of the crew that these additional participants pose no problem, since these professionals are "getting paid to perform certain definite duties at a certain definite time" (43). To ensure that the heist has no hitches, Johnny has mapped out the details, which White includes as a drawing of the racetrack and the positions of each member. Specific actions coordinated with specific temporal moments describe the foundational axes for the mathematics of horse racing and the stock market. In *The Killing*, time correlates to money, but the intrusion of an external temporal order thwarts Johnny's plans. Nearly every moment of Kubrick's film directs attention to a capitalist system of time and money. The voice-of-God narrator introduces each heist gang member in terms of temporal and monetary conditions. At almost every moment in the film, time and money are central visually and diegetically: the racetrack and betting tickets; the chess club where one pays to play; the florist selling remembrances; the motel and its rental rates; the bus station, its lockers, and the special bus to the track; the parking lot; the pawnshop; the airport with its banks of pay phones, waiting cabbie, and cab stand; the extra baggage at the airport, and the yellow cab that zips past Faye as she and Johnny try to escape. When Johnny purchases an extra suitcase, the pawnshop's ironic signs read *Money to Loan* and *Money to Buy*. That shop is located next to a placard announcing Lenny Bruce's stand-up routine at a local burlesque house, which Kubrick includes to point to the dark comedy of the Peattys' domestic and sexual dissolution. When George Peatty returns home after being shot by Val, he pleads with Sherry to call an ambulance, but as she continues to pack her suitcase, she dismisses him, before he shoots her, with "Take a cab!" To paraphrase Adam Smith, the world of *The Killing* is governed by an invisible hand of unintended disasters for individual actions—time.

In the novel, the heist is pulled off without a hitch. The planning, the execution, and the initial result prior to the big payoff follow the rules of managed risk taking accompanying reasonable risk aversion; however, chance or fate, in the guise of Sherry Peatty, upsets the entire scheme. Val and his partners kill and are killed by the heist gang, with the exception of George Peatty, who, with a bullet hole bleeding excessively from his face, makes his way to La Guardia field and there fires rounds into Johnny's stomach when he mistakenly perceives Fay for his adulterous wife, Sherry.

Cruel Gun Story relies upon Kubrick's film for essential features of its heist plot, particularly in the introduction of gang members and the planning stages, including the iconic noir lighting for the heist discussion from *The Asphalt Jungle* (John Huston, 1950). Kubrick mimicked John Huston's use of intense overhead single-source lighting concentrated on the center of the table, as Johnny reveals the heist plan. The sole illumination offers several symbolic readings: the monomania of the heist; the egoistic optimism of the gang members; the self-interest and greed of the characters; and a sense of foreboding. From there, the two films depart in terms of narrative, because Furukawa has broader social critiques in mind: the United States' occupation of Japan, the rise of Yakuza, and Japanese postwar economics.

Postwar Yakuza followed the crony system of capitalist corporations, *keiretsu*, with conglomerates interlaced in enterprises, but Yakuza still maintained a kind of family-controlled *zaibutsu*, or monopoly, even though the postwar constitution forbade such exploitative control in companies. American postwar economic policy in Japan remains evident in the numerous shots and sounds of US Air Force jets, and after the gang's inept miscalculation during the heist, they flee to the remains of an abandoned military post's pleasure district. In the initial scene at Takizawa's (Tamio Kawaji's) Moon Star Bar, black airmen (*kokujin-hei*) represent the otherness of the United States military occupation.[4] These visual cues point to the continued cultural domination of American political and economic policies in postwar Japan.

Mimicking Japanese 1950s market models for success, Yakuza, then, created a hybrid organizational structure with a kind of vertical integration of *oyabun* ("foster father") or *kumicho* ("family chief") at the top with subordinates functioning as ancillary entities in a more or less weak horizontal supplier role for the overall *keiretsu*-like edifice. This organizational configuration also mimics the Japanese national bureaucracy, the *tatewari gyosei* (vertical administration).[5] More precisely for the 1950s–60s recovery period, a pivotal figure in Japanese politics, corporations, and Yakuza emerged, the underworld fixer, *kuromaku*, "black curtain," "a word originated in classic Kabuki theater, in which an unseen wirepuller controls the stage by manipulating a black curtain" (Kaplan and Dubro 62). Emerging into Yakuza prominence were three main groups—the *bakuto* (gambler), *gurentai* (hood or thug from postwar black markets), and *tekiya* (street stall workers with a strict code of loyalty)—all of whom represent major areas that fueled Japan's resurgence: money, muscle, and the marketplace. All three groups find representation in the heist gang of the film: a gambling drug

Togawa (Joe Shishido) and his invalid sister, Rie (Chieko Matsubara), in *Cruel Gun Story*.

user, Saeki (Saburo Hiromatsu), a dim-witted former professional boxer, Okada (Shobun Inoue), and Togawa's faithful ally Shirai (Yuji Odaka).

At the beginning of *Cruel Gun Story*, Togawa is pulled into the heist being organized by a disbarred lawyer, Ito, who works for the Yakuza boss Matsumoto, whose underlings refer to him as *sha-cho*, a term usually applied to corporate or company executives. Togawa agrees to mastermind the heist only in order to pay for surgeries for his paralyzed sister. Togawa blames himself for her condition because he sent her out to the store one night and a truck driver struck her down crossing the street. Togawa avenged that accident by killing the driver and landing in prison. Togawa, even more stoic than Johnny Clay, has no hesitation about killing. Furukawa provides an imagined sequence for detouring the police motorcycle escort and armored van away from an accident, with Togawa using the "gun," an old military rifle, to kill motorcycle cops, which prompts the guards inside the van to exit and also to be killed. Then the gang retrieve the key to the back doors of the armored vehicle, drive it into a large truck, and take off to split the loot. As they are going over the plan, Keiko (Minako Kazuki), Saeki's female partner, is heard outside the door, not unlike Sherry Peatty in *The Killing*. Later, she admits that Ito has sent her to spy on them. Of course, the heist does not follow the plan, since the guards remain in the armored vehicle, deviating from Togawa's expectations of human reactions and emotions.

The gang still take the truck, but with difficulty, because the guards alternate between using the brakes and releasing them in an attempt to thwart them from pulling the vehicle up a ramp into their awaiting truck.

They arrive at an abandoned set of Air Force buildings once used by airmen for drinking and carousing. During the failed attempt to smoke the guards out of the armored truck, Shirai is shot by one of the guards, whom Togawa quickly dispatches. Keiko and Togawa drive off to inform Ito of the new situation, leaving the wounded Shirai to watch over the scheming Okada and Saeki, who overpower Shirai, grab the loot, and attempt to kill him and the remaining guard. Before they can pull the trigger, rifle reports ring out and they fall dead, thanks to Togawa's surprising return. Then, the sound of cars can be heard. Here, Furukawa orchestrates a four-minute-thirty-six-second nighttime shoot-out between Togawa and Shirai and the henchmen of Ito and Matsumoto in forty-five edits, averaging a cut every six seconds. The doors of the garage collapse as the car of the escaping Togawa and Shirai crashes into the car of the Yakuza thugs who are trying to enter. One thug lights a bundle of dynamite and tosses it into the garage. Togawa quickly tosses it back, dispersing the betrayers. With the only escape route being the sewer, Togawa and Shirai narrowly make it, only to be hunted down by awaiting assassins at a river culvert's entrance. Fortunately, Takizawa and Keiko have arrived to save them. The significance of this action remains both the locale, a site once occupied by United States Air Force personnel, and the presence of the Yakuza, whose code of honor is as detrimental as the occupation democracy was for Japan.

Cruel Gun Story sets its critique against not only the Yakuza but also the political corruption of the times. Dating back to the nineteenth century with the strategies of the Dark Ocean Society, a rightist group who served as strong-arms for governmental officials, at least since the mid-1950s the Zen Ai Kaigi (All Japan Council of Patriotic Organizations) extorted money from leading corporations, the largest banks in the country, and major financial brokers (Kaplan and Dubro 102). Two economic booms, the Jinmu of 1955–56 and the Iwato of 1959–60, also saw rises in Yakuza labor and business expansion (Hill 45). Both booms resulted in recessions. The Supreme Commander for the Allied Powers began a crackdown on organized crime in the major cities in the fall of 1947, but those efforts were undercut by links between "occupation reconstruction efforts and gang-affiliated labor" to such a degree that the occupation actually helped to consolidate crime syndicates (Friman 102). In 1963, the conservative LDP (Liberal Democratic Party or *Jiyu-Minshuto*) that had formed in 1955 publicly committed itself to rapid urbanization and expansion of industrialization with appeals to wage earners, as Miki Takeo, chair of the Research Committee on Organization, set forth that "a party that makes workers its enemy has no future" (quoted in Garon and Mochizuki 160). Reinterpreting that statement in the context of Yakuza expansion into corporate and labor structures, as well as conservative politics, reveals a kind of social hypocrisy and collusion among economic institutions, the government, and the criminal underworld. Commenting on the American occupation era, film director Sato (*Story of Military Cruelty*) recalled the condition of "democracy" under the new regime and the association with corporations and Yakuza:

> But, as I grew up, it seemed to me that the democracy was only supported by American power, American dominance. To stem the tide of violence, the government tried to go along with it. But the *yakuza* were very much against the idea of American democracy. Also, the corporate entities felt threatened by it, almost the same as the *yakuza* gangs. There was a huge underground black market that supported Japan's economy after the war, and there were many *yakuza* conflicts based around market competition. You also had the American-led democracy force influencing and manipulating things. (quoted in Desjardins 81–82)

Clearly, in a similar fashion to other *zankoku* films, *Cruel Gun Story* serves as an allegory for the interrelationships among Japanese postwar politics, economics, and crime.

Cruel Gun Story's critique of native and foreign economic schemes plays out in the gang's inability to assess risk in a heist plan that does not foresee uncertain action by the armored truck guards. The heist rests upon a great economic fiction that men will act rationally in accordance with predictable outcomes, when, in fact, just the opposite holds true. As with horse racing, the heist makes a probability bet that such an action will occur with positive benefits and lower risk. That type of reasoning eschews fundamental uncertainty, which means that chaos can occur at any unpredictable moment, and the remainder of the heist relies upon two motivating factors: self-regard in terms of sustaining an untenable situation to avoid regret or admission of error, and recalculating for further risk avoidance.[6]

Common to both films remains the overarching concept of time and its persistent disruption of human plans. For *Cruel Gun Story*, two forms of temporal experience intersect: the human, mechanical time of plots, deadlines, schedules, and ransoms and the transcendent, indifferent, and almost predetermined time of a universal force. This latter time is associated with the subplot concerning Togawa's invalid sister recuperating from unsuccessful operations in a Christian hospital. In one scene, she reads to a group of children from Maurice Maeterlinck's fantasy, *The Blue Bird*, a tale that emphasizes spiritual happiness instead of material pleasures of luxuries and wealth. Furukawa's irony is readily apparent.

In the elaborate final gun battle in the Moon Star Bar between Togawa and the corrupt Ito, two mistaken killings mirror one another: because of the complete darkness of the bar, Ito shoots the arriving Keiko; then, because of his inability to see clearly due to Ito's fatally wounding him, Takizawa shoots Togawa, thinking he is Ito, and mortally wounds him. Togawa stumbles out of the room, tripping over and spilling kerosene, which ignites and engulfs the entire bar in an inferno. In Togawa's hand is the symbol of unseen power, a cross. It is not a Christian ending so much as it is an ironic one, because Togawa has no salvation, no redemption. The cross is simply a symbol of death.

The Killing concludes with risk aversion and risk taking. At the airport, Johnny tries to take his overly large suitcase packed with money as carry-on luggage. The desk agent advises Johnny and Faye to send it through as checked baggage, but Johnny calls for the supervisor, Mr. Grimes, who offers to rebate their tickets, even though the plane is just about to board. Johnny resigns himself to chance and lets the suitcase go through. Johnny's transaction relies upon trust and luck; moreover, it depends upon timing, catching the plane to elude capture. The irony remains that Johnny's risk avoidance is the riskiest maneuver in the film. An obnoxious, fat, bourgeois woman's dog runs out onto the tarmac, causing the luggage cart driver to swerve, thereby overturning the stacked bags, one of which is the recently purchased suitcase with the broken locks. Of course, the money spills out and scatters into the air because of the prop wash of the arriving plane. As Johnny and Faye exit the airport, Mr. Grimes and two detectives spot them. The moment that Faye cannot flag down a passing cab the detectives close in, guns drawn. In utter disgust and resignation, Johnny mutters the summation of the temporal, existential, and economic conditions of gambling, robbery, and capitalist speculation: "What's the difference?"

Notes

1. Mather also makes other connections between that film and Kubrick's later work, such as Weegee working on the stills in *Dr. Strangelove*, Ted de Corsia appearing in both *Naked City* and later *The Killing*, and the clandestine camerawork from a van following de Corsia walking along a sidewalk being used in *Killer's Kiss* (1955).

2. McCloskey quotes Adam Smith from *The Theory of Moral Sentiments* on the instinct value of rhetorical persuasion: "The desire of being believed, the desire of persuading, of leading and directing other people, seems to be one of the strongest of all our natural desires" (232).

3. For an insightful and lucid discussion of the history of utility theories and the detractors, see Heukelom 28–70.

4. For a discussion of Japanese literary and media portrayals of African American military men in the 1950s, see Molasky.

5. For an account of this ineffectual bureaucracy, see Maclachlan.

6. See Schimd 45, 124–28.

Heists and "Eye-sts"

Sense and Sensuality
in the Aesthetic Experience
of the Heist Film

◇◇◇◇◇◇◇◇◇◇◇◇◇◇◇◇◇◇◇◇◇◇◇◇

Andrew Clay

What makes the heist film work, or not work? This question is addressed by adopting a mainly phenomenological approach to film theory that reflects on five British heist films from the period 1970–2010, *Perfect Friday* (Peter Hall, 1970), *Bellman and True* (Richard Loncraine, 1987), *Face* (Antonia Bird, 1997), *Sexy Beast* (Jonathan Glazer, 2000), and *The Bank Job* (Roger Donaldson, 2008), as aesthetic experiences. There are a number of sources in this field that are linked in their titles by reference to the "eye" of cinematic technology and experience, "eye-sts," if you like: phenomenological (Vivian Sobchack's "address of the eye," Jennifer Barker's "tactile eye"), pragmatist (Jon Boorstin's voyeuristic, vicarious, and visceral "Hollywood eye"), and constructivist (Dziga Vertov's "film-eye"). While the titles of these works and ideas explicitly invoke cinema as "seeing," they do so only as shorthand for a wider interest in the felt experience and sense-making of cinema. This essay investigates the phenomenology of heist films, seeking to establish what we experience or feel about them and how heist films can be seen as embodied or enworlded.

Most of us will not have any direct subjective experience of participating in a heist as professional criminals or amateurs. We may have stolen something or taken something without permission willfully or inadvertently, but this is far from the experience of driving a getaway vehicle or jimmying open a security deposit box. Our experience of heists is normally secondhand, apperceived vicariously through media such as film and print. Phenomenologically, major robberies are objective events that exist in the world independently of our viewing them on-screen and upon which the art of filmmaking can be brought to bear to create an experience. So, what is the heist film as an "aesthetic experience"?

In *Technology as Experience* (2004), McCarthy and Wright are concerned with the design and evaluation of technology as experience via a pragmatic approach informed by the works of John Dewey and Mikhail Bakhtin, whose accounts of activity and experience are "not constrained by the demands of analytic philosophy or positivist science" to consider the "livedness and feltness of experience" (52). Accordingly, a differentiation is made between the quotidian, often unnoticed, "flow of events" and "aesthetic experience"—the satisfying, enlivening, or challenging events or activities where "the aesthetic quality of the event reflects the way in which person and event relate to each other" (88). Aesthetic experience, then, is framed by effort and thought, giving it structure and meaning particularly as a transactional act in which "the elements of experience so interpenetrate each other that we lose our sense of the separation of self, objects and events" (90–91).

To assist with the analysis of aesthetic experience such as in relation to film, where "we are part of the film and the film is part of us," McCarthy and Wright use four ideas, four "threads of experience." These threads are about the relationships between the parts and the whole of an experience ("compositional thread") and about the quality of time and space that are produced in an experience ("spatio-temporal thread"). To these relational aspects are added an interest in the feltness ("emotional thread") and activity ("sensual thread") of lived experience. The emotional thread focuses on the values, goals, and desires that are ascribed to other people or things to make them meaningful, while the sensual thread refers to the participation, action, engagement, or absorption through which the immediate sense of a situation is actualized in the quality of the experience.

The Heist Film and "the Hollywood Eye"

In relation to film, McCarthy and Wright turn to Jon Boorstin's *The Hollywood Eye* in order to illustrate how the threads of experience might be applied to actual technology. Boorstin is a writer and filmmaker whose aim in *The Hollywood Eye* is to "look at the theoretical issues from a practical point of view, to show why quality pays, why the work works" (8). He does so by identifying three competing pleasures that can be produced in the work and "read" as effects of the film, pleasures that McCarthy and Wright map onto three of their own threads of experience: "The Voyeur's

Eye" (compositional thread), "The Vicarious Eye" (emotional thread), and "The Visceral Eye" (sensual thread). The voyeuristic pleasure is about "chasing a good story through a fresh new world" (136). More than that, it is seen as a self-conscious act of recognizing novelty or beauty or being satisfied by the credibility or plausibility of the story. The vicarious gratification is of characters and performances—the "cathartic insight into human nature and the human condition, which is the movies' real claim to higher meaning" (136). Lastly, the visceral sensuality is sensations rather than emotions, the "thrill of motion, joy of destruction, lust, blood lust, terror, disgust" (110).

McCarthy and Wright aim to understand aesthetic experience in everyday life in order to facilitate the successful use of technology in design. Similarly, Boorstin's interest is diagnostic in terms of a textual analysis of the formal properties of film linked to the aesthetic experience of the viewer. Despite Boorstin's pragmatic turn away from the theory of filmmaking, his theory is that a movie is actually three movies running at once (9), and the movies that work are the ones that combine the three pleasures of the text in a harmonious way. Above all, according to Boorstin, a successful film must combine such elements as novelty and plausibility, emotional empathy, and sensuality with an "emotional theme" and "larger meaning" that empower the action, inextricably bind up the plot, drive the story, and give a film its direction (163–66).

Of my selected films, *Sexy Beast* is the most successful film under the lens of "the Hollywood eye." The film's totally engrossing and novel story about a retired professional criminal, Gal (Ray Winstone), forcibly torn away from his Spanish villa to take part in a high-value security deposit box robbery in London requiring access to the vault through underwater tunneling, is formed of explainable and thought-provoking sequences, with characters eliciting strong emotional empathy. Because he is the central person of intentional objectification, we experience Gal's inner life, in particular, as a vital essence that drives our understanding of his aversion to being recruited for the job by Don Logan (Ben Kingsley) in a series of tense scenes of menace and intimidation. Gal and his girlfriend, ex–porn actress Deedee (Amanda Redman), have taken a redemptive path to retirement from murky London to the bleaching sunlight of southern Spain. The emotional theme of *Sexy Beast* is the restorative power of love, and the larger meaning is in the belief that the past can be another country.

The Bank Job is less successful than *Sexy Beast* as an aesthetic experience. "Based on a true story" (the robbery of the security deposit vault at Lloyd's Bank, Baker Street, London in 1971), the film's heist narrative is thickened with other historical references from the same period, such as to the alleged existence of sexually compromising photographs of the Queen's sister, Princess Margaret, and to porn racketeering coupled with police corruption. As a consequence, the film means to be revelatory about a story that can now be told beyond the establishment suppression that was in operation at the time. The story is expressed with a credible sense of time and place, such as through attention to historically accurate sets, but without a sense of cleverness or newness, and the tying together of an opportunist robbery under the scrutiny of both the intelligence services, "porn kings," and "bent coppers" stretches the credibility of the action. Vicariously, the characters are emotionally consistent, and we care about the likeable robbers, but Jason Statham's gang leader role (Terry Leather) lacks a forceful sense of identification with his predicament. Viscerally, there is some humorous dialogue between the gang members and some tension around our emotional involvement with the gang's success, but it is not an action film with memorable thrills or moments of great jeopardy.

Face, in many aspects, is a successful heist film in "Hollywood eye" terms. It has the rarity of equating professional crime ("being bent") with ordinary work ("going straight") contributing to its larger meaning of political critique of the power and corruption of money and its damaging effects on society. The depiction of a London professional criminal milieu in *Face* is credible and the story is also convincing up to the point of the overblown shoot-out at the police station when the remnant of the gang attempt to retrieve the loot from the locker of the corrupt policeman, Chris (Andrew Tiernan). Ray (Robert Carlyle), as the leader of the heist, is presented with inner turmoil in coming to terms with his lack of success as a career criminal and the abandoning of his youthful years of socialist protest. The love for his girlfriend, Connie (Lena Headey), and the belief that they can make a new start together is the powerful emotional theme of the film. The rest of the characters are more caricatured than Ray and Connie, but it has a compensating depth of visceral physical violence and action thrills.

In *Bellman and True*, Hiller (Bernard Hill) is the "inside man" sourcing information and providing technical expertise, but only under a threatening state of bribery and coercion in which he is held captive with his young stepson (Kieran O'Brien) by the gang in a situation that stretches plausibility. Hiller and "The Boy" are well-rounded characters in the misery and hopelessness of their predicament, and the gang's roles are drawn

Face: The gang members count the haul and find it is much less than they anticipated.

convincingly from the London professional criminal milieu, including the safecracker ("Peterman" in criminal slang) and alarm specialist ("Bellman" in criminal slang). The heist itself is elaborate and technical, and there are plenty of associated thrills of action and chase, near miss and jeopardy. In terms of emotional themes and larger meaning, the family melodrama elements do not always mesh satisfyingly with the crime narrative. Hiller and his stepson are abandoned by their wife and mother. Hiller, highly skilled but ground down by his misfortunes, seems like a man out of sync with the consumer values and the veneer of "happy families" that has fed his cynicism about modern life. However, Hiller's self-harmful attempts to protect his stepson and return to a "normal family life" amount to a miserable situation that ultimately undermines the film as an entirely successful aesthetic experience in "Hollywood eye" relations.

Of all the films in my sample, *Perfect Friday* is the only one that is not set in the cultural verisimilitude of professional crime. Graham (Stanley Baker) is a deputy under manager at a London bank who sits in his panopticon-like glass-walled cubicle of an office contemplating how he can steal from his employers and say farewell to his boredom at work. He recruits an aristocratic married couple, Nick (David Warner) and Britt (Ursula

The thieves force Hiller (Bernard Hill) into participating in the heist by threatening his stepson in *Bellman and True*.

Andress), Lord and Lady Dorset, and waits for the "perfect Friday" when his feckless manager will absent himself from the office and they can implement his plan. As a film it lacks empathetic depth of characterization, but the performances of the actors are engaging and credible. The emotional theme is a playful permissiveness built around multiple double-crossing plot lines and a mobile and dynamic ménage à trois, but with coyly teasing female nudity. Its larger meaning linked to emotional detachment from identification with characters is life as a "cool" game that seems beyond significant consequence. At the end of the film, at the airport when Britt has doubled-crossed both Graham and her husband, Nick turns to Graham and wonders if they couldn't do it again next year. Graham tells Nick to "Call me." It is as if the only impact is like having lost a game of cards that can be played again. The mutual antipathy between the characters and their position of having been robbed of the proceeds that have been gained through a stressful and elaborate confidence trick are forgotten and put aside. However, in "voyeur's eye" respects, it succeeds through a stylish appeal with arresting framings of characters and objects, exaggerated camera movements, momentary freeze-frames, and elliptical editing.

Banker Nick (Stanley Baker) and aristocrat Nick (David Warner) vow to try again after Britt flies off with the money at the end of *Perfect Friday*.

The Heist Film and Phenomenology

The "Hollywood eye" approach to film experience rests mainly on the phenomenon of the film as a pleasurable object that can be analyzed as such. The approach of McCarthy and Wright and Boorstin to aesthetic experience leans toward phenomenology, with their concerns for the interpenetration of the film and viewer as an embodiment of subject and object addressed through intellectual, emotional, and physical properties and effects of the film experience, but without any philosophical interest in phenomenology's attempt to reflect upon the structures of experience and consciousness. How does phenomenology expand on this pragmatic approach to the formal qualities of the aesthetic experience of film?

Put simply, given the many variants, phenomenology as a philosophical movement seeks to reflect upon the structures of experience and consciousness. Foundationally, Edmund Husserl suggests that consciousness is being conscious of something beyond the mind to something other than itself (the intentional object) in a process described as "intentionality" or "aboutness." Intentionality, then, refers to the notion that consciousness is always the consciousness of something. Husserl's particular approach to phenomenology is transcendental in terms of the study of the essence of consciousness as a subjective experience as a starting point to reflect on the essential features of experiences (feelings, perceptions, memories, daydreams, films) and the core of what we experience to the point of generalization or universality. Allan Casebier tries to correct what he sees as contemporary film theory's idealism, in which "perceivers only read meanings into what they see" (11). He suggests that representation is not a textual construction but rather something that is discovered and experienced as an act of being aware of the recognition of what is being represented. The experience of representation is one of selective recognition (apperception) in the experience of perception as a "living through" or "passing through" the artwork experience.

In Husserlian phenomenology, consciousness is actional in that it is always doing something and referential in the way that it is always pointing to something. This intentionality "involves a complex interaction between what appears to us and our manner of positioning ourselves in being aware of it" (Casebier 16). Methodologically, the basic belief or "natural attitude" that the reality of our world exists separate from our experience of it has to be "bracketed," set aside in order to turn our attention to the ongoing activity of consciousness through which our experience is constituted. The aim of this reduction is to start to notice how we are actually experiencing things, to search for the features of an experience that are both necessary and invariant, and to identify essences such as what makes an experience an experience. How do we pass through "film"? How do we allow ourselves to reach beyond what appears to us? What perceptual act are we doing when we do this? In relation to the heist film, what objects (events, persons, states, affairs, actions) are being discovered in the activity of watching heist films? How do we "live or pass through" the heist film?

Coincidentally, all of the films in my sample are set in London without necessarily being about London. British heist films point frequently at the professional criminal sociocultural milieu of the East End of London that operates as a powerful referent of verisimilitude circulating in popular culture. As stated earlier, heists are objective events in the world, and they have patterns of events and participants that are being pointed at in film—"work" has to be found, targets have to be identified, plans have to be made, a team has to be recruited, the robbery has to be executed and the aftermath plans implemented, and so on. There are leaders and organizers and specialists who pass through the before, during, and after of the heist according to the same rhythm that is more often than not discovered in the experience of watching the heist film. The criminal acquisition of money is, above all, an action that has to be expressed in the heist film, and negotiating the glamorization or validation of this for the viewer is addressed regularly through the drawing of moral boundaries between good and bad persons, such as through their levels of decency, personal motivations and life circumstances, or attitudes to such things as violence and personal relationships. The perception of the heist through film can also work in the other direction. Bruce Reynolds, one of the lead robbers in the Great Train Robbery of 1963, often reflected that his experience of being a professional thief felt like he was either in or making a film. "I was beginning to see the thief as an artist," Reynolds recalls in his autobiography, "writing the scenario, choosing the cast, deciding the location, acting and directing action" (194).

Following Casebier, we can reflect on the phenomenology of the heist film experience through a consideration of the "objects" that are being pointed at by the film and discovered by the viewer and other aspects of intentionality in terms of what we are doing in this discovery process. From a phenomenological attitude or perspective, how are we actually experiencing heist films? In *Perfect Friday*, for instance, we discover bowler-hatted bank gent Graham outside of any professional robbery context. Graham is a disaffected amateur, whose scheme details remain hidden to us for most of the film prior to the short heist and aftermath sequences. In the extensive preamble to the heist, the film points to the rigid hierarchies of work and social status, and the lethargy, boredom, lying, and deceptions almost to the point of social critique, though perhaps more like a malaise. Above all, we are passing through a game, a "bored game," the playing out of a game that we watch based on disguise, misdirection, and double, double-dealing. Britt is the winner of the game who takes it all, leaving Nick and Graham floundering in her jet stream as she flies away with her handsome Swiss boyfriend and a suitcase full of "lolly."

In all of the other films considered here we discover a professional crime context in which the main male character of identification is a participant in a narrative about the heist as personal ordeal involving varying degrees of suffering. The lightest treatment in this respect is in *The Bank Job*. Terry is involved in a heist as a setup by the intelligence services that inadvertently puts him in further danger when he steals an incriminating ledger belonging to pornography and prostitution racketeer Lew Vogel (David Suchet). The security deposit vault is the hiding place of the compromising royal photographs, and the lengthy, elaborate heist involving a weekend of tunneling, the setup, and the aftermath resolution are leading to the exposure of the "truth." This directs the viewer with little or no sensuality or feeling, like the exposé in the sensational Sunday newspapers, to "putting the records straight" in a more open and less corrupt society.

Above all, *Bellman and True* wants to show us a technical heist in great detail in the middle of the film. The viewer's passage through all phases of the heist is guided by the fate of Hiller and his boy, who does not even have a name. For this broken family and the sake of the child, Hiller, in the preparation and planning of the robbery, has to undergo physical violence, loss of liberty, and forced participation in a dangerously difficult heist. Even the aftermath places him in unrelenting misery, since the death of a security guard threatens the safety of the gang, who need to eliminate the "inside man" Hiller because they will be more likely to be linked to the crime by the underworld and the police. In quiet moments together, the boy asks Hiller to tell him a story. Hiller's stories entwine elements from their own lives with fairy tales, where the absent mother is "The Princess," an odd fantasy combined with social observation of modern and technical life gone awry. The title of the film references the lyrics of the traditional folk song "Do You Ken John Peel," which is sung in the film by the little girl Mo (Kate McEnery). These allusions to age-old tales are linked to the unfolding of a family melodrama and grievous twists and turns of fate and fatality visited on the innocent victims by the criminal gang in need of technical mastery for their greedy and selfish machinations.

Unlike Hiller, who is an amateur sucked into the maelstrom of professional crime, Ray, in *Face,* is discovered as a "face," a known person in the criminal fraternity and experienced leader of riskily intimidating and visceral robberies of the kind that features near the beginning of the film, which we see without the preamble of planning and recruitment. The remainder of the film, after a ten-minute heist sequence of an armed "ram raid" robbery on a security depot, is the double-cross aftermath. The heist is Ray's workplace, but it is not working out as work. Ray's suffering in the aftermath is not only that his friends are being killed and their money stolen but a coming to self-consciousness about the futility of what he is doing as he has to choose the redemptive love of Connie over continuing his life as a thief. It is in the aftermath of the heist that what we are doing is being called to commune with the film as a political parable about the righteous man of protest and activism who became an outlaw and discovered, as spoken by the corrupt policeman Chris, "All there is, is money, and the people who have it." We are shown the aftermath of the heist to be pointed to how the old "face" values and codes have declined in the transformative corruption of money and power and how Ray must become "face"-less through the power of love and a belief that the corruption can be opposed anew.

In *Sexy Beast* we discover not the leader of gang of thieves but a social group of two couples living the "good life" in Spain, a state of grace interrupted when menacingly determined Don arrives to recruit Gal for a London heist led by the equally terrifying Teddy Bass (Ian McShane). This impingement on Gal's present by the past he has abandoned dominates the first hour of the film, leading up to the heist in which Gal has no choice but to take part. The lengthy opening exposition of a battle of wills between Gal and Don, ending with Don being killed and buried under the swimming pool at the villa, sets up how we pass through the heist framed through Gal's extreme anxiety at being involved and possibly caught and sent to prison or killed by Bass for Don's disappearance. What we are doing in the experience of *Sexy Beast* is being positioned in a paradise temporarily lost and then regained, perhaps in a dream state accessed through Gal's subjectivity about the fear of the past and the healing power of love.

What part might subjectivity play in the heist film as phenomenological experience? How does perception of the object (as such) become predelineated by potentialities ("horizons")? Casebier addresses the role of human subjectivity in perceptual experience via the phenomenological terms "co-determination" and "horizon." Perceptual experience of the objects of experience is based on the subjective knowledge and experiences that bring about differing codetermination of the activity of perception. The openness of the perceptive experience is also predelineated by potentialities or horizons that affect the subjective codetermination of the "perceived objects as such" (30) by the activity of consciousness that takes place. One might see genre as an important horizon of codetermination in the perceptual experience of making and watching films.

Conceptually, there is a paradox that films belong to no genre, rather they *participate* in genre "because the frame or trait is not part of the genre it designates" (Culler 196). Thus, when describing films generically, such as, for instance, that "this film is a heist film," this really means that films participate in conceptual generic categories in which specific texts are regarded as being intertextual members—"this film participates in the heist film genre." Genre films as intertextual objects of generic categories such as the "heist film" become objects of our intentionality, part of the experience of watching and making films and the horizon for the codetermination of perception. The aesthetic practice of genre is characterized by modes of representation or organizing modalities that are mechanisms for the formation of conceptual generic categories as part of the production and reception of films. In particular, Gledhill suggests that realism and melodrama are the main organizing modalities at the boundaries between culture and aesthetics, where realism is the "modality that makes a claim on the real" and melodrama is the modality in which aesthetic articulation is to "make the world morally legible" (227–35). Melodrama's rhetoric as a horizon of subjective knowledge and experience affecting expression and perception is a construction of moral legibility in aesthetic form that can be discovered in the experience of film viewing. Melodrama is "structured upon the 'dual recognition' of how things are and how they should be" (Williams 48), an "allegory of human experience dramatically ordered, as it should be rather than as it is" (Booth 14).

Linda Williams (1998) identifies five qualities that are central to the melodramatic mode that we can regard as being "objects" that can be discovered potentially in the experience of watching heist film melodrama. These are the presence of victim-heroes, the dialectic of pathos (suffering) and action (activity), the characterization of good and evil, a loss (of innocence) or tendency to look back, and being up-to-date in order to create moral legibility. *Perfect Friday*'s expression of playful self-interest around the pursuit of money is not framed by a melodramatic mode, but all the other heist films considered here are subjectively melodramatic. *Bellman and True* is classic heist film melodrama in this regard. Hiller's suffering is pathetic until he finally takes action as a "good" father resisting the "evil" thieves. His broken situation governed by "Sod's Law" is the "world as it is rather than as it should be." *The Bank Job* is up-to-date in adding a central female character, Martine Love (Saffron Burrows), as part of the gang. Terry, as a victim-hero, manages to restore his own broken family relationships and actively help bring the corrupt policemen and gangster to justice so that the "world can be as it should be." Ray in *Face* and Gal in *Sexy Beast* are also victim-heroes. Ray's loss is of a sense of purpose in his past world that can be restored only through love. Gal loses his present "things as they should be" when he is visited by Don as the embodiment of "how things are." The film expresses a nostalgic tendency of looking back at the classic conception of London gangland in the 1960s and 1970s, but its glossy style is updated with the feel of the latest advertising and music video.

Further phenomenological reflections upon the aesthetic experience of heist films are possible through the existential phenomenology variant. In contrast to transcendental phenomenology's concern with everyday experience in order to gain insight about its underlying order, structure, and coherence, existential phenomenology is more interested in concrete human existence or the experience of free choice or actions in concrete situations in order to move enquiry away from thought as consciousness of something. Existential phenomenologists such as Maurice Merleau-Ponty shift the constitution of meaning in human experience to the foundational role of perception in this process. Merleau-Ponty's particular emphasis on the body (through embodiment or the "body-subject" and "body-object") and on perception has been influential in film theory and phenomenology (Sobchack; Barker).

The Heist Film and "the Tactile Eye"

Vivian Sobchack's *The Address of the Eye* (1992) gives us a very theoretical explication of film and existential phenomenology. Sobchack stresses the tactile, communicative act of viewing of two bodily objects (human bodies and "film bodies"), an exchange of perception and expression as a perceptive material and plural encounter between two bodies. This notion of a tactile, embodied encounter between the film and viewer is developed more illustratively by Jennifer Barker in *The Tactile Eye* (2009) through a series of textural "handlings" rather than textual "readings" of exemplary films. Barker, staying closer to the existential phenomenology of Merleau-Ponty, shifts attention to a much more visceral encounter between film and viewer where meaning and emotion do not reside in films or viewers but emerge "in the intimate, tactile encounter between them" (15).

The key perspective of film and existential phenomenology is that attention must be given not just to the film and the objects intended in its perception and expression but to the conscious act in which it is perceived. Both the structure of the object and the subjective act of our own looking must be examined together "with the understanding that they cannot exist separately" (Barker 17). For Sobchack the act of viewing is the "address of the eye" that "links the spectator *of* a film and the film *as* spectator" (129). The film experience is more than a representation constituted by the viewer, it is an encounter between "the film's lived-body" and the spectator's uniquely situated and embodied existence (308), "an *object of vision*, an *act of viewing*, and a *subject of vision* in a dynamic and transitive correlation" (49). A film is "at the same time a *subject* of experience and an *object for* experience, an active participant of both perception and expression" (Barker 8).

The fundamental conception here is that the film is also a "body," "a concrete but distinctly cinematic lived-body, neither equated to nor encompassing the viewer's or filmmaker's body, but engaged with both of these even as it takes up its own intentional projects in the world" (Barker 7–8).

The spectator and film are mutually engaged in intentional acts of perception and expression, but differently enacted. Film is "perception and expression in motion" (Barker 8), where what we see is *the film seeing: we see its own (if humanly enabled) process of perception and expression unfolding in space and time"* (Barker 9).

Barker's particular take on the existential phenomenology of film as "the tactile eye" is to conceive of a cinematic experience where degrees of "touch" are part of the intersubjectivity and coconstitution of the biological human body and the technologized film body "entangled" together and not rigidly opposed as subject and object positioned on opposite sides of the screen. In the liminal space created in this mutual experience of seeing and being seen, "we are inside the film and outside at the same time" (Barker 160), not sutured but "caught up in a constant oscillation, drawn like a thread back and forth, through the fabric of the film experience" (161). Barker suggests that cinema "in-spires" in situations in which film so captures our attention that reversibly we are drawn in by the film's body opening onto ours, inhaling us so that "we might even feel its pulse and breath as our own" (147).

Barker divides this "in-spirational" structure of cinematic experience in terms of the proximity of various parts of the human body to potential contact with the film's body in three categories—"skin," "musculature," and "viscera"—in order to reflect on "the tactile and tangible patterns and structures of significance" (25) and shift attention from "gaze" to "touch." The first level of contact is "skin to skin." The film's "skin" can consist of technical, stylistic, and thematic elements that amalgamate as perceptive and expressive parts that present a material presence of the image in the form of a "haptic visuality" as "a kind of looking that lingers on the surface of the image rather than delving into depth and is more concerned with texture than with deep space" (35), a "first contact" with the film's style (its external structure) and our own external surface.

"Musculature" coconstitution refers to such things as body language, comportment, gesture, motion, and physicality where we move *with* the film's body while being in two places at once, a cohabitation of "here and there," body and image. This is not so much identification with characters as "kinaesthetic empathy," such that in action films, for instance, we are driven by a need "to act, to move, to *do something*," and, "whether the narrative goal is a bank heist or a risky rescue, the primary impetus in both the film's body and our own is to *move*" (Barker 109).

Finally, "viscera" refers to the vital internal organs and the experience of gut reactions, feelings, emotions, or intuition when cinema "gives us a feel for our own deep rhythms, reminding us what we're made of" (Barker 129). In particular, Barker highlights continuity and intermittence, stillness and motion in reference to both the illusion upon which cinema lives and the vital rhythms of our own mortality, which are grasped by our visceral bodies—"with every breath the perpetual possibility of stillness and death" (144).

It is worth at this point comparing Barker's "tactile eye" with Boorstin's "Hollywood eye" to draw out the difference between pragmatic and phenomenological approaches to film experience. Boorstin considers the properties of a successful film text that can produce certain audience effects in a causal relationship constructed by the formal properties of a film. This is based on a simple differentiation between the film as an object and the viewer as a subject. In contrast, Barker posits multiple subject-object relations in which the experience on the part of the human body and film's body enables "us not only to see but also to feel the film as an embodied subject who is like us but also different in fundamental ways" (145). Accordingly, Barker's "skin," "musculature," and "viscera" do not map straightforwardly onto Boorstin's voyeuristic, vicarious, and visceral pleasures in the text. "Skin" could be associated with "the voyeur's eye" where there is wondrous or novel curiosity engaging the viewer in the materiality of surface texture of a film, but "the voyeur's eye" is more an appeal to the "head" than to the intimate haptic visuality Barker experiences in the surface materiality of the image.

Similarly, Barker's "musculature" could be aligned with "the visceral eye," but Boorstin's bodily sensation of thrill, joy, or action cannot be entirely equated with the "muscular empathy" or "sensual understanding" in muscular terms that doubly situates the viewer in two places at once, moving *with* the film's body. Nor is this sensation similar to the empathetic identification with characters of Boorstin's "vicarious eye." Again, Barker's "viscera" might be associated with the emotional "inner space" of "the vicarious eye" and more directly with the sensual aspects of "how a film gets you" in relation to "the visceral eye," but Barker's stress on the act of viewing as the experience of two bodies reminding ourselves of what we are made of (129) is unlike merely experiencing the world vicariously or being sensually manipulated by film.

Perfect Friday holds us at a distance, trying to maintain a gap between the viewer and the film's body. The characters are on display or in disguise, frequently stilted in framing and lack of movement, comported, framed, and settled. In the absence of eliciting a strong sense of gut reaction, feelings, or emotions, *Perfect Friday* is a film of mainly skin-to-skin tactility of surface textures. The occasional freeze-frames are so momentary that they could be glitches rather than deliberate motion interrupted by stillness. These seconds of stasis do not operate in relation to the vital rhythms of visceral bodies but more as part of the expressive stylistic surface of the film's "skin," such as the postcoital embraces between Britt and Nick and Britt and Graham, especially—and the way that the actors are positioned and choreographed within the setting. For instance, in the opening sequences at the museum when Nick and Graham are posed between barred gates or wired sculptures, and also when the three managers are aligned in (un)harmonic hierarchies of seniority in their glass office boxes.

In contrast, *The Bank Job* lacks any great sense of being "in-spired" by surface texture or style, or indeed with any of the three aspects of Barker's "tactile eye." Its "skin" is limited to a concern for creating a convincing sense of period accuracy channeled into sets, costume, wigs, and pop music. The film also falls short on high levels of kinesthetic empathy typical of "musculature" connection with bodily movement. In a situation where the gang are imperiled simultaneously by operatives from the intelligence services and a desperate porn racketeer and his corrupt police associates, there is a disappointing lack of a sense of anticipation about their fate or relief at their extrication from the danger. We are not offered any vital rhythms of falling between being boxed in or blunted and liberated, as one would expect from the setup of the film's heist.

Similarly, *Bellman and True* has little surface texture or style with which to be touched, but it is multifaceted in terms of touching, handling, and bodily empathy, linking "skin" to "musculature." Hiller relieves his anxiety and pain through whisky, and he is constantly reaching for the comfort of the bottle, whose contents dull his senses and stop his hands from shaking. This is essential for his technical skills to be utilized in the robbery and so give him any chance of being released by the gang. Hiller's mastery of technology and his dexterity in making devices is an area of bodily function where he can potentially excel and ultimately free himself with an improvised bomb fashioned from a gas canister. However, Hiller's body is also vulnerable to the violence of tormentors who cut and assault him on numerous occasions. His body lets him down when he soils himself in response to one particular assault. There is a great deal of bodily jeopardy. Gang member Gort (Ken Bones) is fatally injured during the heist when he can't outclimb the rising lift in the shaft, and an excessive use of force during the escape leads to the death of one of the guards. Most tactile of all, perhaps, is the vital rhythm of the anticipation and expectation that bad things will happen according to "Sod's Law," to which Hiller often refers in his stories and conversations with the boy. Accordingly, we grasp the implication of being mocked by fate, so that at any moment the illusion of our "robust vitality" can be exposed by things going wrong.

At times *Face* has a tactile surface texture created by low-contrast lighting in night and interior scenes. In the opening sequence, the lights of a tunnel zip over the bodywork of Ray's car as he drives to rob a drug dealer ahead of the heist itself. Limited tonal ranges of clothing of black, gray, and white mean that we have to search for definition in the surface of the screen. Ray touches Connie, the men grab their weapons, and for the heist they dress in counterpoint bright custard yellow boiler suits so that they can easily see each other in the gloom and under the strip lighting. The gang move confidently through the city, physically handling guns and their fists. There is a visceral sense of control and then loss of control; the power and vulnerability of the body is a visceral rhythm. Ray's inner turmoil is textured through a slow-motion subjective recollection of his protest past juxtaposed with the speeded-up sensation of his gun battle in the present.

As *Sexy Beast* makes contact with us in the opening sequence, we are pointed at Gal, who is nearly all skin, roasting, sweaty skin at the poolside. A bird's-eye view flattens his body against the bright white floor where he is lying. Skin touches hard surface, hands cradle drinks and cigarettes. A huge boulder falls from the hillside above the pool, narrowly missing Gal as it plunges into the water. In the heat, Gal moves around slowly, whereas more muscularly Don sweeps in, the "second boulder" that nearly kills Gal, a force of nature who urinates hands free, allowing his "piss" to touch the pristine bathroom floor. The vital rhythms of the life and death of the heist are slow and fast motion. Slowness is the love of an embrace, a heart-shaped smoke ring blown from Gal to Deedee as she moves in slow motion toward him, while the quickening of time is the viscera of the rapid heartbeat of approaching death.

Conclusion: The Heist Film and Embodiment

Jennifer Barker (7) asks how films can be said to be like bodies. This is clearly an important question for film and phenomenology, particularly for the existential variant. Barker dismisses the symbolism of the Vertovian "kino-glaz" (film-eye) in this regard, but Dziga Vertov's conception of a "mechanical eye" facilitates a further and closing discussion of the aesthetic experience of film and phenomenology. Vertov's "film-eye" is by analogy partly an embodied device, but also an idea about an anthropomorphic object underpinning a manifesto about political filmmaking. Kino-glaz is neither a theoretical nor a pragmatic analysis of the experience of making and viewing films but more a fetishizing of a device capable of delivering the expression of perception of the world as truth ("pravda").

However, phenomenologically, the "embodied vision" of film is not merely anthropomorphic prosthesis or cinematic apparatus, and the "film-eye" offers less (in relation to taste, smell, and limited field of vision, for instance) as well as more (such as the use of close-ups) in relation to the direct lived-body engagement with phenomena. As discussed earlier, the film's body is a "technologically mediated consciousness of experience" (Sobchack 168) realized primarily through sight, but amplifying "the tactile capacity of the filmmaker's vision, his or her eyes through the camera informed by a capacity to touch the world, to intend *texture* through this machine-mediated vision" (Sobchack 185).

In a film experience, the film and viewer are simultaneously both subjects and objects—the film and viewer see and are seen in a process of "being seeing," "seeing being," and "being seen" (Sobchack). Barker's *The Tactile Eye* is an unconventional conceptualization of a cinematic experience where degrees of "touch" are part of the entanglement of human and film bodies. As such, Barker's framework is very helpful for reflecting upon a film experience as being more than just a representation constituted by the viewer. A film as an aesthetic experience is one in which the spectator and film, as differently enacted bodies, are jointly occupied in purposeful acts of perception and expression, and this in terms of phenomenology is "how a film works."

As a concluding note on films as bodies, I offer some final thoughts about heist films not just as being embodied but as being enworlded as particular types of persons. For me, *Perfect Friday* is perhaps a television sports presenter hosting the game in which the rules, according to Graham, are "freedom equals money." *The Bank Job* is a journalist on a popular newspaper supplying us with enough well-written facts and titillating revelation to be convincing about the indiscretions and misdemeanors of the past. *Bellman and True* is a teller of folk tales, spinning a story in which the hero is visited by the "big, bad thieves," and "Sod's Law" mocks *almost* his every turn, since happy endings are always possible and desired. *Face* has to be an earnest socialist activist clinging to the hope and belief that the flow of money and power can be diverted to those in need. Finally, *Sexy Beast* is a professional thief, an "old lag" who has been in and out of prison, a "face" in a former time, but now possibly a bit of a celebrity. As his head lies on the pillow at night, he dreams about what might have been if things had been different, the nightmarish times when the "hare-man" came looking for him and the "good times" when the thieves' farewell of "be lucky" touched his heart, and that is why *Sexy Beast* "works" for me and "through" me in Barker's sense of "in-spiration." *Sexy Beast* creates a satisfying aesthetic experience grounded in the cultural verisimilitude of professional crime. It entangles me as both a subject who sees and an object who is seen by the film, which is also both a subject ("the dreamer") and an object ("the dream") so that I feel truly "touched" by the experience.

The *Galerie Imaginaire* of Steven Soderbergh's *Ocean's* Trilogy

Modernist Painting in the Contemporary Heist Film

◇◇◇◇◇◇◇◇◇◇◇◇◇◇◇◇◇◇◇◇◇◇

Daryl Lee

Heist films may be read as aesthetic parables of creative processes and failures. They foreground rule-breaking bravado, imaginative problem solving, balletic physicality, technological ingenuity, and poetic redirections of people, instruments, and behavior for criminal ends. Here the heist allegorizes the aesthetic through criminal activity itself—the crime *is* the work of art. More literally, however, how and why might the heist thematize aesthetic experience or the history or work of art? After all, while thieves in heist movies rob banks, armored cars, casinos, racetracks, diamond exchanges, and villas for cash, gold, precious stones, jewelry, and investment instruments, their intentions for stealing or surrounding themselves with works of art may go beyond the object's exchange value. Such is the case in *The Good Thief* (2002), Neil Jordan's adaptation of Jean-Pierre Melville's *Bob le flambeur/Bob the Gambler* (1956). Bob (Nick Nolte) plans to rob a Monte Carlo casino of its paintings. The director says that Bob—a "good" thief who takes Picasso to be the "best" of them all for his deft borrowings from an Ingres or Velasque—"admires the thievery of imagery and influence, and putting them together to make something new" (Fuchs). What are we to make of a criminal subgenre that revels in stealing other forms of visual art, that, like Bob, values the "thievery of imagery and influence"?

If works of art from virtually every period and place are pinched in heist films, it would seem that the heist of late has constructed a special relation to modernist painting. I have in mind the Cezannes, Gauguins,

Klimts, Manets, Modiglianis, Picassos, Renoirs, and Van Goghs that appear in post-1980s heists, such as John McTiernan's *The Thomas Crown Affair* (1999) or Steven Soderbergh's *Ocean's* films. What is the debt this subgenre apparently owes to modernism, this late-nineteenth- and twentieth-century critical rupture so "dismayed . . . with the cultural cheapening and creative decline of [its] era" (Adamson x)? Evidence for a bond to modernism writ large exists in the postwar emergence of the subgenre. Having learned from mingling in avant-garde circles, German exile Robert Siodmak exploited the powers of montage, expressionist set design, and alienating camera angles in his Hollywood studio films *The Killers* (1946) and *Criss Cross* (1949). Jean-Pierre Melville's eponymous hero in *Bob le Flambeur* lives in a painter's studio in Montmartre, a deft nod to one of the bohemian haunts of Belle Époque modernism and Picasso's Parisian home until 1912, a turning point in the history of cubism; Bob's protégé Paolo says that not everyone can live as an "artist" like Bob does. Alexandre Trauner's involvement in modernist circles—he was Jules Dassin's production designer for *Rififi/Du Rififi chez les hommes* (1955)—shows in the scene where the safecracker César (played by Dassin himself) dies in the prop room of the cabaret *L'Âge d'Or*, an allusion to Luis Bunuel's surrealist silent (featuring Dadaist-surrealist Max Ernst). Other props include a guitar that recalls Picasso's cubist period and a "bric-a-brac of surrealist" mannequins and masks (Rolls and Walker 155). From its inception, then, the heist film intimates a relationship to visual modernism, through its earliest practitioners and motifs.

The heist film, I maintain, is still entwined with aesthetic modernism, whether it knows it or not. The economic dimension at the heart of the heist film links it to a long-standing philosophical debate that revolves around a productive tension between commercial and autonomous aesthetic interests distilled in the broad cultural meaning of modernism. Yet many contemporary heists seem to have dismissed, dissimulated—or dis-*regarded*—this persistent tension. Postmodern pastiche and play, influence and theft in the remake, these are not enough to acknowledge this lineage or to explain modernist art's role when it turns up in the contemporary heist.

In fact, modernist painting may be a key to unlocking one of the heist film's recent cultural significations, its concern for the salience of art, even mass-produced, in a commercial context. How does modernist art function in the heist as one of many potent social issues the subgenre could address? To track the commercial-aesthetic relation in these moments, I will explore modernist painting in Steven Soderbergh's *Ocean's* trilogy, primarily in *Ocean's Eleven* (2001) and *Ocean's Twelve* (2004). The trilogy displays art other than European modernism, but Soderbergh intuits the subterranean link between the heist and modernism. Still, it's a relationship that is fraught with inter-arts rivalry and shaped by a historical distance from modernism's heyday—a rivalry that reverberates in the heist film's rivalry among thieves and in the form's conscious celebration of stealing from others, and that is actuated self-reflexively in moments where the heist film casts its gaze on modernism, sometimes quite literally by fixing the modernist work of art in its frame. Soderbergh's films have been subjected to film-based inter-textual analysis but less to questions of intermediality or remediation (see Baker 16–27; deWaard; Gallagher 168–93; and R. B. Palmer). I would argue, with an admittedly reductive twist on André Malraux's notion of the *musée imaginaire,* or "museum without walls," that in the *Ocean's* films Soderbergh creates a *galerie imaginaire*—a virtual cinematic gallery for market or private consumption that keeps its eyes trained primarily on modernist art (Allan 255–74).

My narrow focus on Soderbergh is a gamble, to be sure. But in a sense it's one Soderbergh initiated, having directed five heist films, from indie, low-budget works like *The Underneath* (1995) and *Out of Sight* (1998) to his high-concept studio blockbusters, the *Ocean's* films. Many directors have tried their hand at the heist at least once—Christopher Nolan, Barry Levinson, Spike Lee, Guy Ritchie, F. Gary Gray, David O. Russell, Tony Scott, Joel and Ethan Coen, David Mamet, Ben Affleck, and the list goes on—so the form is compelling as a malleable vehicle for addressing social questions of all sorts. But for a decade Soderbergh repeatedly drew from this same generic well. The heist has repeatedly allowed him to explore the very tension of his position as an independent and studio director bristling at studio constraint and seeking more freedom to make art. If, as Jon Lewis claims, what is increasingly "at stake in every major film release is less the merit of the picture as a work of art than its measurable value as a product" (87), then Soderbergh has conscientiously attempted to reset the balance, not only in his public denouncements of Hollywood but also in his art. This strain of the heist film matters because it narrates the very commodity structure that brings it into being, a move that reaches back beyond even midcentury conditions for its rationale.

Kant among the Thieves

The debate over economics in aesthetic modernism owes a crucial debt to the aftermath of Enlightenment aesthetics in the nineteenth century, namely, as it regards the heist film, to the celebration of the artist-criminal and the now-commonplace commercialization of art that incited the search for aesthetic autonomy in cultural production. The analogy of the artist as criminal arose in Enlightenment theories of art and nineteenth-century culture and situates the heist film within a larger field of reflection on the nature and role of artists in commodity culture (see Porter; Senelick; and Black). Denis Diderot, for example, confessed, "I don't hate great crimes, first because they make for great paintings and fine tragedies; and also because grand, sublime actions and great crimes have the same characteristic energy" (97). For the sake of hypothesis, let me suggest that the post-Kantian framing of the aesthetic and then subsequent market dynamics determined the heist film's incipient take on art and money when the subgenre was born on the heels of modernism. If Slavoj Žižek can talk of the "Kantian background of the Noir Subject" ("The Thing" 199), then here we can talk of a post-Kantian aesthetic economy in the heist film.

In *Critique of the Power of Judgment,* Kant argued that fine art was the product of genius, a "talent" for creating something that is wholly original and "exemplary," something for which there is "no definite rule" and that consequently eludes imitation (186). By organizing his theory around rule breaking, Kant opened subsequent art to critical evaluation and rivalry in terms of originality. By extension, this laid the groundwork for artistic rivalry between criminals; the genius distinguishes himself not by copying a model but by creating something original. At the very same time, the dissolution of "traditional hierarchies of pictorial types" (Prettejohn 49) that resulted from Kant's theory of taste also prepared the terrain not only for modernism disputing the claims of tradition but for high modernism itself being challenged by mass culture.

The heist film frequently involves the theft of fine art. Kant distinguished *fine art* from *handicraft* on the grounds that fine art is autonomous from economic incentive, the product of unrestrained activity or free play—something "agreeable in itself" (183); craft, on the other hand, is the disagreeable product of drudgery and labor and has its end only in economic compensation. Heist thieves want economic gain, but their endgame is always more complex and generally eludes mere monetary value. This post-Kantian dynamic gives the lie to Stuart Kaminsky's axiom that "the one essential element of big caper movies, the essential which defines them, is the plot concentration on the commission of a single crime of great monetary significance—a crime always directed at monetary gain, at least on the surface" (Kaminsky 76–77). Historically, Kant's dissociation of monetary from aesthetic interests would govern the search for artistic purity that began in the nineteenth century—compelling a retreat into the doctrine of art for art's sake and giving birth to the concept of aesthetic autonomy (Buchloh 23)—and fuel early modernism's vociferous reaction to commercial forces wreaking havoc on visual and literary markets.

Following Adamson (18), modernism's practitioners perceived a "civilizational crisis" born of commodity culture's expansion; they were convinced that modernity could be "reconfigured," and pursued a "self-consciously modern art" to resolve or ameliorate the crisis, sometimes through avant-garde activity. In its fullest array of cultural production and thought, modernism flourished in Europe in the first half of the twentieth century, but it gained currency with close ties to painting in the nineteenth century, in Baudelaire's critical essay "The Painter of Modern Life" and in Manet's "painting of modern life" (Clark). The rupture with a classical *cinema* encompasses distinct "screen" (Kovács), "film" (Rohdie), or "cinematic" (McCabe) modernisms that also critique commodity culture and engage with medium specificity, reflexivity, unconventional narrational strategies, and montage. And Miriam Bratu Hansen has taught us to expand the reach of American formulations of modernism into the transcultural "vernacular modernism" afforded by Hollywood (332): "the juncture of classical cinema and modernity . . . [was] the single most inclusive, cultural horizon in which the traumatic effects of modernity were reflected, rejected or disavowed, transmuted or negotiated" (334). In a narrower sense, Bordwell and Thompson present film modernism as a reaction to mainstream Hollywood (412), which makes it structurally homologous to how I am reading Soderbergh as an independent and auteur attentive to crises of "global capital" (deWaard and Tait 131).

As I have argued elsewhere, one function of the heist film came to be its exploration of aesthetic value within the context of capitalistic structures (Lee 10). In one of its key formulations as a social issues film, the heist film operates as an aesthetic parable of sorts, setting up hierarchies of the criminal-artist, lauding creativity, and allegorizing processes of artistic creation in the narrative structure of the planning and execution of a major robbery. As a self-reflexive, vernacular modernism and mass-market wish fulfilment that frequently thematizes art and its spaces of exhibition, the heist film is uniquely situated to tell us about the postwar modernist residue to which I am referring. The subgenre formulates a myth very much inspired by modernist preoccupations in which fine art and economic interests are set in relation to each other—often as opposing values, yet just as often in subtle cooperation with each other. This has always been at the heart of modernism and it reappears in the heist film. "Even the most contestatory positions," Adamson writes of high modernism, "will not be wholly antagonistic to the modern institution of art, since those engaged in them are necessarily also self-interested (and often actively self-promoting) players within the mainstream practices of the institution, which of course include the production for sale of works of art" (19).

Contemporary Hollywood heists know they can "get away with" (see Soderbergh and Lester) making money as part of the culture industry while reinscribing the hierarchy of aesthetic autonomy over commercial corrosion— it's all part of the "commerce of auteurism," as Timothy Corrigan identified it (101). Hollywood has exploited one of cinema's modernist moves, using the auteur as "a *commercial* strategy for organizing audience reception, as a critical concept bound to distribution and marketing aims" that creates the "cult status of an auteur" (Corrigan 103; Corrigan's emphasis). Soderbergh, whom Corrigan identifies as an "auteur of commerce," is acutely aware of this tension or dilemma, which became a singular focus in his "State of the Cinema" talk at the Fifty-Sixth San Francisco International Film Festival. The speech may declaim how money is increasingly destructive for film art, but taken in the context of the long-term debates around aesthetic modernism, it comes across as part of the choreographed dance, the ritual of modernist aesthetic economy. DeWaard and Tait defend Soderbergh by arguing the director has managed his celebrity status to gain capital within the industry while breaking barriers for "commercially unfriendly subject matter" (46–47)—he can be both an "indie impresario" (37) and a "corporate revolutionary" (57). My purpose here is not to resolve this open debate over Soderbergh's auteur status, but I do hope to use his films to reconnect the heist film to aesthetic modernism.

Cinema and Painting in Soderbergh's *Ocean's* Trilogy

Filmmakers avail themselves of paintings in their mise-en-scène and cinematography, from their use as props to inspiration for set design, color composition, or framing. Angela Dalle Vacche writes that "the history of art is *in* film, even though, by evoking high art and creativity, rather than technology and mass culture, painting for the cinema constitutes a forbidden object of desire" (1). Since films "meditate on what is at stake in the encounter between painting and cinema, art and technology, tradition and modernity" (Dalle Vacche 3), the prominence of modernist artwork in all three of Soderbergh's *Ocean's* trilogy cannot be accidental or overlooked.

Their semiotic, social, economic, and other functions deserve attention as potentialities built into the subgenre.

We encounter a predilection for modern visual art from France in an *Ocean's Eleven* montage set in the fictive Bellagio gallery and again in an *Ocean's Twelve* montage of the private art collection of rival thief François Toulour (Vincent Cassel), aka the Night Fox. The relation of painting to the marketplace and the flow of capital among the elite is surely part of Soderbergh's intentions. The films tackle high stakes as a "utopian allegory of America" in the early part of the first decade of the twenty-first century, in which social values need to be "renegotiated in the face of globalized and multinational business practices" (deWaard and Tait 132). What happens in the Las Vegas of the *Ocean's* films doesn't just stay there; it's emblematic of socioeconomic trends affecting the entire globe. For deWaard and Tait, Soderbergh's critique of capital envisions a world with a "different set of moral and monetary rewards" (133–34). These first two films allegorize a complex global economic landscape marked by "competing" modes of capital (deWaard and Tait 132), and *Ocean's Thirteen* (2007) wraps them up by expressing nostalgia for a postwar "modern (American) capital" betrayed by its "postmodern and globalized counterpart" (deWaard and Tait 137). The utopian alternatives function on an interpersonal level—the films celebrate the solidarity and friendship of the crew and the love of Danny and Tess—and on an institutional level in *Ocean's Thirteen*, by advocating "philanthropy, corporate responsibility, and the redistribution of wealth" (deWaard and Tait 132). The members of Ocean's team labor together to create a community in opposition to globalized finance. Although global flows of people and capital have changed quantitatively and qualitatively since the prewar zenith of aesthetic modernism, Soderbergh's utopian revaluation nevertheless sounds strikingly resonant with modernism's sense of civilizational crisis and the conviction that a self-conscious art widening its appeal to a larger audience could reconfigure the values necessary for alleviating the crisis.

I would like to reintroduce the aesthetic into the value equation in terms consistent with deWaard and Tait's analysis of capital in the *Ocean's* trilogy. The films associate fine art with Terry Benedict (Andy Garcia) and Toulour, though not unambiguously—Ocean's team seems indifferent to art but Tess, the object of Danny's (George Clooney's) intentions, stands in for fine art. (When we first see Tess [Julia Roberts], Linus [Matt Damon] says she comes from "that museum [in the Bellagio], she's a curator.") What is the economy of exchange between Soderbergh's cinema and painting? Do the films establish a relation of admiration or condescension, of adoration or dismissal—are they "plagued by a cultural inferiority complex" or are they "self-confident enough to move beyond this state of dependency" (Dalle Vacche 3)? Do they classify painting as fine art in opposition to their own status as "popular culture or industrial technology" (Dalle Vacche 2) or do they meld into a mutually supportive and integrated modern iconography? Dalle Vacche explains the "collusion" between cinema and painting that dissolves traditional hierarchies: "By blurring the distinction between high art and popular culture, the cinema has always had a tendency to challenge not just painting in isolation but rather the whole system of the arts, thus disclosing the possibility of new configurations, hierarchies, alliances, and hostilities" (3). Naturally, for a critically self-aware auteur such as Soderbergh, these questions play into the way films define themselves in relation to other arts. What comes of this particular challenge or alliance between the (heist) film and painting is less a direct engagement with pictorial possibilities and more a reflection on value, aesthetic and commercial, and on institutional credibility.

Montage and Cubist Portraiture in *Ocean's Eleven*

The central robbery sequence in *Ocean's Eleven* involves footage surreptitiously fed through Terry Benedict's closed-circuit surveillance system. That footage, a montage of sorts, portrays Ocean's team breaking into the vault—from a soundstage built adjacent to the Bellagio and to the exact specifications of the actual vault. Benedict, thinking his vault has already been breached, lets the team waltz in, disguised as a SWAT unit, to take the gold at their leisure. In other words, Danny Ocean pulls his job off as a filmmaker, the director of an elaborate set piece—a stand-in for the film creator, if not Soderbergh himself. Danny's visual creation serves two purposes. Ocean not only profits from Benedict buying the illusion of the staged theft, he also reclaims Tess's heart with a kind of digital realism: he broadcasts a confidential conversation with Benedict regarding Tess through the hotel feed to show her that Benedict is willing to sacrifice her to recover his money. Danny's dual motives—coming not only to steal money but to use the theft itself to win back his ex-wife—have already led an exasperated Rusty (Brad Pitt) to say, "Now we're stealing two things!" This duality—Tess and money—condenses the aesthetic-commercial pair I raised earlier in ways that directly link to modernist painting.

Ocean's Eleven pays its debt to aesthetic modernism in a montage of Tess and Benedict in the Bellagio gallery, a space where art is exposed for contemplation but also circulates as a commodity in the marketplace. The brief scene (1'02") is, as it should be, about visual contemplation and observation, seeing and the gaze, with an impressionist Renoir, a postimpressionist Cézanne, and, centrally, a cubist Picasso in view. The montage consists of three parts: Tess looking at a painting and its purchase, without diegetic sound; Tess and Benedict discussing the painting in shot/reverse shot; Benedict walking away through the gallery in far shot. The first shot frames Tess in a medium shot, posed sculpturally in an Asian coat, tightly buttoned to her neck with hair tightly pulled back. She is looking offscreen in a slow reverse tracking shot. As the frame recedes, she's staring past the spectator (at the painting, it turns out). There is no diegetic sound yet, only David Holmes's sleek jazz overlay, favoring Tess's internal disposition as she focuses intently on the painting. We cut to a tracking shot moving toward the canvas, as if a POV shot, until the widescreen frame cuts off the top and bottom of the vertical canvas. Benedict arrives and shakes hands with a man, implying a transaction for the painting (and still no diegetic sound). Then a cut shifts the axis of action to a view well behind Tess and Benedict as they both contemplate the painting, a bust separating them in the frame and blocking the painting. Only then does the dialogue ensue: the cubist portrait pleases Tess, but for Benedict, it is merely an object to be bought or sold. In their shot/reverse-shot conversation, two paintings frame Tess and self-reflexively evoke elements of the heist: Renoir's *Acrobats at the Cirque Fernando* (1879, oil on canvas, Art Institute of Chicago) and a Cézanne from the painter's series, *The Card Players* (early 1890s, oil on canvas, Musée). Cézanne's image of gaming complements the casino context in which Ocean's "play" against Benedict will take place, while Renoir's anticipates the acrobatics the "Greaseman" Yen (Shaobo Qin) was required to do in order to pull off the caper. The dialogue ends with Benedict turning down Tess's kiss because a surveillance camera is recording their interaction.

The Tess/Picasso montage concludes a series of segments with her as the object of narrative causality, after Linus and Rusty watch her descend the stairs, and then Rusty complains to Danny when he finds out that the heist is not about the money but Tess. This sequence is thus organized around Tess, looking at her descending the staircase as an object of the gaze no less than the painting, talking about her as an aesthetic object (Danny: "How'd she look?" Rusty: "She looked good!"), then looking at her looking at the painting. Tess is thus aestheticized in the dialogue and the staging: she stands inert, like a statue, her steely monochromatic suit making her statuesque. The film feminizes the aesthetic while maintaining two registers

Tess (Julia Roberts) and Terry Benedict (Andy Garcia) contemplate Picasso's *Woman with a Guitar* in *Ocean's Eleven*.

of masculinity: Tess is the object of the rivalry, a commodity for Benedict, an object of love and metonymically (as a curator) of aesthetic attraction for Danny, a living work of art.

Picasso's cubist canvas *Woman with a Guitar* (1914, oil, sand, and charcoal on canvas, Museum of Modern Art) provides little mimetic pictorial inspiration to the montage or film at large. Instead, the editing and mobile frame draw a generic parallel between Picasso's portrait and the film's own cinematic portraiture. As with Picasso's many cubist paintings of bodies (Karmel 49–97), *Woman* presents the body as overlapping colored strips and superimposed transparent planes. Muted, seemingly unfinished, the portrait's color palette includes blue, blue-gray, red dots, green, browns, and black matches, with undulating parallel black bars—*un*like the erotic palettes and curvilinear features of his *Woman with Chemise in an Armchair* (1913), painted only months before (Karmel 92–95). The painting hints at the ubiquitous guitar (and violin) of the period of the painter's "rupture" with his own preceding cubist work that, with the help of Braque, ushered in a new "cubist semiology" (Bois 187). Though not a papier collé—the pasted paper, ink, integrated newsprint, and charcoal of his most radical cubist collages—it does incorporate flatness, geometric abstraction, and Cyrillic text, and deploys bold textural experiments with sand and charcoal like his works in the fall of 1912. Cubist flatness is no model for the film, generally, or the Tess/Picasso montage, which conveys depth of field by the twin tracking shots and the sharp foreground focus that accentuates the planes. On the other hand, the effect of the long shot of Tess and Benedict looking at the painting, taken from the surface of a table, is of a blurred, oblique plane that occupies the lower half the frame. If anything, it recalls Cézanne's practice of *passage*, a brushstroke used by Picasso, Braque, and others to "ease and disguise the transition from shallow to deep space in a picture, or to soften the contour boundary between solid and space" (Cottington 21). There is a play in volume and geometric shapes abutting each other, blending at the upper edge of the table because of the reflection off its polished surface, but the result is depth instead of flatness.

Nor are the reduced representational qualities typical of cubist painting of interest to the film. Production designer Philip Messina (with another regular Soderbergh collaborator, set decorator Kristen Toscano Messina) created a space rife with impressionist painting and modernist sculpture in their fictional gallery. But it was screenwriter Ted Griffin who selected *Woman with a Guitar* for the scene. Griffin recounts in an extra on the DVD that he had "looked up some Picasso paintings on the internet . . . and just saw the title of it, *Woman with a guitar*, and thought, okay, it's a painting of a woman, [Tess and Benedict] can comment on it. And then I saw it and I thought, oh!" Presumably Griffin was expecting something more representational and straightforwardly feminine.

Soderbergh's cinema does not toy with cubist semiology, where word, image, and object had combined in new ways that challenged the spectators of early modernist art. For one thing, the *Ocean's* films are high-concept studio work intended for a mainstream audience—the emphasis is on character (star appeal) and narrative. In this sense, the "rhythm and release" of the Tess/Picasso montage matches David Bordwell's definition of montage as a "highly overt mark" (49) of narrative summary that tames by converting "dramatic and visual patterns into an intelligible story" (16). Soderbergh does experiment within his mainstream films. The *Ocean's* films, for example, enjoy "aberrant scenes of unexpected delirium" (deWaard and Tait 16, 19). In their scale of Soderbergh's stylistic departures from classicism, deWaard and Tait discriminate between what they call "chaotic" elements—such as "stunted framing, handheld camera and digital video, non-linear and jarring editing, witty postmodern banter"—and "paradoxical" ones that emphasize highly "reflexive" and "modular" editing, "hyperbolic" performances, and independent production practices (17–19). Nevertheless, here montage is brought to heel, absorbed into contemporary Hollywood storytelling.

Still, deWaard and Tait's singling out of Soderbergh's aesthetic of "mo-saic" and "collage"—an allusion to cubism's innovation between 1912 and 1914, the very period of *Woman with a Guitar*—based in his experiments encompassing "raw" camera work, coordinated visual textures and color palettes, and postproduction frame manipulations, calls for some comment. Soderberghian "collage" represents no equivalent cinematic rupture in his high-concept studio fare; his innovation is in some sense a composite effect of introducing "guerilla" practices into mainstream fare. Soderbergh him-self believes that little innovation in the cinema has occurred since the late 1970s or so, with the exception, perhaps, of Godard's films in the 1980s. But, says Soderbergh, with an unmistakable reference to painting as less costly than filmmaking, "what's the audience for that? Like, how many people are interested in watching somebody make that attempt? This is not an inex-pensive hobby—it's not something that you make and then hang on your wall. It's a public artform" ("In Conversation with Steven Soderbergh"). The director understands intimately the aesthetic-economic tension, which becomes an emblem in his high-concept heists, just as he is aware of the "substantial viewer distance" provoked by a Godard or a Resnais (Gallagher 62)—not unlike that of cubism in its day. But he doesn't resolve the aes-thetic challenge of modernism: "I'm frustrated by my own inability to break through to somewhere else" ("In Conversation"). The problem may result from the simultaneous "stimulation and intimidation" that comes with a profound sense of "belatedness," of arriving late to a party at which most of the tricks modernism already invented—not merely in terms of cinema, as Bordwell is addressing (23), but also in terms of a long-duration engage-ment with visual modernism dating to the invention of cinema itself. The belated arrival proves critical for Soderbergh's relation to film.

Unlike Soderbergh's film intertexuality, the *Eleven* montage leans more on the cult value of modernist art in popular culture than on drawing pic-torial inspiration from it. Modernism's role as a rare commodity in high-end art markets and public auctions figures in the scenario. Filmmaking, as Soderbergh says, is not an "inexpensive hobby"—yet Benedict invests in a Picasso and hangs it on his gallery wall precisely because of its spec-tacular market value. (In *Ocean's Thirteen*, Gustav Klimt's *Portrait of Adele Bloch-Bauer I* hangs in Benedict's office [1907, oil on canvas, private col-lection but displayed in the Neue Art Gallery, New York]; it sold in 2007 for $135 million, then the highest auction price paid for a painting.) More-over, the filmmaker resigns himself to referring to the cubist period that marked a break in the history of painting without itself breaking with the commodity structure of film in the cultural context of the first decade of the twenty-first century. To put it as Kovács might, the film recognizes that "modernism as an *ideological project* belongs to a historical moment in the past" (45; Kovács's emphasis). Only Tess seems interested in looking at the Picasso in a contemplative mode. Significantly, in the parallel tracking shots of Tess and the painting we contemplate the painting and Tess, engaging, however briefly, with both cubist and cinematic portraiture. In sum, the Tess sequence simultaneously stages exhibition value (the gallery), barters in exchange value (the handshake transaction), hints at aesthetic value (Tess contemplating the painting), and cues a cult value (cubist modernism) that reinscribes aura in contemporary mass culture. Like Bob in Jordan's *The Good Thief*, Soderbergh relishes the thievery of imagery and influence—the prerogative of the heist film.

Ocean's Twelve: Montage as Disappearing Act?

Soderbergh's dynamic approach to montage may still fit with the spirit of how the avant-garde generally favored an aesthetic that dissuaded contemplation. This seems true when the director once again turns to montage in *Ocean's Twelve* to link his film to modernist painting. In truth, the montage I'm referring to is rather brief and ancillary to the plot. In *Twelve*, Benedict has tracked down Ocean's crew and wants his money back. In order to repay the money they stole, they will have to steal it back. Meanwhile, a rival thief, François Toulour (Vincent Cassell), knowing their predicament, proposes a challenge. He and Ocean's team can face off in a competition to steal the Fabergé Coronation Egg from a museum in Rome. If Ocean wins, Toulour will pay their debt to Benedict. If not, they will pay the consequences of their inferiority. Since both Toulour and Danny were trained by the master thief Lemarque, competing to steal the same object appears to be the only reasonable way to determine which thief is best. The first such competition heist is for a valuable rare document held by a collector in Amsterdam; Toulour steals the document from under their noses to announce the game. In retaliation, Ocean's crew nick several of Toulour's paintings from his luxurious Lago Maggiore villa. The main heist is a simulacrum in at least three senses: the apparent plan is to substitute a hologram of the (golden) egg, using Tess playing the Julia Roberts persona as a diversionary tactic in the gallery where it's exhibited. Toulour betrays Ocean's team to the police, who take them into custody, and assumes the egg is his to take. But it's all a sham, because the team let themselves be caught—the real egg had already

Edgar Degas, *Blue Dancers*, ca. 1899.
(Courtesy of Pushkin Museum,
Moscow, Russia / Bridgeman Images)

been stolen from the beginning, as revealed in a deus—or fur—ex machina montage that rounds out the film. The frustrating climax, then, reveals that the central robbery was never to be the most important theft; the film had always intended to misdirect our attention.

In that spirit, I would suggest that while the first two thefts seem narratively inconsequential, generically speaking they are much more important. In the first, the document to be stolen is a rare (and fictional) stock certificate, historically "the first ever issued." The document no longer has currency—it cannot be cashed in. But it does have value to collectors and historians, because, symbolically, it launched a new form of capitalism. Thus the document has little value within the very system it brought into being and yet bears an extravagant value outside of it. Here, in this play of competing value systems, the heist film evokes the importance of alternative value systems (social, sacred, amorous) to mere capitalist or exchange value. In this sense it relates to the questions I have thus far raised, including that of the supposed devaluation of the aesthetic in commercial culture, and thus subtly ties to the second rivalry theft of Toulour's art collection—another set of objects whose values defy classical utility in the name of aesthetic, cult, or cultural value.

Among Toulour's paintings that go missing is a prized Degas pastel, "my *Blue Dancers*," he laments. The clever, kinetic montage building up the prowess of Toulour, voiced over by Danny and overlain with the French psych rock *Dynastie Crisis*'s song "Faust 72," paints the gentleman thief as a worthy rival. Toulour's criminal résumé and lifestyle are sutured together in an ambiguous time frame with references to his thefts at the Louvre, Tate, and Prado. Rapidly cut images of his playboy lifestyle don't match the narration with any certainty until the end, when the montage shows Toulour walking through his villa as the voice-over claims the Ocean team will steal his art, just as Toulour discovers the frames emptied of his most precious canvases.

The compositional aspects of Degas's *Blue Dancers* (c. 1899, pastel on paper, Pushkin Museum, Moscow) were based on three individual photographs the painter took, experimenting with the medium, during a short period between 1895 and 1896. Degas quickly abandoned his interest in photography, but the images he created from this brief interlude influenced several important works in the late 1890s, including his bold *Four Dancers* and the luminescent *Blue Dancers*, a composite image overlapping the pastel renderings of three photographed models into a single frame (Kendall and Devonyar 192, 197). It's hard not to contrast Degas's uneasiness behind the camera with Soderbergh's ease, since he doubled as director and cinematographer on the *Ocean's* films. Soderbergh describes his creative process by evoking the role of painter in ways germane to our discussion: "It's become a very organic process for me. . . . It's really about creating the canvas piece by piece, and I'm willing to reconcile the fact that I'm not a world-class cinematographer for the moment" (qtd. in Bankston 38). Degas was apparently wary of his place behind the camera, in part because of his skepticism over how this technological art immobilized visual subjects whose movement he was trying to express in lively pastel. In their study of Degas's pursuit of movement in his pictures of ballet, Kendall and Devonyar conjecture that Eadweard Muybridge's photographic studies of bodily movement and Etienne-Jules Marey's chronophotographs (published in *La Photographie du mouvement* in 1892 and *Le Mouvement* in 1894) were a "revelation" (200) to Degas in his late career, one that they link directly to Degas's *Study of Dancers* from this same period. For them, Degas's fin de siècle work emphasized movement, if not as a rebuke to photography then at least in relation to photographic experiments seeking to capture and analyze movement. They cannot help but read *The Greek Dance* (ca. 1887–92), for example, "as a representation of a single figure traversing the stage from right to left, rotating slightly as she advances," or similarly *Three Dancers in Violet Tutus* (c. 1985–98) in a "Marey-like progression of a single model" rather than three (207). The latter's texture, "energized" and made "restless" by repetitious pastel strokes and the juxtaposition of warm and cool tonalities, conveys blurry, vibrant movement (208).

Las Vegas color connects the palette of the *Ocean's* films to a Degas pastel. The vibrant colors of Degas's late pastels, functioning in tandem with their matte surface, are a testament to the painter's mastery of subtleties of light and texture in movement. Degas was fascinated by the effect of artificial lighting on dancers' legs, and he found in pastels a medium for his pursuit. The tulle fabric of tutus allowed for marvelous light effects, its layers capturing light and shadows and creating a dazzling atmosphere. Degas's craft relied heavily on process, in the tactile application of individual strokes and layers of pastel, each fixed with glaze before moving on to successive layers that created a chromatic harmony (Lloyd 280). What distinguishes Degas is the "almost alchemical skill with which [he] blended his colors that produced such memorable results—rosy pinks, sparkling violets, almond greens, iridescent blues, vibrant oranges, striking yellows, russet reds, warm browns—all varying, sometimes saturated and often acidic, hues" (Lloyd 280). Soderbergh's palette differs from Degas's, but his technical prowess with color and light is undisputed. With his veteran lighting specialist on *Ocean's Eleven*, James Plannette, Soderbergh shot for the "natural" feel of their colorful Las Vegas casino milieu (Planette qtd. in Bankston 44).[1] The director-cinematographer selected film and print stocks that captured contrast and "grit" without getting "too glossy" and that offered "tight grain control, inky blacks, deep shadow detail and bold colors" (Soderbergh qtd. in Bankston 42). He looked for the "clash of colors" and experimented by "mix[ing] color temperatures . . . like those on the casino floor" (qtd. in Bankston 42). But these elements must align with the dramatic function of story—"All of the cinematographers I love have always embraced color and used it as a way to enhance mood and drama" (qtd. in Bankston 42).

Soderbergh's respect for Jean-Luc Godard shaped his appropriations for the richly layered auditory and visual worlds his films create, if not his jumbled chronology, kaleidoscopic color palettes, and eclectic cutting, all part of Soderbergh's "chaotic" practice (deWaard and Tait 17).[2] Godard's films are heavily citational, as he constantly "collects already existing images in order to observe their relationships, their powers and their limitations" (Berenz 235). This principle of "collection" takes on special valence in a genre whose central narrative crux is the crime of theft. Paradoxically, Godard may be iconophobic. In a playful montage in his black-and-white deconstruction of the heist film, *Bande à part* (1964)—apparently Soderbergh had a poster of the film in his office (A. Thompson 95)—his protagonists run through the main galleries of the Louvre in record time, taking no time to identify, let alone contemplate, the works hanging there.) A more lyrically crafted image aversion may structure *Pierrot le fou* (1965), his vivid "collage of words and images, graphics and colors, lines and volumes" (Dalle Vacche 10). In Dalle Vacche's subtle reading, after the excessive citational stimulation of most of the film, an "intense antipictorial[ism]" takes over when

Godard "abandon[s] the visual register for the sake of an empty canvas, a blank sky, a colorless sea, or a black screen—voids where the mind, through language, can project all its abstractions" (11). In these films, Godard dispenses with looking at other images.

With those readings of Godard in mind, it is a telling aspect of *Ocean's Twelve* that we never actually *see* the stolen painting, Toulour's prized *Blue Dancers*. In *Twelve's* verbal allusion to the Degas, painting functions by reputation as part of the aesthetic tradition, a marker of independent wealth and a figure of international art auctions, in much the same way Picasso's *Woman with a Guitar* did in *Eleven* and Klimt's *Portrait of Adele* does in *Thirteen*. Angela Dalle Vacche writes of this function of painting as decoration that projects financial might; art "prevails over the law of the marketplace" and becomes "implicated in the establishment" (2).[3] Terry Benedict and François Toulour are both associated with this function of artwork as financial investment.

But what other games are at play here? What takes the place of the image of the *Blue Dancers*? Toulour is a dancer. His elected method for beating the deep pastel blue laser field of the Galleria dell'Arte of Rome (a fictional space, like the Bellagio gallery) is an intricately choreographed capoeira routine. Soderbergh substitutes the montage of Toulour's own blue dance for Degas's stolen *Blue Dancers*. If Soderbergh has, in effect, erased the modernist image in *Ocean's Twelve*, is it because he doesn't need the object anymore? Has he absorbed the principle in a moment of Hegelian *aufhebung*, a sublation that carries on the spirit of modernist innovation for a new cultural context? Or, in an iconophobic gesture akin to Godard, has he eclipsed the modernist visual reference?

Toulour says at one point that it is impossible to compare two thefts. We face a related challenge here in comparing two modern moments and media separated by a century of change. But the relationship between cinema and painting begs for commentary, since the *Ocean's* films deliberately cast their gaze upon art. What is the connection to modernism in the trilogy? I believe the paintings reassert the heist film's links to the social and aesthetic preoccupations of modernism—Soderbergh's imaginary gallery gives a nod to the subgenre's origins. In this case, the heist film references modernist avant-gardes as models for institutional positioning vis-à-vis Hollywood. In addition, as modernist art's intricate links to the development and fluctuation of modern art markets, with extravagant prices that elude classical utility—ones that hover in the same scale of revenue grossed by the *Ocean's* films—painting inscribes the aesthetic-economic tension of modernism itself. The heist film steals modernist painting and uses it as a visual currency, as a guarantor of meaning and aesthetic credibility. It calls upon it less as a direct visual or mimetic model and more as a marker of rule-breaking institutional aesthetics vying for attention in a post-Kantian world that values originality, genius, and the *ideal* of art untainted by commercial corrosion. But here the mass-market film allegorizes creative release from institutional constraint while not necessarily lapsing into hermetic forms associated with high modernism. Soderbergh needs the heist film to tell the story of the break he would like to make with the current state of cinema, what he'd like to get away with—to explain as a belated artist the break he wishes he could make but cannot fully realize from his position within the commodity structure. The heist film affords this market reflection.

Notes

1. If ever there were a town other than Degas's native City of Light known for its own artificial luminosity and color variations from garish neon to the blinding white of the American desert, it would be Las Vegas. It is a town also known for its economy of sex on dancerly display—a parallel to Paris, where Degas's interest in the social life of dancers highlighted the predatory nature of bourgeois men waiting in the wings of theaters for their mistresses, the ballerinas. Soderbergh desexualizes the venality of Las Vegas in the *Ocean's* films, emphasizing instead gaming and real estate, other modes of global capital (deWaard and Tait 131).

2. Soderbergh embodies the "belatedness" (Bordwell 75) American directors in the 1990s felt toward Godard and other modernists (Morton 189; Gallagher 45).

3. Degas's role in the creation of an international art market was central; see Patry. At auctions Degas pastels and oil paintings regularly sell in the millions of GBP, www.artsy.net/artist/edgar-degas/auction-results.

September 11 as Heist

⬡⬡⬡⬡⬡⬡⬡⬡⬡⬡⬡⬡⬡⬡⬡⬡⬡⬡⬡⬡⬡

Hamilton Carroll

In this chapter I discuss two films, James Marsh's *Man on Wire* (2008) and Spike Lee's *Inside Man* (2006). Despite their manifest differences—Marsh's film is a documentary account of a real-life event and Lee's is a fictional crime thriller—I read both films as symptomatic responses to the terrorist attacks of September 11, 2001. In particular, I examine how each film makes recourse to the thematic and formal conventions of the heist genre to work through post–September 11 cultural anxieties. The conventions of the heist film, I argue, help make sense of September 11 by producing a different set of relations to time and space that draw on the uncanny, rather than the traumatic, nature of the events. The heist allows a different point of access to the events of September 11 that moves beyond the representation of trauma, thereby producing new meaning for the events by placing them in a different set of psychological and emotional contexts. They do not ask, as much post–September 11 culture does, how the events can be represented. Rather than locating September 11 outside of narrative, each film mobilizes a particular form of narrative contextualization for the events. Recasting the events of September 11 as uncanny, rather than traumatic, these films move beyond questions of representability and place the events within history.

As a cinematic genre, the heist film contains features of the uncanny that are evident in its formal structures, recurrent tropes, and plot devices. With antecedents dating back to the earliest days of narrative cinema in the United States, the genre gains its current form with the noir films of the 1940s and 1950s. Classic heist films include *The Asphalt Jungle* (John Huston, 1950), *Bob le flambeur/Bob the Gambler* (Jean-Pierre Melville, 1956), *Rififi/Du Rififi chez les hommes* (Jules Dassin, 1955), and *Ocean's 11* (Lewis Milestone, 1960). More recent examples include *Reservoir Dogs* (Quentin Tarantino, 1992), *Ocean's Eleven* (Steven Soderbergh, 2001), and *Heist* (David Mamet, 2001). Usually revolving around an elaborate plot to

steal something, heist films typically follow a three-act formula: preparation and planning, heist, aftermath. While the genre typically follows a
three-act formula with a clear temporal progression of before, during, and
after, it also relies on troubled or confused spatial, temporal, and interpersonal relationships. The crime that stands at the center of any heist film is
frequently the work of a group of criminals (rather than of a single individual), intergroup tension is a common feature, and the double cross is a
frequent plot device. In both its spatial and its temporal representations,
the heist further reflects the uncanny in its representation of complex psychological drama in which doubling is a constitutive feature. The heist's
uncanny aspects frequently reflect or allegorize the transformed relationships of the human subject to the social, technological, and cultural conditions of late modernity.

As the singular transformations of modernity have radically altered subjective perceptions of both time and space, the uncanny has become a mode
of perception. In his foundational essay on the uncanny, Freud suggests that
the term "applies to everything that was intended to remain secret, hidden
away, and has come into the open," and he wonders, "under what conditions
the familiar can become uncanny and frightening?" (132, 124). The relationship between these two aspects of the uncanny—the familiar rendered
unfamiliar, the unfamiliar discovered at the heart of the familiar—produces
what is perhaps the most uncanny effect of all: its ambivalent and mutable
nature. "*Heimlich*," Freud suggests, "becomes increasingly ambivalent, until
it finally merges with its antonym *unheimlich*" (134). What was presumed
familiar is revealed to be—or transformed into—the unfamiliar. These two
central aspects of the uncanny—the familiar made strange and the hidden
being revealed—correspond to the key plot devices of the heist film: the
elaborate planning of the heist, on the one hand, and the collapse into uncertainty that inevitably follows its execution, on the other. The one thing
the viewer knows as he or she sits down to watch a heist film is to expect
the unexpected. Because the unexpected is couched within the confines of
a clearly recognizable set of genre conventions and is thus familiar (even
expected), the heist film also produces a complicated relationship between
the known and the unknown. What is familiar frequently becomes unfamiliar, what is unfamiliar becomes familiar, and the double and the double
cross are constitutive devices of the genre. It is this uncanny relationship
between the known and the unknown that makes the heist a particularly
rich genre for the cinematic representation of post–September 11 anxieties
in US culture.

The uncanny is most clearly manifest in the heist film in relation to fraught spatial and temporal relations. Problems of proximity and of the fraught relationship between the inside and the outside, the near and the far, haunt the heist film and account for many of its uncanny aspects. Anthony Vidler calls the uncanny "a dominant constituent of modern nostalgia" and "a significant psychoanalytical and aesthetic response to the real shock of the modern" (x, 9). Refracted through the miniaturizing lens of an elaborate bank robbery or "one last job," the heist film provides a location for the working through of cultural anxieties about spatial and temporal relations. A frequent feature of the heist genre, for example, is the act of gaining access to a building by subterranean means, and the successful execution of the heist often involves approaching the target object by tunneling under, through, or around buildings. Much of the action typically takes place underground, under water, or inside enclosed spaces. The criminal act is typically one of attempting to gain access to a forbidden space (the bank vault, the safe, the locked display case, the bedroom dressing table). Time, moreover, is always of the essence, and the heist almost always takes place against the clock. A race against time, the heist is a representation of the conflict between movement and stasis. Confinement is both a temporary working condition for the criminal and, with the risk of capture and imprisonment, a potential future condition.

In its penetration of forbidden spaces, the heist draws on one of the constituent features of the uncanny: fear of invasion, and of the home in particular as a violable space. Displaced to the bank vault or the jewelry store, the genre draws on fears of domestic invasion and anxieties over the porous relationship between the public and the private. Vidler argues that the "favorite motif" of the uncanny is "precisely the contrast between a secure and homely interior and the fearful invasion of an alien presence; on a psychological level, its play was one of doubling, where the other is, strangely enough, experienced as a replica of the self, all the more fearsome because apparently the same" (3). The uncanny not only names the disquieting intrusion of the foreign into the domestic that has become a pervasive feature of modernity but also names the radical transformations of domestic space itself. Viewed in this way, the uncanny aspects of the September 11 terrorist attacks become clear. As a series of attacks on public buildings, the events were uncanny precisely because of their nondomestic locations. The home was palpably absent on September 11. This is why, at least in part, the events of September 11 were such a shock: separated from the realm of the domestic in almost every way, they refused the sorts of sentimentalization that typically undergird responses to disaster. As the almost immediate reclamation of the term "homeland" in US discourse after September 11 shows, the domestic was a vital symbolic location for the production of meaning about the events. Thus, what many responses to September 11 attempt is to transform the scale of the attacks into something manageable, legible, or comprehendible. Their incomprehensible scale is collapsed through a process of domestication.[1] The heist film enables this transformation by reframing the events within the contours of a familiar cinematic genre, thereby enabling a working through of the events' uncanny aspects. As *Man on Wire* and *Inside Man* each attempt to make sense of the incomprehensible, to represent the unrepresentable, it is in their uses of the heist genre that they find the representational space to make such transformations possible.

Man on Wire

In its nostalgic representation of a spectacular event, recast as a heist, *Man on Wire* reclaims the symbolic space of the World Trade Center (WTC) from the space of terror as it constructs a useable past from the extraordinary act it documents. A joint production of Discovery Films, the BBC, and the UK Film Council and directed by British filmmaker James Marsh, *Man on Wire* takes as its subject matter Philippe Petit's famous highwire walk between the North and South towers of the as-yet-unfinished World Trade Center on August 7, 1974.[2] Adapted from Petit's memoir of the event, *To Reach the Clouds* (2002), the film is comprised of a mixture of interviews with Petit and his fellow conspirators, archival film footage and photographs, and dramatic reenactments. Following the artist's own descriptions of the event, *Man on Wire* presents Petit's act as a daring heist and constructs a tense and compelling account of the planning, execution, and aftermath of the event. As Annie Allix, Petit's former girlfriend and accomplice, suggests, part of the appeal of the wire walk was its illegality. "It was like a bank robbery," she points out in the film, "and that pleased him immensely." Using the three-act formula typical of the heist genre, in particular a long planning and preparation sequence, the film provides tension and a sense of the unexpected to an event whose outcome is already well known. The audience of *Man on Wire* knows from the start how events turn out: Petit's wire walk is successful, he is arrested and then freed, he does not die in the attempt. The audience knows what, and it is given a version of the how and the why.[3] The film stages a relationship between the known and the unknown that is cut through with uncanny resonances that form a central part of its meaning-making apparatus. Recast as heist, a minor historical event gains meaning through its uncanny resemblance to the historical events that took place in the same location almost thirty years later. Although *Man on Wire* does not directly reference the terrorist attacks of September 11, 2001, the film nevertheless draws a clear series of parallels between that event and Petit's earlier transformative act. The parallels produce the film's meaning as the evocation of September 11 provides the film with a powerful set of contextual references. At the same time, the story of Petit's act is reclaimed in order to make sense of the present.

Finding a symbolic origin point for the World Trade Center in Petit's act, the film attempts to counteract the uncanny status of the Twin Towers as the "shock of the modern" by humanizing them. For, if the attacks of September 11 were unimaginable, the building itself was no less difficult to comprehend.[4] The Twin Towers of the WTC were always already uncanny objects, provoking fear, awe, and a sense of time and space out of joint with human cognition. They were later-day examples of the technological sublime that features so prominently in twentieth-century American life and culture. The uncanny nature of September 11 is often tied to the buildings' disturbing double nature. Twins, doubles, mirror images, the Twin Towers already evoke the uncanny. Their overwhelming proportions further unsettle. Even before September 11, the World Trade Center was a contested site at which the relationship between the human inhabitants of Manhattan and the increasingly inhuman scale of modern life came into conflict. Vast in scale and doubled in number, the Twin Towers dominated the New York skyline and refused the human by existing out of all proportion to human scales of perception.[5] That after September 11 the signature buildings of the World Trade Center were transformed from the Twin Towers to Ground Zero merely confirms their already uncanny status: a monstrous double, endowed with the mythic force of an origin point at the moment of its destruction, the World Trade Center transcended the limits of human cognition while also signifying the triumph of human endeavor.

A eulogy of sorts, *Man on Wire* uses its celebration of Petit's "coup" not only to memorialize the Twin Towers but also to rescale them for human consumption. Because Petit's act took place at the moment of the Twin Towers' creation, it serves as a symbolic bookend and inaugurates the thirty-year-long life of the World Trade Center as a signature feature of the Manhattan skyline and the tourist life of the city of New York. Petit, the film suggests, "introduced" the Twin Towers to the city and the world. Through an extraordinary act of daring, bravery, and superhuman physical prowess,

After breaking into the World Trade Center, Philippe Petit sets out on his illegal walk between the two towers in *Man on Wire*.

Petit performed the magical act of transforming the inhuman scale of the towers into something altogether more manageable for the citizens of Manhattan and of the world. By stringing a wire between the two towers, he made them one. Joined and conquered, the Twin Towers were reduced to a human scale, and their uncanny doubleness was transformed into an irreducible singularity. As two became one, the World Trade Center became a familiar, and therefore mournable, object.[6] The film manages this transformation through its mix of interview footage and reenactment, which gives human scale to the buildings by placing them within the familiar confines of genre. As Petit and his accomplices provide information about their heist in the form of filmed interviews, the events they describe are illustrated on screen. Moving from documentary footage shot by an early accomplice to reenactments using actors, the action sequences of the film split the mammoth undertaking into a series of vignettes that emphasize the criminal aspects of the undertaking. Shot in grainy black and white, the reenactments seamlessly blend with the film's archival footage and photographs. They show Petit and his accomplices planning the heist, practicing the various skills they will need to carry it out successfully, acquiring the necessary tools and equipment, and, finally, carrying out the coup.

The heist that *Man on Wire* describes constitutes a criminal act conceived as a public spectacle. Petit's act was described as the "artistic crime of the century," a naming that can now invite comparison only with the crime of the century that was September 11 and that Karlheinz Stockhausen called the "biggest work of art there has ever been."[7] The relationship between art and criminality often is a central feature of the heist. The genre typically elevates the criminal act to an artistic one, and the criminal is frequently likened to an artist or, at the very least, a craftsman. The skills required to carry out the heist are often shown in loving detail, and the criminals, each with a particular specialization, come together to form the perfect team. At the same time, these characters often are presented as artists as well, and the skills required to break into a bank are often the same as those required to repair watches or build antique sailboats, for example. Such legitimate skills often serve as a front for the criminal enterprise, but they also serve to humanize and build sympathy for the criminal and to blur the distinctions between criminal and legitimate enterprise. The film finds in Philippe Petit a perfect example of the criminal as artist. A young man in 1974, Petit is presented in *Man on Wire* as an artist whose amazing physical dexterity and sense of showmanship gave him the ability to rebel against the conventions of a staid society in spectacular ways and to offer the citizens of Manhattan a superhuman spectacle beyond their wildest imaginations. In Petit's performance, however, art and spectacle transcend criminality.

By encoding Petit's criminal act in the confines of the heist genre, the film mobilizes a series of conventions through which criminality can be recoded. Narrated as a magical tale of youthful transgression by the now-old participants of the original event, Petit's actions are placed in a nostalgic frame. As a work of nostalgia, the film is about time and the transformation of the past into a useable fiction in order to make sense of the present. Since September 11, the nostalgia that the film promotes stands as a form of memorialization in which the later act becomes encoded in the former. When, in an interview clip given early on in the film, Petit says of his nascent desire to join the Twin Towers, "the object of my dream doesn't exist yet," the audience cannot but be reminded that they exist no longer. Petit's desire for a future moment, the completion of the Twin Towers, is recast in the face of a now-past moment, that of their destruction. While the film's meaning derives from two past events, Petit's wire walk and the terrorist attacks of September 11, Petit's original act gains its full meaning only retrospectively. After September 11, its time has finally come and its proper meaning is made clear. *Man on Wire* offers the viewer an alternative answer to the common question asked about September 11, articulated by Slavoj Žižek in the rhetorical question, "Where have we already seen the same thing over and over again?" (*Welcome* 11). While, for Žižek, as for many others, the answer to this question is in that other staple of Hollywood genre cinema, the disaster film, *Man on Wire* provides a different answer: in Petit's sublime performance. The suicidal fantasy of the disaster film is replaced by the awe-inspiring spectacle of Petit's performance. What *Man on Wire* represents in its performance-as-heist is an act of giving and not an act of theft. Nevertheless, when Petit plays down the risk of death inherent in his feat, his almost boastful claim—"if I die, what a beautiful death. To die in the execution of your passion"—is voiced after September 11 and with full knowledge of the terrorists who *did* die in the execution of *their* passion, and of the innocent victims who died with them. As the spectacular collapse of the Twin Towers—which could not have been planned by the terrorists but which must have fulfilled their wildest fantasies—instantly turned an act of terrorism into a global media event, Petit's earlier transformative act gains meaning retroactively as it signals a birth, the proper meaning of which becomes clear only after the towers' destruction and symbolic death.

When the film transitions to the execution of Petit's act after a long planning and preparation sequence, the resonances with September 11 become clear. Looking at the still photographs and the brief snatches of black-and-white film footage of the crowds standing on street corners in lower Manhattan in 1974, stunned into awesome silence as they crane their necks to get a better view of the spectacle that unfolds before them, it is impossible not to see the parallels between that morning and its horrific corollary a quarter of a century later. Photographs of the event, such as one in which Petit is seen walking across the wire suspended between the two towers and a small commercial jet plane can be seen in the upper left-hand corner of the frame, provide an unsettling reminder of events to come.[8] Situating Philippe Petit's playful and mischievous act in implicit comparison to the events of September 11, *Man on Wire* simultaneously recalls the moment of the Twin Towers' inauguration as American icons and rewrites the historical comparison between August 7, 1974, and September 11, 2001. Petit's assault on the Twin Towers both substitutes for September 11 and is its uncanny double. It is the uncanny familiar that rewrites the later event. Viewed in light of *Man on Wire*, the terrorist attack on the World Trade Center becomes a doppelgänger, a monstrous restaging of Petit's earlier act, which is itself rendered uncanny by the comparison.

So striking is the correspondence between Petit's act and that of the September 11 hijackers that it constitutes an example of what Harold Bloom calls, in another context, "*apophrades*, or the return of the dead." The term *apophrades*, Bloom explains, comes from "the Athenian dismal or unlucky days upon which the dead returned to reinhabit the houses in which they had lived." For Bloom it names the moment in a great poet's career when

> the poem is . . . *held* open to the precursor, where once it *was* open, and the uncanny effect is that the new poem's achievement makes it seem to us, not as though the precursor were writing it, but as though the later poet himself had written the precursor's characteristic work. (15–16)[9]

The "uncanny effect" described by Bloom in relation to the art of poetry is the stunning transformation of the original into the copy. In just such a way, Philippe Petit's wire walk in August 1974—despite its originary status—becomes, retroactively, a copy of the terrorist attacks of September 11, 2001, which so fulfils the "object of [Petit's] dream" that it replaces it. What *Man on Wire* attempts to do is reclaim that dream from terror. The film transforms the terror of September 11, 2001, into the sublime wonder of August 7, 1974.

If Petit's triumph is that he *did not* die in the fulfillment of his dream, and the terrorists' triumph is that they *did*, then *Man on Wire* attempts to return life to the site of death. The film performs the ideological work of reclaiming a sense of American innocence, what Amy Kaplan has called "a narrative of historical exceptionalism," that offers an image of what was that can be celebrated (83). In its presentation of the moment of the Twin Towers' symbolic birth, the film offers a nostalgic vision of a forgotten history rendered familiar by its uncanny resemblance to another event. Presenting the audience with the spectacle of a band of foreigners invading New York in order to carry out a criminal act, but offering the spectacle of art not of death, the film performs a recuperative function as it memorializes the absent Twin Towers and those who died within them. The past becomes a possible future as the film substitutes the awesome sublimity of Petit's spectacular performance for the act of terror. The film's utilization of the heist situates Petit's benign spectacle in relation to a series of genre conventions that manage the uncanny correspondence between art and terror. Freud suggests, "we can also call a living person uncanny . . . when we credit him with evil intent . . . realized with the help of special powers" (149). In *Man on Wire*, Petit is presented as the antidote to the uncanny figure of the terrorist, bent on harm. Intent on transporting the spectator to a realm beyond the everyday, Petit transforms the criminal into an artistic act. The criminal becomes an artist, the crime a spectacular performance. As the space between life and death is shown to be infinitesimal, *Man on Wire* reclaims the narrative of the World Trade Center from the terrorists as it tells the story of an event that becomes uncanny in its familiarity.

Inside Man

If the links between *Man on Wire* and September 11 are clearly apparent (albeit left implicit in the film itself), *Inside Man* bears a less obvious relationship to the events. Nevertheless, as *Man on Wire* produces a usable past through which the events of September 11 can be understood, *Inside Man* also uses the heist genre to work through post–September 11 anxieties. The film was marketed and reviewed as a conventional crime thriller and, propelled by a cast of well-known actors, including Denzel Washington, Jodie Foster, Clive Owen, Willem Dafoe, and Christopher Plummer, it was a critical and commercial success. Taken by audiences and critics alike to be a straight genre film, it was seen not as a "Spike Lee film" but merely as a piece of entertainment cinema.[10] However, like *Man on Wire*, the film utilizes the familiar trappings of genre to singular effect, and the conventions of the heist allow the working through of more serious subject matter. The film produces a dialectical relationship between the known and the unknown, the familiar and the foreign, through which the events of September 11 and their effects can be explored.

The plot of *Inside Man* bears many of the hallmarks of the conventional heist film. In it, a team of bank robbers, led by Dalton Russell (Clive Owen), besieges a Manhattan bank and holds a group of bank employees and members of the public hostage for a number of hours. The film opens on a bright and sunny morning in downtown Manhattan as the bank robbers make their way to Wall Street and the fictional Manhattan Trust Bank. The strikingly clear blue skies and early-morning time frame of this opening sequence recall to the viewer's mind, as does the timing of Philippe Petit's wire walk in *Man on Wire*, that the events of September 11 also unfolded as New Yorkers awoke to cloudless skies on a perfect early fall day. As the opening credits end, the viewer follows the criminals' nondescript panel van as it parks behind the bank, and, with a quick cut, the audience is placed inside the bank foyer as a crane shot captures from above a view of the early-morning patrons of the bank, who are, as of yet, unaware of what is about to transpire.[11] In this opening scene, the film's complex production of disorientation becomes clearly apparent. While the first-time viewer has no reason to believe that anyone other than the boiler-suit-wearing criminals

A power broker (Jodie Foster) tries to manage the actions of Detective Frazier (Denzel Washington) as they stand in front of a wall commemorating the victims of 9/11 in *Inside Man*.

are involved in the heist, later events in the film make clear that easy distinctions between victim and perpetrator are unsettled from the very outset. Characters who appear to be victims turn out to be gang members, and the everyday frictions between strangers cast together side by side in a line at the bank become far more sinister. The criminals' target is a cache of diamonds in the possession of bank owner Arthur Case (Christopher Plummer) that are stored in a safe deposit box in the bank's vault. The plan for the theft calls for Russell to be hidden behind the wall of a storage room in the basement of the bank and for his accomplices to be set free by the police alongside their victims. After things have died down, Russell frees himself and leaves the bank by the front door with the diamonds. It is this eventuality that the hostage taking is designed to facilitate. The diamonds that Russell and his accomplices steal from Case are the remaining spoils of the banker's dealings with the Nazis during World War Two, crimes that Russell has evidence of. Because Case does not wish for his own history as a war criminal to become public knowledge, he does not reveal to the police that he has lost anything during the robbery, and attempts to have the investigation halted. The film ends with Russell and his accomplices at liberty and the police investigation all but dead. The film's use of the uncanny conventions of the heist genre is clear: doubling, interment, hidden knowledge, and uncertainty are all constitutive aspects of the film's plot.

The criminals execute their heist through a cunning use of subterfuge and obfuscation: they force their hostages to strip down to their underwear and to don dark blue jumpsuits, white facemasks, and dark sunglasses identical to the ones that they themselves wear; they refer to each other using only variations of the name Steven—Steve, Stevie, Steve-O; they fake the execution of a hostage; they bug the police command trailer and deliberately mislead the police; and they appear to all leave the bank mingled among the hostages when the police storm the building. In their execution of a hostage taking that is in reality a piece of theater designed to enable another criminal act to take place unnoticed (Russell's interment and subsequent theft of the diamonds), the criminals produce a fake or a double of the real event. The spectacular event disguises the actual crime, and the film stages a conflict between the real and the unreal. A crime has taken place, but it is not the one that the police believe has been perpetrated or that the film's audience has watched unfold on the screen before them. As it becomes clear that the criminals have orchestrated the whole event and have repeatedly manipulated the police, questions arise about who is watching whom, and for what reason. Such questions are made explicit in the film as the hostage crisis immediately produces an audience of onlookers, who are shown standing behind police sawhorses and eager to see how events will unfold. Describing the filming of one of these crowd scenes, Lee points out that there is also a second level of audience visible on the film: the crowds of real New Yorkers watching the filming take place. Television news crews film the events, and they are broadcast live on air. There is in these displacements a doubling, almost a tripling, of the order of spectacle and performance. Real New Yorkers watch fictional New Yorkers watch a fictional hostage crisis develop. As *Man on Wire* does when it shows images of the crowds watching Petit walk between the Twin Towers, Lee's film foregrounds the staging of spectacle and repeatedly calls up the uncertain status of the real. In both films, a spectacular and theatrical event precedes a real crime, which is itself a work of spectacle.

In *Inside Man*, the relationship between the real and spectacle is also evoked in the film's narrative framing. The film utilizes a double time frame that shifts between the events of the hostage taking and interwoven scenes, set after a siege of the building by the police, in which detectives Keith Frazier (Denzel Washington) and Bill Mitchell (Chiwetel Ejiofor) interview the survivors. Because of the success of the criminals' subterfuge, the police are unable to tell criminal from innocent victim. The triumph of the robbers' plan (and, to a lesser extent, of the film's plot) lies in the success of this subterfuge. Neither the police nor the audience know who is a criminal and who is a victim, and, in the confusion, the criminals are able to disguise the fact that they have left one of their own concealed in the basement of the bank. Because the later scenes are inserted within the action of the heist, the audience knows almost from the outset that all is not right, but does not know precisely how or why. Part of the pleasure to be derived from watching the film is that of trying to solve the riddle of who is who. While at the end of the film the audience finally sees all of the criminals together and out of disguise and is thus given the satisfaction of a neat resolution, the police, pressured by Case, have concluded that there is no crime to solve. What is known to the audience remains unknown to the police. These breakdowns in distinction between criminal and victim, between crime and performance, reflect the uncanny status of the known and the unknown, the inside and the outside, after September 11. Like the suicide bomber trained in US flight schools and living in suburban Florida, *Inside Man*'s representation of criminals hidden in plain sight reflects post–September 11 anxieties of proximity.[12] At the same time, the film's staging of crime as carefully orchestrated spectacle mirrors the September 11 attacks and the news media's live reporting of the collapse of the Twin Towers.

Inside Man is a film about seeing. Nowhere is this clearer than during the film's opening sequence, in which New York is represented as a site in which what is absent gains an uncanny and destabilizing presence. As the opening credits of the film begin to the accompaniment of the hypnotic and compelling beat of the song "Chaiyya" by famed Indian film score composer A. R. Rahman, the viewer watches the members of the criminal gang make their way, first individually and then together, to Wall Street and the bank in which the heist takes place. The audience travels with the criminals through the outer districts of New York, from Coney Island, to Brooklyn Heights, across the Brooklyn Bridge, through Chinatown, and finally to the intersection of Wall Street and Broadway, where they park behind the fictional Manhattan Trust Bank building and the criminals, who are disguised as painters, begin to unload their supplies. In this opening sequence, the audience is given the familiar sights of the city, but it is a familiarity that is now marked by an uncanny absence: that of the Twin Towers.

Offering a virtual tour of the city, the sights of New York and Manhattan that the film establishes here are already familiar to the audience from other films, television shows, and tourist visits: the Coney Island Cyclone roller coaster, Chinatown, the view of lower Manhattan from Brooklyn Heights, the Statue of Liberty, the sweeping expanse of the Verrazano-Narrows Bridge, the towering pillars and immense suspension cables of the Brooklyn Bridge, the stone gargoyles of Wall Street, and, in a reminder of the film's post–September 11 context, the massive stars and stripes now suspended from the external facade of the New York Stock Exchange. In this opening sequence, Lee creates a tourist's-eye view of Manhattan and the outer boroughs. The easy familiarity conjured by the New York City sights that appear on-screen, however, is belied by the various shots of the Manhattan skyline in which the absence of the Twin Towers of the World Trade Center still, five years later (at the time of the film's release), serves as a stark reminder of their destruction. The serialization of New York tourist attractions and signifiers is haunted by the absence of the Twin Towers, which remain startlingly present in their absence.[13] Radically transformed, the broken skyline of Manhattan symbolizes loss, and its representation at the start of the film contextualizes the action that follows.

The heist that the elaborate hostage taking is designed to obfuscate—the interment of Dalton Russell behind the wall of a storage room in the bank's basement and the subsequent theft of Case's diamonds—calls to mind what is perhaps the most uncanny aspect of September 11 and the thing that most haunts the site of Ground Zero: the absence, indistinguishability, and un-representability of human remains. Freud points out that, "to many people the acme of the uncanny is represented by anything to do with death, dead bodies, revenants, spirits, ghosts" (148). He further elaborates that "some would award the crown of the uncanny to the idea of being buried alive, only apparently dead" (150). Buried alive, Russell calls forth the specter of the absent presence of the victims of September 11, innumerable because they literally could not be counted, but-as dust-everywhere in the air of lower Manhattan in the weeks following the attacks. Russell is the double both of the members of the terrorist sleeper cell, poised in waiting for their moment of action, and of the absent victim's body. The victims of September 11 were nowhere and everywhere at once, beyond representation be-cause both invisible and all too present: buried in, and constitutive of, the rubble of the World Trade Center; fragmented and atomized into the air of lower Manhattan; excised from media portrayals of the event like the fall-ing man of Richard Drew's infamous photograph. If, as Vidler suggests, the uncanny is an "intimation of the fragmentary, the morselated, the broken," then *Inside Man*'s representation of the buried subject performs a doubled refraction (70). An "inside man," Russell stands as both the known and the unknown, the proximate and the foreign. At once criminal and victim, thief and agent of justice, Russell becomes an example of the extimate, that which inhabits both the inside and the outside. An uncanny double, Russell, like Petit, haunts the site of mass death.

Russell's interment, moreover, is symbolic of the hidden history of violence in lower Manhattan in relation to which the attacks of September 11 become not singular but part of a series of events reaching back to the turn of the century. While the film explicitly locates itself in a post–September 11 world of US anxiety and global military adventurism, it traces the roots of that world much further back than 2001. Staging a heist at the center of Wall Street, *Inside Man* conjures up the history of the interrelationship between global finance and violence in lower Manhattan that long precedes the events of September 11. As Eric Darton points out in *Divided We Stand*, his cultural history of the World Trade Center, lower Manhattan had been "visited more than once by acts of horrific violence" (5). Linking the failed attempt to blow up the World Trade Center on February 20, 1993, to the explosion on September 16, 1920, outside J. P. Morgan's recently completed bank at 23 Wall Street, Darton excavates a history of violence that also resonates through *Inside Man*'s recasting of terrorism as criminal heist.[14] For if lower Manhattan and the financial and corporate interests that reside there have been the victims of violence before, they have also, as *Inside Man* suggests, been its perpetrators. Questions of criminality here are brought to light by, and in relation to, the film's representation of crime as performance. Moreover, while the global economic collapse of 2007, precipitated by the US subprime mortgage fiasco, came in the wake of the film's release, its shadow falls on the film and informs subsequent viewings.

Linking the terrorist attacks of September 11 to a longer history of terrorism in lower Manhattan, routed through an excavation of the links between global capital and violence, *Inside Man* tells the story of a heist in order to problematize the relationship between criminal and victim and to historicize contemporary fears. What the film offers is a representation of loss. That which is hidden is brought to the surface, in the form of guilty secrets, prior histories, and buried men. Couched in the formal and visual pleasures of a familiar cinematic genre, *Inside Man* produces a spectacle of confusion and obfuscation in which the presence of absence is a constant concern. Hidden deep in the basement of a building that guards its own half-hidden secrets, Dalton Russell stands as an uncanny remainder, that which was thought buried returned to the light of day. That his story is told against the backdrop of absence and the gaping hole where the Twin Towers once stood transforms the film's representation of spectacle into a form of memorialization. Keyed to loss, the film gives absence an uncanny and concrete presence.

The protagonists of *Man on Wire* and *Inside Man* each recast the criminal act as spectacle, one high in the air, suspended between the Twin Towers of the World Trade Center on a filament of wire almost invisible from the ground, one interred in the bowels of a building at the heart of the financial center of the globalized world. Uncanny doubles of each other and of the September 11 terrorists, these two men and the films that tell their stories encapsulate the events of September 11, 2001, in a longer history. Narrating stories of transgression, both films place the horrors of September 11 in another context. Through the genre conventions of the heist, each film offers a view of New York in which the events of September 11 and the destruction of the World Trade Center stand as the center. Not yet complete in one, already destroyed in the other, the Twin Towers haunt these films. In both films, the conventions of the heist provide a way to come to terms with loss. The psychological structures of the uncanny that underpin those genre conventions provide a different mode of understanding. Freed from the questions of representation that typically frame the events as traumatic, these films offer an alternative way of seeing. Placing the events of September 11 in longer histories, both films move beyond trauma. Seeing the present in relation to a usable past, they each, in their own ways, situate the destruction of the World Trade Center in a history of Manhattan that does not deny the horror of that event but situates it within a different context. Through the uncanny conventions of the heist, the towers are reclaimed. Revenants, the Twin Towers are exhumed in order to be laid to rest; given a past, the towers themselves are made history.

Notes

1. For more on this subject, particularly in relation to the figure of the firefighter in US culture after September 11, see Carroll chapters one and two.

2. Petit's act also serves as a plot device in Colum McCann's *Let the Great World Spin* (2009), winner of the National Book Award, and is the subject of Mordecai Gerdstein's Caldecott Medal–winning children's book, *The Man Who Walked between the Towers* (2003), which was made into an animated film narrated by Jake Gyllenhaal.

3. In this way, the film bears comparison to Paul Greengrass's extraordinary film, *United 93* (2006), which sets out with careful precision to document—and, where necessary, imagine—the events that led up to the crash of the fourth hijacked plane, United Airlines flight 93, in a field in Shanksville, Pennsylvania.

4. There is, even in such attempts to describe and discuss September 11, an already complex terminological tension: Is it the event or the events? The attack or

the attacks? Are the World Trade Center and the Twin Towers a building or the buildings? The singular and the plural are in constant and irresolvable conflict. Any decision in the name of consistency leaves out as much as it clarifies, not least the attack on the Pentagon and the plight of United Airlines flight 93, each of which have been all but excised from the public perception of the day.

5. Nicholas Royle suggests of September 11 that, "the appalling apparent accident of a plane flying into a skyscraper [which he calls an "extraordinary double-building"] was followed minutes later by its uncanny repetition, another plane crashing into the other skyscraper, immediately disconfirming (and yet, still, in that moment, incredibly) any sense of the mere 'accidental'" (vii).

6. On an episode of *Larry King Live* that aired in October 2001, Paul Goldberger, architecture critic for *The New Yorker*, claimed of Petit and WTC climber George Willig, "I thought both George and Phillipe did something wonderful, which is they put some of the romance into the towers that the architects had left out. These were—these were not always the most exhilarating buildings. We were proud of them. We believed in their height, we believed in the ambition that they represented, but there was a certain dullness to them, and it was only [when] Phillipe Petit and then later George Willig did their extraordinary things that these towers became actually objects of romance and excitement to so many people." Transcript can be found at www.edition.cnn.com/TRANSCRIPTS/0110/27/lklw.00.html.

7. Petit, one might say, was at the forefront of the now common relationship between corporate power and the culture industries. After his arrest and subsequent release following his wire walk, Petit was rewarded with a lifetime pass to the observation deck of the World Trade Center. He was, in effect, paid for his transformative act. In this way, Petit's own spectacular act fused the still-developing global economy (to which the World Trade Center was intended to be a monument) and the spectacle of art. It was corporate-sponsored art *avant la lettre*. A transcript of Stockhausen's interview, in German, is available in *MusicTexte*, 91 (2001): 69–77.

8. Such is the power of this image that it was chosen for inclusion in Petit's memoir of the events (189).

9. Nicholas Royle devotes useful attention to this passage from Bloom in his discussion of the uncanny nature of being buried alive (146–48).

10. *Inside Man* was Lee's most commercially successful film to date, grossing $88.5 million domestically with total global box-office receipts of $184.3 million (realized from a production budget of $45 million). These totals put the film ahead of the year's two explicitly September 11–themed films, *United 93* (2006) and Oliver Stone's *World Trade Center* (2006), whose domestic grosses totaled $70 million and $31.4 million, respectively. *Inside Man* was also far more commercially successful than Lee's previous film, *25th Hour* (2002), which grossed a mere $13 million (albeit from a production budget of only $5 million).

11. In *Man on Wire*, too, the criminal accomplices, driving a panel van, gain access to the subterranean WTC parking garage by masquerading as construction workers.

12. As Jean Baudrillard suggests, "Adding insult to injury, they even used the daily banality of the American way of life as a mask: these people were two-faced. Sleeping in the suburbs, where they read and studied, with wife and kids, until one day they sprang into action, like time bombs. The faultless mastery of this clandestinity is as practically terrorist as the spectacular act of September 11, because it throws the cloak of suspicion on any individual" (409–10).

13. It is interesting, in this regard, that Lee does not choose to include the Empire State Building in this whirlwind tour, perhaps simply because none of the film's criminals come from that far up the island.

14. On September 16, 1920, J. P. Morgan's bank located at 23 Wall Street (only completed in 1914) was extensively damaged by a massive explosion. Forty-eight people died and over 150 were injured. The blast caused two million dollars' worth of damage to the exterior of the building, much of which is still visible today, and to its interior. The explosion was blamed on anarchists, with some claiming that it was a response to the indictment of Sacco and Vanzetti some days earlier. The cause of the explosion was never confirmed, however, and it has also been suggested that the explosion might have been an accident (Darton 4–7).

Select Filmography

This list includes only the heist films discussed in this book.

Ambush in Leopard Street (J. Henry Piperno, 1962), Britain
American Heist (Sarik Andreasyan, 2014), USA
Armored Car Robbery (Richard Fleischer, 1950), USA
The Art of the Steal (Jonathon Sobol, 2013), Canada
The Asphalt Jungle (John Huston, 1950), USA
The Badlanders (Delmer Daves, 1958), USA
The Bank Job (Roger Donaldson, 2008), Britain
The Bank Raiders (Maxwell Munden, 1958), Britain
Bellman and True (Richard Loncraine, 1987), Britain
Between Friends (Don Shebib, 1973), Canada
The Big Caper (Robert Stevens, 1957), USA
Big Deal on Madonna Street/I soliti ignoti (Mario Monicelli, 1958), Italy
Blue Collar (Paul Schrader, 1978), USA
Bob le flambeur/Bob the Gambler (Jean-Pierre Melville, 1956), France
Cairo (Wolf Rilla, 1963), Britain
Calculated Risk (Norman Harrison, 1963), Britain
The Challenge (John Gilling, 1959), Britain
Charley Varrick (Don Siegel, 1973), USA
La Città si Difendi/Four Ways Out (Pietro Germi, 1951), Italy
Cool Breeze (Barry Pollack, 1972), USA
The Criminal (Joseph Losey, 1960), Britain
Criss Cross (Robert Siodmak, 1949), USA
Cruel Gun Story/Kenjû zankoku monogatari (Takumi Furukawa, 1964), Japan
Date with Disaster (Charles Saunders, 1957), Britain
Dangerous Cargo (John Harlow, 1951), Britain
The Day They Robbed the Bank of England (John Guillermin, 1959), Britain
Dead Presidents (The Hughes Brothers, 1995), USA
Le Dernier Tunnel/The Last Tunnel (Erik Canuel, 2004), Canada
Detroit 9000 (Arthur Marks, 1973), USA

Èchec au porteur (Gilles Grangier, 1958), France
Face (Antonia Bird, 1997), Britain
5 Against the House (Phil Karlson, 1955), USA
Foolproof (William Phillips, 2003), Canada
The Frightened Man (John Gilling, 1951), Britain
Gambit (Ronald Neame, 1966), USA
Gelignite Gang (Francis Searle, 1956), Britain
The Good Die Young (Lewis Gilbert, 1954), Britain
The Good Thief (Neil Jordan, 2002), USA
The Great St. Louis Bank Robbery (Charles Guggenheim, 1959), USA
He Ran All the Way (John Berry, 1951), USA
Heat (Michael Mann, 1995), USA
Heist (David Mamet, 2001), USA
Heist (Scott Mann, 2015), USA
Hell or High Water (David Mackenzie, 2016), USA
High Sierra (Raoul Walsh, 1941), USA
I Died a Thousand Times (Stuart Heisler, 1955), USA
Inside Man (Spike Lee, 2006), USA
The Italian Job (Peter Collinson, 1969), Britain
The Italian Job (F. Gary Gray, 2003), USA
Juice (Ernest Dickerson, 1992), USA
The Killers (Robert Siodmak, 1946), USA
The Killing (Stanley Kubrick, 1956), USA
Killing Them Softly (Andrew Dominik, 2012), USA
Larceny, Inc. (Lloyd Bacon, 1942), USA
L.A. Takedown (Michael Mann, 1989), USA
The League of Gentlemen (Basil Dearden, 1960), Britain
The Lost Man (Robert Aurthur, 1969), USA
Man on Wire (James Marsh, 2008), USA
Naked Fury (Charles Saunders, 1959), Britain
No Road Back (Montgomery Tully, 1957), Britain
Ocean's 11 (Lewis Milestone, 1960), USA
Ocean's Eleven (Steven Soderbergh, 2001), USA
Ocean's Twelve (Steven Soderbergh, 2004), USA
Ocean's Thirteen (Steven Soderbergh, 2007), USA
Odds Against Tomorrow (Robert Wise, 1959), USA
Offbeat (Cliff Owen, 1960), Britain
Palookaville (Alan Taylor, 1995), USA
Payroll (Sidney Hayers, 1961), Britain
Perfect Friday (Peter Hall, 1970), Britain
Picadilly Third Stop (Wolf Rilla, 1960), Britain
Plunder Road (Hubert Cornfield, 1957), USA

Pouvoir Intime/Blind Trust (Yves Simoneau, 1986), Canada
A Prize of Arms (Cliff Owen, 1961), Britain
A Prize of Gold (Mark Robson, 1955), Britain
Razzia sur la chnouf (Henri Decoin, 1955), France
Reservoir Dogs (Quentin Tarantino, 1992), USA
Rififi/Du Rififi chez les hommes (Jules Dassin, 1955), France
Robbery (Peter Yates, 1967), Britain
Ronin (John Frankenheimer, 1998), USA
Le Rouge est mis (Gilles Grangier, 1957), France
The Secret Place (Clive Donner, 1956), Britain
Set it Off (F. Gary Gray, 1996), USA
Seven Thieves (Henry Hathaway, 1960), USA
Sexy Beast (Jonathan Glazer, 2000), Britain
Six Bridges to Cross (Joseph Pevney, 1955), USA
Small Time Crooks (Woody Allen, 2000), USA
The Split (Gordon Flemyng, 1968), USA
The Suspect (Stuart Connelly, 2013), USA
They Came to Rob Las Vegas (Antonio Isasi-Isasmendi, 1968), USA
Thief (Michael Mann, 1981), USA
The Thomas Crown Affair (Norman Jewison, 1968), USA
The Thomas Crown Affair (John McTiernan, 1999), USA
Three Crooked Men (Ernest Morris, 1958), Britain
Three Kings (David. O. Russell, 1999), USA
To Steal from a Thief/Cien años de perdón (Daniel Calparsoro, 2016), Spain
Touchez pas au grisbi/Don't Touch the Loot (Jacques Becker, 1954), France
Victoria (Sebastian Schipper, 2015), Germany
Violent Saturday (Richard Fleischer, 1955), USA
Welcome to Collinwood (Anthony Russo, Joe Russo, 2002), USA
White Heat (Raoul Walsh, 1949), USA
The Wrong Arm of the Law (Clive Owen, 1963), Britain

Works Cited

Acland, Charles R. "Screen Space, Screen Time, and Canadian Film Exhibition." *North of Everything: English-Canadian Cinema Since 1980*. Ed. William Beard and Jerry White. Edmonton: University of Alberta Press, 2002. 2–18.

Adamson, Walter L. *Embattled Avant-Gardes: Modernism's Resistance to Commodity Culture in Europe*. Berkeley: University of California Press, 2007.

Alexander, Michelle. *The New Jim Crow: Mass Incarceration in the Age of Colorblindness*. New York: New Press, 2010.

Allan, Derek. *Art and the Human Adventure: André Malraux's Theory of Art*. New York: Rodopi, 2009.

Allen, Joan. "Playing with Hope and Despair: Bourdieu and the Habitus of Horse Betting." *The Sociology of Risk and Gambling Reader*. Ed. James F. Cosgrave. London: Routledge, 2006. 185–205.

Alpert, Hollis. "The Inexpensive Look." *Saturday Review* 4 Aug. 1956: 32.

Altman, Rick. *Film/Genre*. London: BFI, 1999.

Andersen, Thom. "Afterword." *"Un-American" Hollywood: Politics and Film in the Blacklist Era*. Ed. Frank Krutnik, Steve Neale, Brian Neve, and Peter Stanfield. New Brunswick, NJ: Rutgers University Press, 2007. 264–75.

———. "Red Hollywood." *"Un-American" Hollywood: Politics and Film in the Blacklist Era*. Ed. Frank Krutnik, Steve Neale, Brian Neve, and Peter Stanfield. New Brunswick, NJ: Rutgers University Press, 2007. 225–63.

Baker, Aaron. *Steven Soderbergh*. Urbana: University of Illinois Press, 2011.

Bakewell, Sarah. *At the Existentialist Café: Freedom, Being, and Apricot Cocktails*. New York: Other Press, 2016.

Bankston, Douglas. "Smooth Operators: Steven Soderbergh Goes for Broke with *Ocean's Eleven*." *American Cinematographer* 83.1 (2002): 36–49.

Barker, Jennifer M. *The Tactile Eye: Touch and the Cinematic Experience*. Berkeley: University of California Press, 2009.

Baudrillard, Jean. "L'Espirit du Terrorisme." *South Atlantic Quarterly* 101.2 (Spring 2002): 403–15.

Berenz, Nicole. "Forms: 'For It Is the Critical Faculty That Invents Fresh Forms.'" *The French Cinema Book*. Ed. Michael Temple and Michael Wit. London: British Film Institute, 2004. 230–46.

Bessy, Maurice, Raymond Chirat, and André Bernard. *Histoire du cinéma français: Encyclopédie des films 1951–1955*. Paris: Pygmalion, 1995.

———. *Histoire du cinéma français: Encyclopédie des films 1940–1950*. Paris: Pygmalion, 1997.

Black, Joel. *The Aesthetics of Murder: A Study in Romantic Literature and Contemporary Culture*. Baltimore: Johns Hopkins University Press, 1991.

Bloom, Harold. *The Anxiety of Influence: A Theory of Poetry*. 2nd ed. Oxford: Oxford University Press 1997.

Bois, Yves-Alain. "The Semiology of Cubism." *Picasso and Braque: A Symposium*. Ed. Lynn Zelevansky. New York: Museum of Modern Art, 1992. 169–208.

Bolongaro, Eugenio. "Playful Robberies in *Palookaville* (1995): Alan Taylor, Italo Calvino and a New Paradigm for Adaptation." *New Cinemas: Journal of Contemporary Film* 4.1 (2006): 3–20.

Boorstin, Jon. *The Hollywood Eye: What Makes Movies Work*. New York: Cornelia & Michael Bessie Books, 1990.

Booth, Michael R. *English Melodrama*. London: H. Jenkins, 1965.

Bordwell, David. *The Way Hollywood Tells It: Story and Style in Modern Movies*. Berkeley: University of California Press, 2006.

Bordwell, David, and Kristin Thompson. *Film History: An Introduction*. New York: McGraw-Hill. 1994.

Bould, Mark. *Film Noir: From Berlin to Sin City*. London: Wallflower Press, 2005.

Brecht, Berthold. *Die Dreigroschenoper* (1931 print version). In *Ausgewählte Werke in Sechs Bänden*. Frankfurt am Main: Suhrkamp Verlag, 1997.

Browning, Mark. *George Clooney: An Actor Looking for a Role*. Santa Barbara, CA: ABC-CLIO, LLC, 2012.

Bruzzi, Stella. *Undressing Cinema: Clothing and Identity in the Movies*. London: Routledge, 1997.

Buchloh, Benjamin H. D. "The Social History of Art: Models and Concepts." *Art Since 1900: Modernism, Antimodernism, Postmodernism*. Ed. Hal Foster, Rosalind Krauss, Yves-Alain Bois, Benjamin H. D. Buchloh, and David Joselit. Vol. 1. 2nd ed. New York: Thames and Hudson, 2011. 22–31.

Buhle, Paul, and Dave Wagner. *Hide in Plain Sight: The Hollywood Blacklistees in Film and Television, 1950–2002*. New York: Palgrave Macmillan, 2003.

———. *Radical Hollywood: the Untold Story Behind America's Favorite Movies*. New York: New Press, 2002.

———. *A Very Dangerous Citizen: Abraham Lincoln Polonsky and the Hollywood Left*. Berkeley: University of California Press, 2001.

Campbell, Donald E. *Incentives: Motivation and the Economics of Information*. Cambridge: Cambridge University Press, 2006.

Canby, Vincent. "'Italian Job' and 'Ace High.'" *New York Times* 9 Oct. 1969: 55.

Carroll, Hamilton. *Affirmative Reaction: New Formations of White Masculinity.* Durham, NC: Duke University Press, 2011.

Casebier, Allan. *Film and Phenomenology: Toward a Realist Theory of Cinematic Representation.* Cambridge: Cambridge University Press, 1991.

Chibnall, Steve. "Ordinary People: 'New Wave' Realism and the British Crime Film 1959–1963." *British Crime Cinema.* Ed. Steve Chibnall and Robert Murphy. London: Routledge, 1999. 94–109.

———. "Travels in Ladland: The British Gangster Film Cycle, 1998–2001." *The British Cinema Book.* Ed. Robert Murphy. 3rd ed. London: BFI, 2001. 375–86.

Clark, T. J. *The Painting of Modern Life: Paris in the Art of Manet and His Followers.* Princeton, NJ: Princeton University Press, 1984.

Clay, Andrew. "Men, Women and Money: Masculinity in Crisis in the British Professional Crime Film 1946–1965." *British Crime Cinema.* Ed. Steve Chibnall and Robert Murphy. London: Routledge, 1999. 51–65.

———. "When the Gangs Came to London: The Postwar British Crime Film." *Journal of Popular British Cinema* 1 (1998): 76–86.

Corrigan, Timothy. *A Cinema Without Walls: Movies and Culture After Vietnam.* New Brunswick, NJ: Rutgers University Press, 1991.

Cottington, David. *Cubism.* Cambridge: Cambridge University Press, 1998.

Crisp, Colin. *The Classic French Cinema, 1930–1960.* Bloomington: Indiana University Press, 1997.

———. *French Cinema: A Critical Filmography Volume 2, 1940–1958.* Bloomington: Indiana University Press, 2015.

Crowther, Bosley. "'Ocean's 11': Sinatra Heads Flippant Team of Crime." *New York Times* 11 Aug. 1960: 19.

———. "Recruiting Jewel Thieves." *New York Times* 18 Sept. 1964: 25.

Culler, Jonathan D. On Deconstruction: Theory and Criticism after Structuralism. Ithaca, NY: Cornell University Press, 1982.

Dalle Vacche, Angela. *Cinema and Painting: How Art Is Used in Film.* Austin: University of Texas Press, 1996.

Darton, Eric. *Divided We Stand: A Biography of New York's World Trade Center.* New York: Basic Books, 1999.

Davies, Jude, and Carol R. Smith. *Gender, Ethnicity and Sexuality in Contemporary American Film.* Edinburgh: Keele University Press, 1997.

Delaney, Marshall. "Artists in the Shadows: Some Notable Canadian Movies." *Take Two: A Tribute to Film in Canada.* Ed. Seth Feldman. Toronto: Irwin Publishing, 1984. 2–17.

Desjardins, Chris. *Outlaw Masters of Japanese Film.* London: I. B. Tauris, 2005.

deWaard, Andrew. "Intertextuality, Broken Mirrors, and *The Good German.*" *The Philosophy of Steven Soderbergh.* Ed. R. Barton Palmer and Steven M. Sanders. Lexington: University Press of Kentucky, 2011. 107–19.

deWaard, Andrew, and R. Colin Tait. *The Cinema of Steven Soderbergh: Indie Sex, Corporate Lies, and Digital Videotape*. London: Wallflower Press, 2013.

Di Carmine, Roberta. "Comedy 'Italian Style' and *I soliti ignoti* (*Big Deal on Madonna Street*, 1958)." *A Companion to Film Comedy*. Ed. Andrew Horton and Joanna E. Rapf. Chichester: Wiley-Blackwell, 2013. 454–73.

Diderot, Denis. *Diderot on Art*. Vol 1: *The Salon of 1765 and Notes on Painting*. Ed. and trans. John Goodman. New Haven, CT.: Yale University Press, 1995.

Dimendberg, Edward. *Film Noir and the Spaces of Modernity*. Cambridge, MA: Harvard University Press, 2004.

Durgnat, Raymond. *A Mirror for England: British Movies from Austerity to Affluence*. London: Faber, 1970.

Dux, Sally. "Allied Film Makers: Crime, Comedy and Social Concern." *Journal of British Cinema and Television* 9.2 (2012): 198–213.

Dyer, Richard. *Only Entertainment*. London: Taylor & Francis, 2002.

Elsaesser, Thomas. *The Persistence of Hollywood*. New York: Routledge, 2012.

Epstein, Richard A. *The Theory of Gambling and Statistical Logic*. 2nd ed. Burlington, MA: Elsevier, 2008.

Felson, Marcus. *Crime and Everyday Life*. Thousand Oaks, CA: Sage, 1998.

Forshaw, Barry. *British Crime Film: Subverting the Social Order*. Basingstoke: Palgrave Macmillan, 2012.

Fothergill, Robert. "Coward, Bully or Clown: The Dream-Life of a Younger Brother." *Canadian Film Reader*. Ed. Seth Feldman and Joyce Nelson. Toronto: Peter Martin Associates, 1977. 234–50.

Fraterrigo, Elizabeth. *Playboy and the Making of the Good Life in Modern America*. New York: Oxford University Press, 2009.

Freud, Sigmund. *The Uncanny*. Trans. David McLintock. London: Penguin, 2003.

Frijters, Paul, with Gigi Foster. *Economic Theory of Greed, Love, Groups, and Networks*. Cambridge: Cambridge University Press, 2013.

Friman, H. Richard. "The Impact of the Occupation on Crime in Japan." *Democracy in Occupied Japan: The U.S. Occupation and Japanese Politics and Society*. Ed. Mark E. Caprio and Yoneyuki Sugita. London: Routledge, 2007. 89–119.

Fuchs, Cynthia. "*The Good Thief*: Imagery and Influence." *Pop Matters*, 2002, www.popmatters.com/feature/jordan-neil-030505/.

Gallagher, Mark. *Another Steven Soderbergh Experience: Authorship and Contemporary Hollywood*. Austin: University of Texas Press, 2013.

Garon, Sheldon, and Mike Mochizuki. "Negotiating Social Contracts." *Postwar Japan as History*. Ed. Andrew Gordon. Berkeley: University of California Press, 1993. 145–66.

Geraghty, Christine. *British Cinema in the Fifties: Gender, Genre and the "New Look"*. London: Routledge, 2000.

Gilbert, James. *Men in the Middle: Searching for Masculinity in the 1950s*. Chicago: University of Chicago Press, 2005.

Gledhill, Christine. "Rethinking Genre." *Reinventing Film Studies*. Ed. Linda Williams and Christine Gledhill. London: Arnold, 2000. 221–43.

Goffman, Erving. "Where the Action Is." *The Sociology of Risk and Gambling Reader*. Ed. James F. Cosgrove. London: Routledge, 2006. 225–54.

Grant, Barry Keith. "Beautiful Losers: Don Shebib's *Between Friends*." *Take One* 11.38 (July–Aug. 2002): 8–11.

Guérif, François. *Le Film policier*. Paris: Éditions j'ai lu, 1989.

Handling, Piers. "A Canadian Cronenberg." *Take Two: A Tribute to Film in Canada*. Ed. Seth Feldman. Toronto: Irwin Publishing, 1984. 80–91.

Hansen, Myriam Bratu. "The Mass Production of the Senses: Classical Cinema as Vernacular Modernism." *Reinventing Film Studies*. Ed. Christine Gledhill and Linda Williams. London: Arnold, 2000. 332–50.

Harcourt, Peter. "Men of Vision: Some Comments on the Work of Don Shebib." *Canadian Film Reader*. Ed. Seth Feldman and Joyce Nelson. Toronto: Peter Martin Associates, 1977. 208–17.

Harper, Sue, and Vincent Porter. *British Cinema of the 1950s: The Decline of Deference*. Oxford: Oxford University Press, 2003.

Harvey, David. *The Condition of Postmodernity: An Enquiry into the Origins of Cultural Change*. Oxford: Blackwell, 1990.

Hayes, Graeme. "*Rififi*." *The Cinema of France*. Ed. Phil Powrie. London: Wallflower Press, 2006. 71–79.

Hazareesingh, Sudhir. *How The French Think: An Affectionate Portrait of an Intellectual People*. London: Penguin, 2015.

Heukelom, Floris. *Behavioral Economics: A History*. Cambridge: Cambridge University Press, 2014.

Hill, Peter B. E. *The Japanese Mafia: Yakuza, Law, and the State*. Oxford: Oxford University Press, 2003.

"In Conversation with Steven Soderbergh." *The Empire*, Nov. 2009, www.nevpierce.com/wp-content/uploads/2011/03/Steven-Soderbergh-career-interview-Nev-Pierce.pdf.

"The Italian Job." *Independent Film Journal* 19 Aug. 1969: 1095.

Kahan, Dan M. "The Logic of Reciprocity: Trust, Collective Action, and Law." *Moral Sentiments and Material Interests: The Foundations of Cooperation in Economic Life*. Ed. Herbert Gintis, Samuel Bowles, Robert Boyd, and Ernst Fehr. Cambridge, MA: MIT Press, 2005. 339–78.

Kaminsky, Stuart M. *American Film Genres: Approaches to a Critical Theory of Popular Film*. Dayton: Pflaum, 1974.

Kant, Immanuel. *Critique of the Power of Judgment*. Trans. Paul Guyer and Eric Matthews. Rev. ed. Cambridge: Cambridge University Press. 2001.

Kaplan, Amy. "Homeland Insecurities: Reflections on Language and Space." *Radical History Review* 85 (Winter 2003): 82–93.

Kaplan, David E., and Alec Dubro. *Yakuza: Japan's Criminal Underworld*. Berkeley: University of California Press, 2003.

Karmel, Pepe. *Picasso and the Invention of Cubism*. New Haven, CT: Yale University Press, 2003.

Keaney, Michael F. *British Film Noir Guide*. Jefferson, NC: McFarland and Co., 2008.

Keeling, Kara. *The Witch's Flight: The Cinematics, the Black Femme, and the Image of Common Sense*. Durham, NC: Duke University Press, 2007.

Kendall, Richard, and Jill Devonyar. *Degas and the Ballet: Picturing Movement*. London: Royal Academy of Arts, 2011.

Kimmel, Michael. *Manhood in America: A Cultural History*. New York: The Free Press, 1996.

Kirkham, Pat, and Janet Thumim. "Men at Work: Dearden and Gender." *Liberal Directions: Basil Dearden and Postwar British Film Culture*. Ed. Alan Burton, Tim O'Sullivan, and Paul Wells. Trowbridge: Flicks Books, 1997. 89–107.

Kline, T. Jefferson. *Unraveling French Cinema: From L'Atalante to Caché*. London: Wiley-Blackwell, 2010.

Kovács, András Bálint. *Screening Modernism: European Art Cinema, 1950–1980*. Chicago: University of Chicago Press, 2007.

Krutnik, Frank. *In a Lonely Street: Film Noir, Genre, Masculinity*. London: Routledge, 1991.

Krutnik, Frank, Steve Neale, Brian Neve, and Peter Stanfield, eds. *"Un-American" Hollywood: Politics and Film in the Blacklist Era*. New Brunswick, NJ: Rutgers University Press, 2007.

Kuberski, Philip. *Kubrick's Total Cinema: Philosophical Themes and Formal Qualities*. London: Continuum, 2012.

Kynaston, David. *Austerity Britain 1945–51*. London: Bloomsbury, 2007.

Lacan, Jacques. *The Four Fundamental Concepts of Psycho-Analysis*. Ed. Jacques Alain-Miller. Trans. Alan Sheridan. Harmondsworth: Penguin, 1979.

Leach, Jim. *Film in Canada*. 2nd ed. Don Mills, Ontario: Oxford University Press, 2011.

Lee, Daryl. *The Heist Film: Stealing with Style*. London: Wallflower Press, 2014.

Leonard, George. B., Jr. "The American Male: Why Is He Afraid to Be Different?" *Look* 18 Feb. 1959: 95–104.

Letkemann, Peter. *Crime as Work*. Englewood Cliffs, NJ: Prentice-Hall, 1973.

Levy, Emanuel. *Cinema of Outsiders: The Rise of American Independent Film*. New York: New York University Press, 1999.

Lewis, Jon. "Money Matters: Hollywood in the Corporate Era." *The New American Cinema*. Ed. Jon Lewis. Durham, NC: Duke University Press, 1998. 87–121.

Lindstrom, J. A. "*Heat*: Work and Genre." *Jump Cut* 43 (2000): 21–30.

Lloyd, Christopher. *Edgar Degas: Drawings and Pastels*. Los Angeles: J. Paul Getty Museum, 2014.

Loewenstein, George F., Elke U. Weber, Christopher K. Hsee, and Ned Welch. "Risk as Feelings." *Exotic Preferences: Behavioral Economics and Human Motivation*. Ed. George F. Loewenstein. Oxford: Oxford University Press, 2007. 565–611.

"Looking Backward." *Saturday Review* 5 Jan. 1957: 27.

Maclachlan, Patricia L. *Consumer Politics in Postwar Japan: The Institutional Boundaries of Citizen Activism*. New York: Columbia University Press, 2002.

Maltby, Roger. "Censorship and Self-Regulation." *The Oxford History of World Cinema*. Ed. Geoffrey Nowell-Smith. Oxford: Oxford University Press, 1996. 235–48.

Mandelbrot, Benoit B. *Fractals and Scaling in Finance: Discontinuity, Concentration, Risk*. New York: Springer-Verlag, 1997.

Mann, Michael. "Notes for the Coffee Shop Scene." *Sight and Sound* 6.3 (March 1996): 14–19.

Manvell, Roger. "Critical Survey." *Penguin Film Review* 4 (1947): 12–16.

Mason, Fran. *American Gangster Cinema: From* Little Caesar *to* Pulp Fiction. New York: Palgrave MacMillan, 2002.

———. *Hollywood's Detectives: Crime Series in the 1930s and 1940s from the Whodunnit to Hard-boiled Noir*. Basingstoke: Palgrave Macmillan, 2012.

Massonat, François. "The Policier." *Directory of World Cinema: France*. Ed. Tim Palmer and Charlie Michael. Bristol: Intellect, 2013. 206–41.

Massood, Paula. *Black City Cinema: African American Urban Experiences in Film*. Philadelphia: Temple University Press, 2003.

Mather, Philippe. *Stanley Kubrick at Look Magazine: Authorship and Genre in Photojournalism and Film*. Bristol: Intellect, 2013.

McArthur, Colin. "Mise-en-scène Degree Zero: Jean-Pierre Melville's *Le Samouraï*." *French Film: Texts and Contexts*. Ed. Susan Hayward and Ginette Vincendeau. 2nd ed. London: Routledge, 2000. 189–201.

McCabe, Susan. *Cinematic Modernism: Modernist Poetry and Film*. Cambridge: Cambridge University Press, 2005.

McCarthy, John, and Peter Wright. *Technology as Experience*. Cambridge, MA: MIT Press, 2004.

McCloskey, Deirdre (*né* Donald) N. "Metaphors Economists Live By." *Social Research* 62.2 (Summer 1995): 215–37.

Mittell, Jason. *Genre and Television: From Cop Shows to Cartoons in American Culture*. New York: Routledge, 2004.

Molasky, Michael S. 1999. The American Occupation of Japan and Okinawa: Literature and Memory. London: Routledge.

Morton, Drew. "Schizopolis as Philosophical Autobiography." *The Philosophy of Steven Soderbergh*. Ed. R. Barton Palmer and Steven M. Sanders. Lexington: University Press of Kentucky, 2011. 173–93.

Moskin, Robert. "Why Do Women Dominate Him?" *The Decline of the American Male*. Comp. The editors of *LOOK*. New York: Random House, 1958. 3–24.

Munby, Jonathan. "Art in the Age of New Jim Crow: Delimiting the Scope of Racial Justice and Black Film Production since Rodney King." *African American Culture and Society after Rodney King: Provocations and Protests, Progression and Post-Racialism*. Ed. Josephine Metcalf and Carina Spaulding. Farnham: Ashgate, 2015. 283–302.

———. "From Gangsta to Gangster: The Hood Film's Criminal Allegiance with Hollywood." *The New Film History*. Ed. James Chapman, Mark Glancy, and Sue Harper. New York: Palgrave, 2007. 166–79.

———. *Public Enemies, Public Heroes: Screening the Gangster from* Little Caesar *to* Touch of Evil. Chicago: University of Chicago Press, 1999.

———. *Under a Bad Sign: Criminal Self-Representation in African American Popular Culture*. Chicago: University of Chicago Press, 2011.

Naremore, James. "Stanley Kubrick and the Aesthetics of the Grotesque." *Film Quarterly* 60.1 (Fall 2006): 4–14.

Nason, Richard W. "Evaluating the 'Odds': Harry Belafonte Tries Broad Racial Approach in Locally Made Feature." *New York Times* 15 Mar. 1959: X7.

Neal, Larry. "Beware the Tar Baby." *New York Times* 3 Aug. 1969: D13.

Neale, Steve. "Masculinity as Spectacle: Reflections on Men and Mainstream Cinema." *Screening the Male: Exploring Masculinities in Hollywood Cinema*. Ed. Steven Cohan and Ina Rae Hark. London: Routledge, 1993. 9–20.

Newman, Kim. "The Caper Film." *The BFI Companion to Crime*. Ed. Phil Hardy. London: Cassell, 1997. 70–71.

Orr, John. *Cinema and Modernity*. Cambridge: Polity Press, 1993.

Osteen, Mark. "A Little Larceny: Labor, Leisure, and Loyalty in the '50s *Noir* Heist Film." *Kiss the Blood Off My Hand: On Classic Film Noir*. Ed. Robert Miklitsch. Urbana: University of Illinois Press, 2014. 171–92.

Palmer, R. Barton. "Alain Resnais Meets Film Noir in *The Underneath* and *The Limey*." *The Philosophy of Steven Soderbergh*. Ed. R. Barton Palmer and Steven M. Sanders. Lexington: University Press of Kentucky, 2011. 69–90.

Palmer, Tim. "Paris, City of Shadows: French Crime Cinema Before the New Wave." *New Review of Film and Television Studies* 6.2 (2008): 213–31.

Patry, Sylvie, ed. *Inventing Impressionism: Paul Durand-Ruel and the Modern Art Market*. London: National Gallery, 2015.

Peirson, John, and Philip Blackburn. "Betting at British Racecourses: A Comparison of the Efficiency of Betting with Bookmakers and at the Tote." *The Economics of Gambling*. Ed. Leighton Williams. London: Routledge, 2003. 30–42.

Petit, Philippe. *To Reach the Clouds: My High Wire Walk Between the Twin Towers*. New York: North Point Press, 2002.

Pezzotta, Elias. *Stanley Kubrick: Adapting the Sublime*. Jackson: University of Mississippi Press, 2013.

Phillips, Alastair. *Rififi*. London: I. B. Tauris, 2009.

Pitzulo, Carrie. *Bachelors and Bunnies: The Sexual Politics of* Playboy. Chicago: University of Chicago Press, 2011.

"The Playboy Reader." *Playboy* 2.9 (September 1955): 36.

Polonsky, Abraham. *Odds Against Tomorrow: The Critical Edition*. Northridge, CA: Center for Telecommunication Studies, California State University, Northridge, 1999.

Porter, Dennis. *The Pursuit of Crime: Art and Ideology in Detective Fiction*. New Haven, CT: Yale University Press, 1981.

Preda, Alex. *Framing Finance: The Boundaries of Markets and Modern Capitalism*. Chicago: University of Chicago Press, 2009.

Prettejohn, Elizabeth. *Beauty and Art 1750–2000*. Oxford: Oxford University Press, 2005.

Prime, Rebecca. "Cloaked in Compromise: Jules Dassin's 'Naked' City." *"Un-American" Hollywood: Politics and Film in the Blacklist Era*. Ed. Frank Krutnik, Steve Neale, Brian Neve, and Peter Stanfield. New Brunswick, NJ: Rutgers University Press, 2007. 142–51.

Rafter, Nicole. *Shots in the Mirror: Crime Films and Society*. Oxford: Oxford University Press, 2000.

Ramsay, Christine. "Canadian Narrative Cinema from the Margins: 'The Nation' and Masculinity in *Goin' Down the Road*." *Canadian Journal of Film Studies* 2.2–3 (1993): 27–49.

Reynolds, Bruce. *The Autobiography of a Thief*. London: Bantam, 1995.

Richards, Jeffrey. *The Age of the Dream Palace: Cinema and Society in Britain 1930–1939*. London: Routledge and Kegan Paul, 1984.

Riesman, David. *The Lonely Crowd: A Study of the Changing American Character*. New Haven, CT: Yale University Press, 1950.

Rioux, Jean-Pierre. *The Fourth Republic, 1946–1958*. Trans. Godfrey Rogers. Cambridge: Cambridge University Press, 1989.

Robertson, James C. "The Censors and British Gangland, 1913–1990." *British Crime Cinema*. Ed. Steve Chibnall and Robert Murphy. London: Routledge, 1999. 16–26.

Rohdie, Sam. *Film Modernism*. Manchester: Manchester University Press, 2015.

Rolls, Alistair, and Deborah Walker. *French and American Noir: Dark Crossings*. New York: Palgrave Macmillan, 2009.

Royle, Nicholas. *The Uncanny*. Manchester: Manchester University Press, 2003.

Rubin, Martin. *Thrillers*. Cambridge: Cambridge University Press, 1999.

Sartre, Jean-Paul. *Being and Nothingness*. Trans. Hazel Barnes. London: Routledge, 2003.

Scaggs, John. *Crime Fiction*. London: Routledge, 2005.

Schlesinger, Arthur K., Jr. "The Crisis of American Masculinity." *Esquire* 51 (November 1958): 64–66.

Schmid, A. Allan. *Conflict and Cooperation: Institutional and Behavioral Economics.* Oxford: Blackwell, 2004.

Senelick, Laurence. *The Prestige of Evil: The Murderer as Romantic Hero from Sade to Lacenaire.* New York: Garland, 1987.

Server, Lee. "Marc Lawrence: The Last Gangster." *The Big Book of Noir.* Ed. Ed Gorman, Lee Server, and Martin H. Greenberg. New York: Carroll & Graf, 1998. 47–54.

Shadoian, Jack. *Dreams and Dead Ends: The American Gangster Film.* 2nd ed. Oxford: Oxford University Press, 2003.

Sieving, Christopher. *Soul Searching: Black-Themed Cinema from the March on Washington to the Rise of Blaxploitation.* Middletown, CT: Wesleyan University Press, 2011.

Simmons, Garner. "The Generic Origins of the Bandit-Gangster Sub-Genre in the American Cinema." *Film Reader* 3 (1973): 67–79.

Smith, Michael A. "The Impact of Tipster Information on Bookmakers' Prices in UK Horse-race Markets." *The Economics of Gambling.* Ed. Leighton Williams. London: Routledge, 2003. 67–79.

Sobchack, Vivian Carol. *The Address of the Eye: A Phenomenology of Film Experience.* Princeton, NJ: Princeton University Press, 1992.

Soderbergh, Steven, and Richard Lester. *Getting Away With It; Or, The Further Adventures of the Luckiest Bastard You Ever Saw.* London: Faber and Faber, 1999.

Sperb, Jason. "The Country of the Mind in Kubrick's *Fear and Desire.*" *Film Criticism* 29.1 (Fall 2004): 23–37.

Standish, Isolde. *A New History of Japanese Cinema: A Century of Narrative Film.* New York: Continuum, 2006.

"Steven Soderbergh's State of Cinema Talk." Deadline Hollywood, 3 Apr. 2013, www.deadline.com/2013/04/steven-soderbergh-state-of-cinema-address-486368/.

Straw, Will. "Documentary Realism and the Post-War Left." *"Un-American" Hollywood: Politics and Film in the Blacklist Era.* Ed. Frank Krutnik, Steve Neale, Brian Neve, and Peter Stanfield. New Brunswick, NJ: Rutgers University Press, 2007. 130–41.

Studlar, Gaylyn. "A Gunsel Is Being Beaten: Gangster Masculinity and the Homoerotics of the Crime Film, 1941–1942." *Mob Culture: Hidden Histories of the American Gangster Film.* Ed. Lee Grieveson, Esther Sonnet, and Peter Stanfield. New Brunswick, NJ: Rutgers University Press, 2005. 120–45.

Telotte, J. P. "Fatal Capers: Strategy and Enigma in Film *Noir.*" *Journal of Popular Film and Television* 23.4 (1996): 163–70.

Thompson, Anne. "Steven Soderbergh: From *Sex, Lies, and Videotape* to *Erin Brockovich*—A Maverick Director's Route (with Detours) to Hollywood Clout."

Steven Soderbergh: Interviews. Ed. Anthony Kaufman. Rev. ed. Jackson: University Press of Mississippi, 2015. 94–102.

Thompson, Kirsten Moana. *Crime Films: Investigating the Scene.* London: Wallflower Press, 2007.

Thomson, David. *The New Biographical Dictionary of Film.* 4th rev. ed. New York: Little Brown & Company, 2003.

———. "Two Works of Social Criticism Masquerading as Thrillers." *New Republic,* 6 Oct. 2011, www.newrepublic.com/article/95819/film-noir-kubrick-killing-losey-prowler.

Thurow, Lester C. *The Zero-Sum Society: Distribution and the Possibilities for Economic Change.* New York: Basic Books, 2001.

Truffaut, François. "Une Certain tendence du cinéma français." *Cahiers du cinéma* 6.31 (January 1954): 15–29.

Vaggi, Gianni, and Peter Groenewegen. *A Concise History of Economic Thoughts: From Mercantilism to Monetarism.* Basingstoke: Palgrave Macmillan, 2003.

Vertov, Dziga. *Kino-eye: The Writings of Dziga Vertov.* Ed. Annette Michelson. Trans. Kevin O'Brien. Berkeley: University of California Press, 1984.

Vezyroglou, Dimitri, ed. *Le Cinéma: une affaire d'État, 1945–1970.* Paris: Comité d'histoire du ministère de la Culture et de la Communication, 2014.

Vidler, Anthony. *The Architectural Uncanny.* Cambridge, MA: MIT Press, 1992.

Vincendeau, Ginette. "France 1945–65 and Hollywood: The *Policier* as International Text." *Screen* 33.1 (1992): 50–79.

Walker, Alexander. *Hollywood England: The British Film Industry in the Sixties.* London: Michael Joseph, 1974.

Walls, David W., and Kelly Busche. "Breakage, Turnover, and Betting Market Efficiency: New Evidence from Japanese Horse Tracks." *The Economics of Gambling.* Ed. Leighton Williams. London: Routledge, 2003. 43–66.

Watkins, S. Craig. *Representing: Hip Hop Culture and the Production of Black Cinema.* Chicago: University of Chicago Press, 1998.

Waugh, Thomas. *The Romance of Transgression: Queering Sexualities, Nations, Cinemas.* Montreal: McGill-Queen's University Press, 2006.

White, Lionel. *The Killing.* Berkeley: Black Lizard Books, 1988.

Whyte, William. *The Organization Man.* New York: Simon and Schuster, 1956.

Williams, Linda. "Melodrama Revised." *Refiguring American Film Genres: History and Theory.* Ed. Nick Browne. Berkeley: University of California Press, 1998. 42–88.

Wollen, Peter. *Paris Hollywood: Writings on Film.* London: Verso, 2002.

Wood, Michael. "Modernism and Film." *The Cambridge Companion to Modernism.* Ed. Michael Levenson. Cambridge: Cambridge University Press, 1999. 217–32.

Wylie, Philip. *Generation of Vipers.* New York: Rinehart, 1946.

———. "The Womanization of America." *Playboy* 5.9 (September 1958): 51–53, 77.

Yalom, Irvin D. *Existential Psychotherapy.* New York: Basic Books, 1980.

———. *Love's Executioner and Other Tales of Psychotherapy*. Harmondsworth: Penguin, 1991.

Yoshimoto, Mitsuhiro. "Questions of the New: Oshima Nagisa's *Cruel Story of Youth* (1960)." *Japanese Cinema: Texts and Contexts*. Ed. Alastair Phillips and Julian Stringer. London: Routledge, 2007. 168–79.

Žižek, Slavoj. "'The Thing That Thinks': The Kantian Background of the *Noir* Subject." *Shades of Noir: A Reader*. Ed. Joan Copjec. London: Verso. 199–226.

———. *Welcome to the Desert of the Real*. London: Verso, 2002.

Contributors

HAMILTON CARROLL is associate professor of English (American literature and culture) at the University of Leeds. He is the author of *Affirmative Reaction: New Formations of White Masculinity* (2011). He has published widely in the fields of whiteness and masculinity studies, and on contemporary U.S. literature, television, and film, in journals such as *Comparative American Studies, Genre,* the *Journal of American Studies, Modern Fiction Studies, Studies in American Fiction,* and *Television and New Media.* He has co-edited a special issue of *Comparative American Studies* on the subject of "Intellectuals and the Nation State." Current projects include a book-length study of U.S. American fiction in the decade of September 11 and the global financial collapse and a co-edited special issue of the *Journal of American Studies* on the subject of genre and the financial crisis. He is currently the co-investigator on the AHRC-funded research network, "Home, Crisis, and the Imagination."

ANDREW CLAY is principal lecturer in critical technical practices in the Leicester Media School at De Montfort University, UK. He has published articles on crime and masculinity in British cinema and online video. He is currently researching the theory and practice of social media particularly in relation to online video culture and technology.

SCOTT HENDERSON is an associate professor and chair of the Department of Communication, Popular Culture, and Film at Brock University. His research focuses on issues of identity and representation in popular culture, and he is currently investigating the changing nature of music scenes within post-industrial cities, including St. Etienne, France; Hamilton, Ontario; and Glasgow, Scotland. He has published work on Canadian film and television, youth culture, British cinema, and Canadian radio policy.

JIM LEACH is professor emeritus in the Department of Communication, Popular Culture, and Film at Brock University. He is the author of books on filmmakers Alain Tanner and Claude Jutra, as well as *British Film* and *Film in Canada*. He has also published a monograph on *Doctor Who* in Wayne State University Press's TV Milestones Series, co-edited a volume on Canadian documentary films, and developed a Canadian edition of an introductory film studies textbook.

DARYL LEE is associate professor of French and comparative literature at Brigham Young University. His scholarly interests revolve around urban culture in film and literature, film theory, and the history of French and Italian cinema. His analysis of representations of Third Republic Paris in ruins connects silent films such as Cavalcanti's *Rien que les heures* (1926) and Luitz-Morat and Bouquet's *La Cité foudroyée* (1924) to nineteenth-century photography, lithography, and popular literature that fantasized a Pompeian catastrophe befalling the French capital after the 1871 Paris Commune. His introductory genre study, *The Heist Film: Stealing with Style*, appeared in 2014.

FRAN MASON is a lecturer at the University of Winchester where he teaches in film studies and American studies. He teaches and researches in film and culture with particular interests in classical Hollywood cinema, crime films, cyborgs in representation, and postmodernism. He has published books on gangster movies (*American Gangster Cinema: From Little Caesar to Pulp Fiction*), detective films (*Hollywood's Detectives: Crime Series in the 1930s and 1940s from the Whodunnit to Hard-Boiled Noir*), and on postmodernist literature. In addition, he has published articles on gangster films, cyborgs, zombies, postmodernist fiction, and conspiracy culture, and he is currently engaged in research on assassin films, *The Godfather*, and small-time criminals in film.

JONATHAN MUNBY is senior lecturer in the Lancaster Institute for the Contemporary Arts (LICA), Lancaster University in the UK. He is also an alumnus fellow of the W. E. B. Du Bois Institute at the Hutchins Center, Harvard University. He has written widely on the relationship between ethnic and racial outsiders and criminal representation in American popular culture. He is the author of *Public Enemies, Public Heroes: Screening the Gangster from Little Caesar to Touch of Evil* (1999) and *Under a Bad Sign: Criminal*

Self-Representation in African American Popular Culture (2011), both published by the University of Chicago Press.

TIM PALMER is professor of film studies at the University of North Carolina Wilmington. He is the author of *Brutal Intimacy: Analyzing Contemporary French Cinema* (2011) and *Irreversible* (2015), and the co-editor of *Directory of World Cinema: France* (2013). His work has been published widely in book anthologies and in journals such as *Cinema Journal, Journal of Film and Video, Studies in French Cinema,* the *French Review,* and *New Review of Film and Television Studies.* His latest book project, *A Liberated Cinema: Creating the Postwar French Film State, 1946–1958,* has been supported by the National Endowment for the Humanities.

HOMER B. PETTEY is associate professor of English at the University of Arizona. Along with R. Barton Palmer, he is co-editor of two volumes on *Film Noir* and *International Noir* (2014). He is also co-editor of two collections with Palmer of *Hitchcock the Moralist* and *Biopics and British National Identity,* both contracted with SUNY Press. He has several forthcoming chapters: Wyatt Earp biopics for *Invented Lives, Imagined Communities: Biopics and American National Identity,* co-edited by William Epstein and R. Barton Palmer; on violence, the Production Code, and noir for David Schmidt's edited collection on violence in popular culture; and on class in Hitchcock's American noirs for Jonathan Freedman's *Cambridge Companion to Alfred Hitchcock.*

JONATHAN RAYNER is reader in film studies at the University of Sheffield, School of English. His research interests include auteur studies, genre films, Australasian cinema, naval and maritime films, and interactions of cinema and landscape. His publications include *The Cinema of Michael Mann* (2013), *The Naval War Film* (2007), *Contemporary Australian Cinema* (2000), and *The Films of Peter Weir* (1998/2003). He is the co-editor of *Filmurbia* (2017) with Graeme Harper and David Forrest, of *Mapping Cinematic Norths* (2016) with Julia Dobson, and of *Film Landscapes* (2013) and *Cinema and Landscape* (2010) with Graeme Harper.

JEANNETTE SLONIOWSKI is a retired associate professor in the Department of Communication, Popular Culture, and Film and the Graduate Program in Popular Culture at Brock University. She is a series editor, with Barry

Grant, of the TV Milestones Series for Wayne State University Press, as well as the author of numerous articles and co-editor of anthologies on documentary film, Canadian detective fiction, and Canadian popular culture.

GAYLYN STUDLAR is David May Distinguished Professor in the Humanities at Washington University in St. Louis, where she also directs the Program in Film and Media Studies. She has also taught at the University of Michigan, Ann Arbor, and Emory University. She is the author of four books, most recently *Precocious Charms: Stars Performing Girlhood in Classical Hollywood Cinema* (2013) and *Have Gun—Will Travel* (2015), and co-editor of four volumes, including *Reflections in a Male Eye: John Huston and the American Experience*.

Index

CPSIA information can be obtained
at www.ICGtesting.com
Printed in the USA
FSOW03n1329291117
41596FS

9 780814 342244